LIBERALIZATION AND INDIA'S NORTH-EAST

LIBERALIZATION AND INDIA'S NORTH-EAST

GURUDAS DAS
R.K. PURKAYASTHA
Editors

ST. ANTHONY'S COLLEGE
SHILLONG

COMMONWEALTH PUBLISHERS
New Delhi
1998

Liberalization and India's North-East

1st Edition : 1998

ISBN : 81-7169-498-5

Published by :

AJAY VERMA
for **Commonwealth Publishers**
4831/24, Prahlad Street,
Ansari Road, Darya Ganj,
New Delhi-110002
Phone : 3272541
Fax : 91-11-3257835

Laser Typesetting by :
Stylish Laser Typesetter, Delhi-53.

Printed at :
Efficient Offset Press, Shahzada Bagh, Delhi.

FOREWORD

It is with pleasure that I write this brief foreword to the book "Liberalization and India's North-East" edited by Gurudas Das (Department of Economics) and R.K. Purkayastha (Department of Political Science), both of whom are known for their interest in matters concerning the North-Eastern region. The book contains the papers presented at a national seminar on this theme organised by the College.

Although it is going to be a decade since the formal launching of the programmes of economic reforms in our country, no attempt has been made to study the implications of liberalization for the North-Eastern region. This book is the result of an effort to fill this gap.

Ever since independence, the North-Eastern region has remained a place of perpetual concern. Problems of underdevelopment, infiltration, misgovernance, cultural autonomy, ethnic identity, insurgency have agitated the minds of millions, caught between the dilemma of tradition and modernity, poverty and resourcefulness, integration and protection of group identity, insulation and openness.

The structural transformation that India is engineering will only be meaningful for this region when its special characteristics are adequately attended to in the process. What will be the likely implications of the programmes of liberalization for the North-Eastern region ? Will they mean a better deal and better life for 'the sons of the lesser gods' ?

Several eminent scholars on the North-East have applied their mind and contributed thought-provoking ideas in this book that seeks to answer these and other related questions. Though one may not agree with all the observations made by the different authors in this volume, yet the ideas articulated by them are certainly going to enrich our understanding of the local impact of a national and global event.

We hope that this book will be of benefit to those who are interested in India's North-East and concerned with its developmental problems and possibilities.

Fr. Stephen Mavely SDB
Principal
St. Anthony's College
Shillong-793 001

Preface

This book finds its origin in a seminar on "Liberalization, Ethnic Identity and Economic Development of India's North-East" held at, and organized by, St. Anthony's College, Shillong, on April 25-26, 1997. One of the main inspirations for the seminar was the paucity of literature on the impact of economic reforms—the so-called programmes of globalization and liberalization—on, and their implications for, under-developed regions, like India's North-East.

The North-Eastern Region (NER) is known for its richness in natural resources. A question often asked is : In spite of relative abundance of resources, why does the region fail to accrue the benefits of liberalization? The imperfection of the market forces is often cited as one of the major causes of economic backwardness of the region. How the forces of globalization and liberalization are going to affect the industrially backward areas like NER? Will they be helpful in eliminating the market imperfections for which the region is supposed to have remained backward? Or, are they going to add to the duality that has developed under controlled regime? As the programmes of liberalization intend to reorient the economy in favour of market forces, what will be the role of the state in relation to the backward regions as well as lagging communities under the liberalized regime in the long run? As the task of maintaining 'ethnic identity', as it is perceived by the different ethnic groups in the region, not only involves the preservation of cultural symbols, but also the maintenance of group monopoly over the resources of their habitation, can ethnic identity and economic development go together in post-liberalized regime? Or, do the forces of liberalization make them incompatible? These are some of the issues which need to be attended and addressed to in their proper perspectives.

The seminar intended to provide an opportunity for debating on these issues involving individuals cutting across academic disciplines as well as professional boundaries. This seminar, as far as we know, is the first of its kind since the formal launching of the programmes of liberalization in India in 1991. Hence, many of the observations and inferences made by the contributors are impressionistic, conjectural and hypothetical in nature which call for further examination.

To study the implications of economic reforms for NER is to analyze the local impact of a global event as well. This has been attempted here at three levels. Contributors like R.L. Walli, Apurbananda Mazumdar, B.S. Butola, Mahesh Lalwani, Abhijit Choudhury and B. Datta Ray referred to global experiences of the reforms, general process of the world capitalist development, and mechanisms and institutions through which the process works. In the light of the insights gained from the operation of the world capitalist process, inferences have been drawn on the likely implications of this global change for the backward areas like NER. The approach, in a way, looks into the issues from above.

An opposite approach has been adopted by the contributors like Gurudas Das, H. Srikanth, R.K. Choudhury, Sujit Sikidar and Devadas Bhorali, Ranjit De, C. Joshua Thomas, L.S. Gassah, Debasish Bhattacharjee and Sadhan Sengupta. They have studied the different aspects of the socio-economic structure of the region, its resource potentials, the nature of relationship of the regional economy with its national counterparts as well as the cross-border trade potentials of the region. On the basis of the experience of local issues and local processes of growth and development, attempts have been made to assess the likely implications of the economic reforms for the region in the post liberalized era. Contrary to the approach of the first set of contributors, this approach studies the issues relating to the liberalization and economic development of NER from below. The mutual complementary nature of these two approaches, no doubt, helps in better understanding of the concerned phenomena.

Apurbananda Mazumdar's attempt to categorize the present phase of global core-periphery relation as 'super colonial', P.R. Bhattacharjee's attempt to specify the implications of Michael E Porter's theory of Competitive Advantage for NER and Gurudas Das' endeavour to apply the core-periphery model of world-system variety to parts (NER) internal to a country (India) are no doubt provocative. Inspite of their tremendous analytical importance in understanding the implications of economic reforms for underdeveloped regions, the application of these theoretical perspectives in the context of NER leaves much room for future debate.

Contributors like P.M. Passah, Rakhee Bhattacharya and Debjyoti Bhattacharyya followed a third approach. Highlighting the present infrastructural and industrial conditions of the region as well as the causes of slow growth of these key sectors, attempts have been made to prescribe as to what is to be done to tune up the regional economy to the challenges of liberalization. However, these prescriptive studies have not been undertaken, as part of a pre-planned scheme, as a necessary corollary of the first two approaches as, perhaps, it should have been. Obviously much is left in this area to be worked out in detail.

Contributors like Samir Kumar Das, M.N. Karna, M.M. Agrawal, and S.C. Daniel have taken up issues relating to ethno-social and ethno-cultural implications of economic reforms besides their economic ramifications for the ethnically sensitive NER. The ethnic identity being the dominant criterion on the basis of which people are mobilized in the region, attempts have been made to look into the socio-economic aspects of identity formation and interrelationships of identity, culture and development. Based on experience of ethnic situation in the NER, attempts have been made to explore the scope of compatibility of the various ethnic movements with the global economic reforms and to search for the role which probably the different culture groups could play in transcending the developmental reality created out of globalization.

The seminar and this volume owe much to many persons and organizations who contributed in countless ways in making them a success. We gratefully acknowledge the financial support received from the Government of Meghalaya, University Grants Commission, North-Eastern Regional Office, North-Eastern Council, Indian Council of Social Science Research, North-Eastern Regional Centre and the Rapsang Group of Industries.

We would like to express our gratitude to Fr. Stephen Mavely, Principal, and Fr. J. Nellanatt, Vice-principal, St. Anthony's College, for their constant support, guidance and encouragement without which the seminar and this volume would not have been possible.

We are also thankful to our colleagues, office staff and our beloved students of St. Anthony's College for the logistic support they provided in making the seminar a great success.

We wish to thank Rangan Dutta, N.K. Sarkar, H.W.T. Syiem, Basil Koikara, T. Subba and Basab Roy Choudhury for their invaluable support to this endeavour. We also extend our sincere thanks to B.R. Verma, of Commonwealth Publishers, for undertaking the publication of this volume.

Finally, we owe an apology for our inability to include the keynote address to the seminar by B.P. Misra because of a technical fault in the audio-visual used to record the relevant proceedings of the seminar.

Gurudas Das
R.K. Purakayastha

INAUGURAL ADDRESS

—M.M. Jacob

It gives me great pleasure to be here with you this morning in the inaugural session of the National Seminar on Liberalization, Ethnic Identity and Economic Development in India's North-East'. I congratulate the authorities of St. Anthony's College, Shillong for organizing this seminar focussing on the most crucial issues facing the North-East today.

The new Economic Policy enunciated by the Government of India in 1991 aims at liberalizing industrial and trading activities and giving the Indian economy a global linkage. Major changes have been effected since then in trade, credit and industrial policies. As a whole, the new policies have shown a strong preference for and reliance on the market for solving the problems of our economy. The new policy has received wide appreciation in the country and abroad. Still, some doubts have been raised in some quarters about its effects on employment, income disparities and poverty alleviation. In North-East India reservations about the new policy may also arise from what can be broadly described as an identity and compatibility crisis that has plagued the region for quite some time now. These and other issues will no doubt be discussed threadbare in the seminar to follow.

Since the second world war, the nature of competition between nation states has undergone a sea change. Control over world market share has become more important than control over territory. States like Japan and South Korea, having small territorial boundaries are controlling a significant share of the world market. The success of a nation thus no longer depends so much on the size of its population or on the size of its territory as on the economic competitiveness of the people. It depends on how fast a people can change their orientation, how quickly they can respond to the opportunities arising out of scientific and technological changes and how accurately they can visualize the different dimensions of future change.

Since the launching of the programmes of liberalization, vast opportunities have been opened up before the people of our country. Spectacular achievements made in the fields of science, technology, industry, agriculture and other sectors of our economy during the era of planned development have empowered our people to compete with their global counterparts. The transition from state-led growth to market-led growth has created additional space for private initiative.

The North-Eastern Region is rich in natural resources and has a tremendous potential for growth. As global capital is gradually being attracted to India, there is every reason to believe that the North-East will also attract such capital. Indeed, given certain conditions, the North-East may prove to be a favourable destination for both Indian and foreign investors. The region is receiving increasing attention from the Centre. The Package announced by the then Prime Minister of India, Shri H.D. Deve Gowda in October, 1996, to accelerate the pace of development in this region aims at developing basic infrastructure and human resources in this part of the country. Congenial socio-political environment and investment-friendly atmosphere are, however, required for these initiatives to bear fruit.

For many historical reasons the North-East societies have lived in comparative isolation. Many of them have their own peculiar land tenure systems, under which acquisition of land by an outsider is not permitted. Some of the states of the region have restrictions on the entry of outsiders and on business and trade by them. Some of these isolatory mechanisms are inherent in the socio-cultural ethos of these societies while others were invented by the British to protect them from exploitation. For a hundred years or more the smaller ethnic groups in this region have suffered from the fear of being submerged by other societies from outside. These fears and perceptions should not be made light of. They are real and deserve our serious attention. At the same time, it is also true that the new climate of liberalization and globalization will not enter the economic life of these societies unless they are able to come to terms with the new realities and face the future with courage and determination.

I recall the great economic depression of U.S.A. in 1920s and early thirties. America, then, was facing almost the same situation as we face today. Late President Roosevelt while assuming office, realized the mistake of the "isolationist policy" followed by the U.S. He opened up the U.S. to the world and the result was economic recovery and prosperity to Americans. So I want the people of the North-East to take lesson from history and work hard to catch up with the rest of India in development and progress.

The problems of economic development facing the North-East cannot be solved by economics alone—of whatever brand. A multi-disciplinary and multi-dimensional approach will have to be adopted to address the issues involved. Economists, Anthropologists, Sociologists and people's representatives have to work together to devise a reform package for the North-East which has validity, coherence and acceptability. There is no alternative to participatory and people centred approach to development. People want to be consulted, involved and taken into confidence. Without their participation and involvement no policy or package can succeed.

This brings me to the need for consensus on the new economic policy. It is heartening to note that already a broad consensus on liberalization has emerged, cutting across party lines and social groupings. Even so, much remains to be done. Doubts still persist on many counts some of which I have noted already. These doubts have to be removed by the process of give and take. Confrontation will hamper, not facilitate, development. People may be prepared to accept hardships and overcome fears as a price for prosperity and well-being in the long run. However, they have to be convinced of the soundness of the programme and should be able to see, as one author puts it, "how long the long-run is going to be". For, as Keynes said somewhat whimsically, "in the long-run we are all dead. And in the world of the dead there is no crisis, economic or any other, it is only the curse of the living".

I do not intend my foregoing remarks to be in the nature of a dissertation on socio-economic theory of one kind or another. I have only tried to encapsulate some of the things that I have observed myself. If my remarks are of some relevance to the deliberations in this seminar, I shall feel pleased and gratified.

With these few remarks, I have great pleasure in inaugurating this seminar on 'Liberalization, Ethnic Identity and Economic Development in India's North-East'. I wish your deliberations all success.

Contents

PART TWO

LIBERALIZATION : ECONOMIC IMPLICATIONS FOR INDIA'S NORTH-EAST

PART THREE

LIBERALIZATION : IMPLICATIONS FOR IDENTITY AND ETHNIC SITUATIONS IN INDIA'S NORTH-EAST

PART FOUR

LIBERALIZATION : IMPLICATIONS FOR BORDER TRADE

PART FIVE

LIBERALIZATION : REFLECTIONS ON NORTH-EASTERN SITUATION

CONTRIBUTORS

M.M. AGRAWAL is Professor of Philosophy, North-Eastern Hill University, Shillong.

DEBASISH BHATTACHARJEE is Reader in Political Science, Assam University, Silchar.

P.R. BATTACHARJEE is Professor of Economics, Assam University, Silchar.

RAKHEE BHATTACHARYA is Lecturer in Economics, Shillong College, Shillong.

DEBJYOTI BHATTACHARYYA is Assistant Commissioner, Central Excise, Shillong.

DEVADAS BHORALI is Professor of Commerce, Guwahati University, Guwahati.

B.S. BUTOLA is Reader in Geography, North-Eastern Hill University, Shillong.

ABHIJIT CHOUDHURY is Lecturer in History, St. Edmund's College, Shillong.

R.K. CHOUDHURY is Professor of Public Finance and Fiscal Policy, Guwahati University, Guwahati.

S.C. DANIEL is Reader in Philosophy, North-Eastern Hill University, Shillong.

GURUDAS DAS is Lecturer in Economics, St. Anthony's College, Shillong.

SAMIR KUMAR DAS is Reader in Political Science, Calcutta University, Calcutta.

B. DATTA RAY is Secretary, North-East India Council for Social Science Research, Shillong.

RANJIT DE is Senior Auditor, Office of the Accountant General, Shillong.

L.S. GASSAH is Professor of Political Science, North-Eastern Hill University, Shillong.

M.M. JACOB is Governor of Meghalaya, Shillong.

M.N. KARNA is Professor of Sociology, North-Eastern Hill University, Shillong.

MAHESH LALWANI is Professor of Economics, North-Eastern Hill University, Shillong.

APURBANANDA MAZUMDAR is Reader in Commerce, Assam University, Silchar.

P.M. PASSAH is Professor of Economics, North-Eastern Hill University, Shillong.

SADHAN SENGUPTA is Senior Anthropologist, Anthropological Survey of India, Shillong.

SUJIT SIKIDAR is Professor of Commerce, Guwahati University, Guwahati.

H. SRIKANTH is Lecturer in Political Science, Assam University, Silchar.

C. JOSHUA THOMAS is Deputy Director, Indian Council of Social Science Research, North Eatern Regional Centre, Shillong.

R.L. WALLI is Professor of Political Science, North Eastern Hill University, Shillong.

PART ONE

CONTEXTUALISING GLOBALIZATION FOR INDIA'S NORTH-EAST

Chapter 1

NEW WORLD DISORDER AND INDIA'S MARKET DRIVEN REFORMS

—R.L. Walli

Those who take the meat from the table
Teach contentment
Those for whom the taxes are destined
Demand sacrifice
Those who eat to their full speak to the hungry
Of wonderful times to come
Those who lead the country into abyss
Call ruling too difficult
For ordinary folk.

—Bertolt Bretch

India's economic liberalization has to be seen against the background of the sweeping changes underway at the international level. The saracens of free market and profiteering had commenced their assault on the third world much before the conclusion of the Uruguay round of the GATT negotiations which created the new international trade regime under the World Trade Organization (WTO)*, the successor to GATT.

---

* Agriculture and intellectual property rights have been brought under the ambit of the new international trading arrangements. Product and process patents make it more stringent. Bio-piracy (Genetic imperialism), however, has been given a free reign. It may be recalled that nineteenth century U.S. uninhibitedly pirated the inventions of Britain, the then technological leader.

Beginning with 1980s (Poland, 1980) more than 70 countries have been compelled to go in for the structural adjustment programme (SAP) under the now infamous conditionalities of the International Monetary Fund in conjunction with the World Bank. These global changes have been facilitated by the dismantling of the Soviet system and the eventual dissolution of the Soviet Union in December 1991, the on-going capitalist transformation in Russia, other former republics of the USSR, Eastern Europe, China and Vietnam. This has opened vast new areas to international capital.

I

The post-war II structure of the international system was essentially designed by the U.S. which had emerged from the II World War with its economic and military power not only intact but far more prosperous and powerful. At a time when the Soviet Union, Europe and Japan were reeling under colossal human and material destruction of the World War II, the U.S. emerged as the only post-war world power.[1] Its industry working all the three shifts a day and with near full employment, the U.S. GNP had skyrocketed from $91 billion to $166 billion. This was a historic opportunity for Washington and President Truman could talk about twentieth century being the "American Century".

The U.S. shaped the Bretton Woods institutions and the U.N. system. Bretton Woods Conference of July 1944 set up the International Monetary Fund (IMF) whose responsibility was to maintain a fixed exchange rate system with provisions for dealing with temporary balance of payments problems of member nations, and the International Bank for Reconstruction and Development (IBRD), popularly known as World Bank (WB) to provide long term capital requirements. The two international agencies were set for the first time followed by a third, the General Agreement on Tariffs and Trade (GATT) which was established in 1948 to ensure "a freer and fairer trade" through reduction of tariffs and diminution of other barriers though enough exceptions were made, for instance, to keep agriculture entirely out of its purview at the instance of U.S. and European countries. The acceptance of the U.S.

Dollar as the international reserve currency was predicated on Dollar-gold convertibility which was snapped by President Nixon in August 1971 in the wake of pressure on Dollar caused by U.S. prosecution of the war in Vietnam. The differential weightage of the voting power in the IMF, WB and the veto power in the U.N. Security Council reflected the cruel reality that decision making power corresponds not to legal equality but to the actual distribution of power in the world.

Apart from the "Containment" policy towards the Soviet Union, the U.S. went in for the economic revival of Western Europe through the infusion of massive economic assistance of $13 billion (about $90 billion at the current rate) during five years from June 1947—something the U.S. has been reluctant to do for the impoverished World. Japanese revival was done under the Dodge Plan. The U.S. administration in Japan under Gen. McArthur began with radical land reforms—something India has failed to do during half century of its post-colonial existence.

The strategic Cold War compulsions of the U.S. persuaded it to help not only Japan but also South Korea and Taiwan to emerge as economic success stories. In the latter two countries, *inter-alia,* literacy was accorded a high priority (in contrast to India where the promise of universal compulsory primary education within ten years still remains a pipe dream and 100+ million bonded child labour force is a standing mockery of the various meaningful freedoms so thoughtfully consigned to the dustbin of non-enforceable section of Directive Principles of the Indian Constitution).

A policy mix of a high degree of State intervention, protectionism, and easy access for exports to U.S. and some other Northern markets ensured the speedy economic recovery of Japan, Taiwan and South Korea. This set of policies is diametrically opposite to the current IMF-WB policies in the Third World.

For nearly two decades till the end of the 1960s, the U.S. and other metropolitan States registered such a boom period that some ideologies of Capitalism (Daniel Bell *et al.*) came out with the short lived "end of Ideology" thesis in early late fifties and early sixties.[2] But the inherent logic of Capitalist business cycle—its booms and busts—made its presence felt by the beginning of 1970s. The OPEC's oil price hike and drought in some parts of the world aggravated it.

By the beginning of the decade of 90's, three develop-ments had taken place which have triggered an epochal change in the global politics and economy—the Soviet collapse, new technology and Multinational Corporations (MNC) as ever more powerful players.

The collapse of the Soviet Union has changed the global correlation of forces in economics, political and military spheres. The Third World states have lost the space available to them in the bi-polar world of the Soviet days. Non-Aligned Movement (NAM), the demand for a New International Economic Order (NIEO) and the Group of 77 (G-77) have withered away with the U.S. as the only super power. Incidentally, the strategic shift in India's negotiating position between 1987-89 at the Uruguay round of negotiations is explained by this development.

Among the member States of the OECD and its core group, the G-7, the United States is the lone hegemon in the post-Soviet era.* This was made amply clear to the third world through the

---

* The imperial clout of the lone hegemony is evident from the fact that though practically whole world supported Bhutros Ghali for a second term as U.N. Secretary General, Washington not only blocked the move but had its own choice (Kofi Anan) appointed as his successor. The U.S. is dictating the reform plan for the U.N. including the making of Security Council broad based. The White House bypassed the U.N. in embattled Bosnia via NATO. It violated the U.N. arms embargo by allowing Saudi Arabia, Turkey, Iran, Pakistan, Malaysia and Brunie to supply arms to Bosnian Muslims. The War Crimes Tribunal at the Hague is packed up with U.S. selected judges, funded by Saudi Arabia, and witnesses are coached by Bosnian Muslim secret police. The U.S. overruled its European allies in deciding that presently only Poland, Hungary and Czech Republic be admitted to NATO for the present. It played the central role in designing the WTO and it is deciding the agenda for international relations.

Gulf War. The avoidable* Gulf War demonstrated that the U.S. had lived down the "Vietnam War Syndrome", that it could wreck destruction on the third world through hi-tech warfare**

---

* As per official information leaked to a section of the national press, the CIA had advance information about Iraqi attack on Kuwait. But instead of taking steps to pre-empt it, a U.S. diplomat in Baghdad, April Price, encouraged Saddam Hussain to walk into the trap by assuring him that the U.S. would keep out of Iraq-Kuwait dispute. The U.S. wanted an opportunity to destroy Iraqi power base, the military component of which was, in the first place, built up through Western supplies when the West used Iraq against post-monarchial Iran during the 1980-88 first Gulf (Iran-Iraq) War. Washington does not want democratisation of Iraq because that will have "adverse" political demonstration effect on the populations of its medieval feudal aristocratic regimes in the Persian gulf whose oil wealth it is vastly profiting from. It merely desires the replacement of Saddam Hussain by a pro-U.S. dictator to use Iraq as a counterpose to Iran. While exploiting Kurdish political aspirations, the U.S. is against the grant of self determination to the Kurds in the North and the Shia population in Southern Iraq.

** The International War Crimes Tribunal met in New York in 1991 to investigate nineteen separate charges against President Bush, civilian and military government officials, of crimes against peace and humanity in violation of U.N. Charter, the 1949 Geneva Convention and other International Laws. In a unanimous verdict on 22nd Feb 1992, the 22 member tribunal found the U.S. guilty of all the nineteen charges. The U.S. media blacked out this news. Ramsay Clark, a former U.S. Attorney General was also associated with this multinational probe. Amnesty International's silence on the U.S. crimes and Human Rights violation in Iraq is deafening. It may be recalled that the U.S. refused to accept the jurisdiction of the ICJ which held it guilty of subversion against the Sandinesta Government of Nicaragua.

Beginning with the mid night of 16th January 1991, the U.S. led coalition had already bombed Iraq back into pre-industrial age. Yet the war with its savage bombing was continued for 42 days. Ninety three percent of the 88,000 tons of bombs (equivalent to seven Hiroshima type bombs) through 1,10,000 air sorties were directed at civilian targets killing one lakh to

(Cont...)

without U.S. casualties, and that it had hijacked the U.N.*

Further, it is pre-mature to invoke Paul Kennedy (*Rise and Fall of Great Powers*) and dismiss the U.S. as a declining power in relation to European Union and Japan. It is outspending the rest of the world in basic R&D, has made up for the lag in electronics, and it is leading in the development of new ("Frontier") technologies. It is likely to remain the sole super power in the years to come as the world moves into the third millennia. Yet Francis Fukuyama's (a former State Deptt. and RAND Corporation official) celebration of the collapse of the Socialist world as the "End of History" is as slippery as the earlier "End of ideology" thesis. Fukuyama believes that the victory of capitalism is irreversible. Capitalism and competitive electoral system (Political Democracy) was the end stage of history.[3] "Minor" conflicts over such issues as ethnicity, identity, trade, or market share would go on but the great conflict would no longer be capitalism versus alternative. However, this is an unhistorical view. Issues like the struggle between the stranglehold of exploitative class power and its victims, between predatory market economy fundamentalism and survival rights of people, and between alternative visions of a wider social organization will continue in the long historical struggle for building a humane society.

(Cont...) two and half lakh people. Destruction of such civilian targets as power plants disabling water treatment plants (which caused outbreak of epidemics of gastro-intestinal diseases), hospitals, fertilizer factories, poultry farms is sought to be masked as "collateral damage." The crippling economic blockade has cost the lives of half a million Iraqi children and one lakh others, thereby punishing the ruled and not the ruler.

* Sanctions against Iraq are in violation of the U.N. charter which authorises collective security action for restoration of status quo ante, *i.e.*, vacating of aggression and not for imposition of debilitating sanctions of reparations reminiscent of those imposed on Weimer Germany under the Versailles Treaty.

For Strategic implications of the U.S. intervention in the Gulf War, see *Pax Americana* (Review of this month), *Monthly Review (New York)*, pp. 1-24.

The new technology is highly capital intensive. Though highly productive, the "job liquidation" technology gives "jobless growth". The leading sectors of capitalist economy like software and bio-technology require far fewer workers. The retrenchment of hundreds of thousands of workers ("Down-sizing"/"Re-structuring") all over the first world is taking place in the wake of employment of these "state of art" technologies. In many other cases, this firing of white and blue collar workers on mass scale is taking place in spite of high profits, *e.g.*, Goldman Sachs, a private mega-corporation rewarded each of its partners with $5 million bonus while freezing the salaries of the workers, and laying off many of them. While announcing the phased redundancy of over 30,000 workers, the ATT has given hefty salary increases to its top brass.

In U.S., millions of new jobs have been generated but these jobs are mostly low wage, insecure, or part-time jobs (euphemistically called "carry home work", "flexible working hours") like "work on call with McDonald's chain". Workers are hired on part-time basis to do full time job as was highlighted by the two week (August, 1997) strike of the United Parcel Service Workers. 75 percent of the company's two hundred thousand workforce is engaged as part-timers working 40 hour week shifts without leave, pension, and welfare benefits. Over 20 percent of the U.S. workers are part-timers. Labour movement is dampened with only one in eight workers is a member of any union. President Clinton's proposed fast track authority for NAFTA will inflict another blow on to labour. All this is happening at a time of zooming corporate profits and soaring payments to their Chief Executive officers. The real wages give them a standard of living which existed 10 to 15 years ago. More than one third of the work force has wages lower than the unemployment dole in Germany. In France, Germany, Italy and some other developed states "restructuring" is "shedding" thousands of jobs. The projected merger of two steel giants Krupps and Thysen, in Germany will result in retrenchment of 9000 workers. The withdrawal of state subsidy to coal mines had to be put in abeyance in the face of workers' protest. The French automobile giant Renault, is closing down some of its plants and shifting a few to low wage areas like Spain. Unemployment in Germany is largest (4.6 million) since the economic depression. Over 18 million are unemployed in the European Union.

In the developed world, there is a social welfare system for the unemployed to fall back upon. In the underdeveloped world, the jobless and the working poor do not have the advantage of such a social safety net. The use of the highly capital intensive technologies in the third world, already reeling under high levels of unemployment, will be a recipe for disaster.

Although, Multinational Corporations (MNCs) have been around for sometimes, they have emerged as powerful non-state actors on the international scene by the beginning of the 1990s. They are the key players in the international economic integration. They are the main instrument of on-going globalization as also its principal beneficiaries. According to United Nations Conference on Trade an Development's (UNCTAD) World Investment Report,1995, there are 40,000 MNCs operating worldwide through a global network of 250000 affiliates. But, it is the MNCs from the North which dominate. The revenue of the top 15 corporations exceeds the combined GDP of 120 under-developed countries (UDCs). Again, of the top 25 MNCs, 11 are from the U.S., 8 from Western Europe, and 6 from Japan. Further 100 largest are all from the developed world. Even a tiny state like Switzerland has eight. 172 of the 200 mega corporations are from the first world. This is reflective of the extent of inequality in the world. The top 200 corporations doubled their revenue from $3 trillion to $5.9 trillion from 1982 to 1992 when the world economy was in a down turn.

The ever expanding sweep of their activities spans transnationalization of manufacturing, capital movements, technology transfers, movement of goods and services, increasing penetration of agricultural sector, and lastly, fusion of transnational bank (Finance capital) and MNCs (industrial capital). 80% of patents in the world are concentrated in the MNCs which further enhances their monopoly power and profits. The collapse of the pre-conference Southern solidarity at 1996 WTO Conference at Singapore in opposing the Northern move on investment liberalization (Trade Related Investment Measures-TRIM) will further enhance the colossal power of MNCs. One third of the world trade ($1.6 trillion) is intra-firm (between the parent firm and its affiliates) and another one third is inter-firm, *i.e.*, between transnational companies. Thus, two thirds of world trade is done at rigged prices and not as per free market and free trade principles.

Third world states have weak safeguards and weak mechanism against the malpractices of transnationals. Even these are over-looked by the host governments in their scramble for attracting ("improving investment climate") foreign investments. In their single minded pursuit of quick and maximum profits, the transnationals find it easy to target the UDCs as victims of their notorious practice of transfer pricing which deprives the host state of foreign earnings and tax revenue. Just before it was abolished under U.S. pressure, the U.N. Centre for Transnational Corporations (UNCTNC), in its last analytical reports for an un-named African country, shows how the MNC outflows from the country far exceeding its national debt.[4] A U.S. Congressional Committee gave the indication of the extent of damage done by 36 MNCs which used transfer pricing to avoid paying $100 billion in taxes during 1980s.[5]

Backed by the powerful Developed Countries (DC's), especially the G-7, in the imperialist fashion, the mega corporations have stalled all attempts, within and outside the U.N., to hammer out a mandatory code of conduct for the transnationals. The rules adopted by the U.N. General Assembly in 1980 to prevent, *inter-alia*, the practice of transfer pricing proved to be a non-starter for want of credible enforcement mechanism. They thwarted renewed attempts on this score at the 1996 WTO Conference at Singapore. No wonder, the MNCs have been given the sobriquet of "New Sovereigns"[6] and have been described as the unstoppable totalitarian monsters of corporate capitalism.[7] The environment protection laws and safety regulations in the DC's are stringent but in the UDCs these are practically non-existent. The world's worst industrial disaster of Union Carbide at

Bhopal in December 1984 is a grim reminder of this. Nearly 10,000 people were killed at the time of the occurance and in its immediate aftermath, apart from hundreds of thousands having been affected subsequently.

II

The surplus petro dollars generated by the hike in oil prices in early 70s were funneled into international, largely Western Banks, which, in turn, re-cycled these as loans to third world countries from mid seventies. This sparked off the debt crisis of 1980s (begining with Poland in 1980 and Mexico in 1982) which the hangmen of the G-7, the IMF and the WB, used to restructure the indebted economies to subserve the economies of the North.

IMF loans are tough with harsh conditions which are painful. The IMF dictated reforms (conditionalities) together with those of the WB impose a heavy burden on the vast majority of the people in the unorganized sector. It involves a drive towards the establishment of a minimalist state. These reforms include reduction in the role of the state (deregulation, liberalization, reliance on market), drastic cut back in expenditure (including "reform of the social sector"), devaluation of currency, etc. The reforms encompass giving free play to market forces involves across the board increase in the prices of goods and services. Budgetary austerity with heavy cuts in government's social spending further restricts access to basic social services such as health, education, public transportation, water supply, electricity in the name of user-financing, or, privatization; declining wages and compression of incomes, spiraling food prices and mounting unemployment aggravated by job losses due to privatization of state enterprises, tax cuts for the rich which worsens income distribution. There is an increase in the casualisation of work. Employers employ part time workers to do full time job. Most of the new jobs come up in the service sector, particularly, in the tourism and hotel industries which, in the third world, thrive on large scale child prostitution as in Thailand, Cambodia, South Asia and some South American states. Asia is reported to have one million child prostitutes. Service sector jobs tend to be low wage and part time and the loss of public sector jobs are not matched qualitatively and quantitatively, by job creation in private sector. There is a tendency towards internationalization ("Dollarisation") of the prices of goods and services.

Thus cheap labour (with depressed and declining real wages) is the main input in the third world exports in a cut throat race to stay competitive with exports targeted at mostly the same OECD markets. The MNCs playing off one low wage island against another by threatening to shift to other low wage countries, thus further accentuating domestic and international inequalities. Actually, these states have no control over bulk of their import-export trade because of "transfer pricing" by the MNCs. Of course, the MNCs aim at capturing the internal market albait narrow of a large country like India.

Liberalization-Globalization gives priority to export markets and ignores internal markets. Further, in the name of promoting agricultural exports, agri-business diverts best land for exports to the detriment of domestic consumers who are hit hard by the price rise of staple foods. This is what happened in sub-Saharan Africa since early 1980s though it did not make sense that thousands of hectares of best land in Ghana, Senegal, Mali, Chad and Central African states continued to stay tied to export related production of cocoa, cotton, and groundnuts fetching ever declining prices while millions of Africans suffer food deprivation.

What is the track record of these reforms in the under developed world? The East Asian Tiger economies were being flaunted as economic success stories.* However, these

* The post-cold War problems of South Korean economy are underlined by the 1996 Christmas eve draconian anti-labour legislation which was pushed through in Parliament in just a few minutes time with opposition boycotting. The legislation deprives workers of job security, social security benefits and other rights. However, this legislation had to be put on hold in the face of workers strike and compulsions of OECD membership. The slow down in the economy and the $6 billion Hambo Steel Company scandal are further signs of this. Double digit growth has declined to single digit, and export of electronics (dependent on imported technology) has fallen. Even otherwise, the "tiger" economies contribute no more than 3 percent of world's GDP and are confronted with economic downturn.

"dragons" under authoritarian regimes, pursued economic policies which are strikingly opposite to those being imposed on indebted countries by the IMF and the WB. The economic growth of these countries was characterized by land reforms, high spending on elementary education, protectionism, state intervention, and pivotal concessions (including market access) given by the U.S. out of Cold War compulsions.

Mexico is a prototype of third world countries. Fifty percent Mexicans are poor today compared to thirty percent 15 years ago when the reform process began. Distance between the rich and the poor is growing. Unequal division of spoils is paralleled by regions left behind and regions which have prospered. Today, Mexico has 22 billionaires against only three a few years ago. The Gini Coefficient (which measures income inequality) in Mexico increased from 0.43 in 1984, *i.e.*, before IMF-WB reforms, to 0.48 in 1992. It symbolizes the global economic crisis. The spurious U.S. projection of Mexico as the ideal reform country (from the time of its debt crisis of 1982)

(Cont...)

By November 1997, the South Korean economic crisis had spinned out of control thereby forcing the world's eleventh largest economy to seek IMF bail out to escape bankruptcy. At the 18th nation APEC summit at Vancouver, the US secretary of state, Medelene Albright, voiced apprehension that the East Asian economic miracle may turn into an Asian melt down with knock on effect on global economy. While the US and other developed countries want to stem the tide of the crisis from overwhelming the East Asian economies (Thailand and Indonesia have already sought IMF rescue in the wake of crisis which has been building up since July 1977), they insist that even bilateral loans will be given with the usual tough IMF conditions.

One third of the US exports go to Asia. Washington is fearful that the ailing East Asian economies will not only affect its exports to Asia but may also flood the US market with still cheaper exports from that region.

The gut issue is that most of the 3 billion Asians have no spending power. It is a case of over investment, over capacity, and limited retail market. South Korea has been producing more micro-chips, videao recorders, automobiles, etc. than can be absorbed by the world market, *i.e.*, a case of over production and under consumption. It is more a case of "zero sum game" than a "win-win" situation is global trade.

and as a role model for rest of the south, was ripped open by the December 1994 near collapse of the Mexican economy when the Peso nose dived losing 35 percent against the U.S. dollar. Mexico had proclaimed itself to have graduated out of the third world into the first world and had been admitted to the OECD. But the Zapatista rebellion close on the heels of the signing of the North American Free Trade Agreement (NAFTA) reminded the world of the continued impoverishment of the Mayan Indians in the southern state of Chiapos and the continued electoral fraud through which the ruling Institutional Revolutionary Party (PRI) had hijacked power for the past 68 years. Former Mexican President, Carlos Salinas, whom Washington had hailed as the wizard of the Mexican "economic miracle" and had supported his candidature for the prestigious post of the Secretary General of the newly created WTO, has fled to the U.S.*

Mexican economic collapse would have discredited first world's sale of free market as something positive for the south, created a "Chernobyl" in the international financial markets, and sent shock waves across the world. President Clinton, bypassing the Congress, extended to Mexico a $20 billion loan out of economic stabilization fund and the IMF decided in a record time of just a few hours on its biggest ever loan to Mexico. This bail out also rescued foreign investment and foreign creditors. But even the U.S. Congressional critics say that the day of reckoning has only been postponed and will again haunt and explode in the face of Washington.

In the ex-(bureaucratic) socialist states, people have lost the security of jobs and full employment, paid holidays, and social wages like free health care, education, subsidized housing albeit with a consumer technological base which was lagging behind that of the West. The leadership (Gorbachev) induced dismantling of Socialist economy ("perestroika") in the USSR and Yeltsin's dismemberment of the Soviet Union**

---

* Salinas is reported to have pocketed $300 million through under priced sale of state assets under privatization programme, and parked the loot in Swiss Banks.

** In a referendum held in 12 out of 15 republics in March 1991, an overwhelming majority voted for retention of the Soviet Union. However, three leaders—Yeltsin of Russia, Kravchuk of Ukraine and Saskovich of Belarus—decided to dissolve the Soviet Union in December 1991.

appropriately christened as the "Great Criminal Revolution" by a post-Soviet author—has brought about a precipitous fall in the living standards of the anti-commonist population. Mounting unemployment with millions of employees not getting paid for months on end, including miners and sections of the army, high inflation, destruction of basic social services such as health, education, low cost housing. Hunger, deprivation (in the face of abundant availability of imported but unaffordable consumer goods), and rising infant mortality rates, have stalked the land. Avoidable diseases unknown in the Soviet era, have reappeared on a large scale because of malnutrition and decaying public health care with declining population, a ten year decrease in male longevity, and increasing suicide rate. Corruption is massive and endemic. The only powerful and fast growing "industry" is the mafia—including the old nomenklatura and of which the proliferating juvenile criminal gangs are a part—in the on-going "third worldisation" of the former super power.

The outcome of economic liberalization in the third world has been grim. The economic growth achieved remains confined to the elites and the top docile of the middle class. Though quality of utilities like telephone and electricity services improves, majority cannot afford access to these. The poor majority loses out in the "free" market with no share and stake in the economic growth. The structural adjustment programme (SAP) results in further mounting debts, declining terms of trade and high social cost which are very painful for the masses. This leads to social unrest and political explosion which invites state repression and "state terrorism" as happened in Peru under Alberto Fujimori, Tunis in January 1984, Bolivia in August 1985, Caracus in February 1989 when 2000 demonstrators were gunned down by the government, and Nigeria in May 1989. Thus these economic reforms are subversive of democracy and human rights.

No wonder, IMF's own study of the impact of its policies in the third world is a damning indictment of their counter productive nature :

> *Although there have been a number of studies on the subject over the past decade, one cannot say with certainty whether programmes have "worked" or not... on the basis of existing studies one certainly cannot say whether the adoption of*

> *programmes supported by the fund led to an improvement in inflation and growth performance. In fact, it is often found that programmes are associated with a rise in inflation and a fall in the growth rate.*[8]

Commenting on the socially explosive nature of IMF conditionalities, Sally Shelton, a former U.S. ambassador to the Caribbeans, observes :

> *This years' crisis will develop because, not in spite of, the conclusion of IMF agreements by the major debtor countries; because, not in spite of, the difficult transition to democracy in several Latin American Countries. The dilemma is how to reconcile the stiff austerity programmes required by the IMF with rising popular demands for relief from negative economic growth and wide spread distress. The austerity programmes have had high social costs: double digit unemployment, reduced public spending and an absolute decline in per capita income in countries with virtually no social safety net. The harsh adjustments required by the IMF and foreign bankers have hit all social classes and called into question the ability of even the new democratic regimes to avoid pressure for extremist solutions.*[9]

The chasm of global inequality is getting widened. In 1800, the share of world's poor was 44 percent. Today, this has slumped to one fifth. According to the 1997 Human Development Report, of the $23 trillion global GDP in 1993, $18 trillion was in the industrialized countries. Only $5 trillion was in the developing countries with 80 percent of world's population. According to the report, global growth in income has spread quite unequally during the past 30 years and this inequality is deepening . Between 1960 and 1991, the share of the richest 20 percent has gone up from 70 percent of world's income to 85 percent while that of the poorest fell from 2.3 percent to 1.4 percent. The ratio of the shares of the affluent and the poorest soared from 30:1 to 61:1. The income share of all but the richest quartile fell so that by 1991, 85 percent of the global population received only 15 percent of income. Currently, the net worth of 358 richest people (Dollar Billionaires) equals the combined income of 45 percent of the world's population of 2.3 billion people. The inequality between states are super-imposed on gross inequalities within states. The report notes that international or national increase in income inequalities is a major constraint to sustaining both economic growth and human development. According to the UNDP HDI report of 1991, 20 percent of population in the UDCs consume 60 percent of the national income and at least well over 100 million live below the poverty line in the first world. Globally top 20 percent earns 70 times that of bottom 20 percent of population.

Paradoxically, it is the impoverished population of the periphery who are financing the affluence of the people of the north. The third world is the net exporter of capital to the first world, *e.g.*, between 1984 and 1988, there has been a net economic reverse out flow of $41 billions per annum on account of debt related payments from the indebted south to the industrialized north.[10] This excludes the loss to the former on account of deteriorating terms of trade, "transfer pricing" and other back door methods of repatriation of capital by foreign investors. The above said annual debt related payments is equivalent, in real terms, to two Marshall plans. There was negative lending by the IMF between 1986-88.

From early 80s, Africa has been net exporter of capital to the West. Since 1984, African states have paid nearly $150 billion to creditors abroad and the IMF itself has been a major recipient of this perverse flow. In 1993, African governments have paid $300 million more to the IMF than they received from it. The nutritional, health, and educational needs of impoverished Africans are being ignored to pave the way for debt repayment. In 1995, for example, Uganda spent $2.60 per person on health but $30 per person on debt service.[11]

The first world is also squeezing the UDCs by providing safe heaven to fugitive capital accumulated by third world elites through rampant corruption, tax evasion, and infraction of currency laws. The southern elites can keep the loot in numbered accounts as anonymous depositors.

According to the estimates of some Swiss NGOs, one fourth of this fugitive capital, amounting to $160 billion, is in Swiss banks. The rest is stashed away in Panama, Cayman Islands, Luxemburg, and Bahamas. In case of some third world states, the external debt approximates the money parked abroad by their elites. India's foreign debt of $90 billion is slightly less than the IMF estimate of capital flight of atleast

$100 billion from India. This unofficial estimate by the IMF has been substantiated by findings of a research study by three U.S. economists. They have concluded that capital flight from India to the U.S. alone in 1994 and 1995 ranged from a maximum of $11,300 million to a minimum of $3875 million due to over-invoicing and under-invoicing of imports from and exports to that country respectively. India's trade with the U.S. was $7598 million in 1994 and $9032 million in 1995. Considering that U.S. accounts for 20 percent of India's foreign trade and with other hard currency areas accounting for another 35 percent, this implies that India's trade gap is artificially deficit. Had India's exports earnings been correctly reported, India would be enjoying trade surplus and not a trade deficit.[12] As per another earlier (1990) conservative estimate, the outgo of fugitive capital from India between 1971-86 was of the order of $21.2 to $28.6 billion.[13] The recently (mid 1997) ousted dictator of impoverished but mineral rich Zaire (Democratic Republic of Congo), Mobutu (who was installed in power by the United States Central Intelligence Agency after the assassination of Patrice Lumumba and whose 30 year authoritarian and corrupt rule was backed by Washington and other Western powers)[14] is said to have $5 to $6 billion in foreign banks which is higher than that country's foreign debt. Similarly, Marcos family's $5 billion cash kept abroad equals the foreign debt of the Philippines. Argentina and some other states fall in this category. This practice of the Western Banks to play host to the third world's fugitive capital is nothing short of subversion of third world economies. This problem is not being addressed by the north, whereas the problem of drug use inside the U.S. has been imposed as a global problem on the world and all countries are being pressurised to stop its cultivation and also its being carried through their territories. Interestingly, Washington is reluctant to combat the demand for drugs within the U.S. for that will involve facing uncomfortable issues of poverty, racial discrimination and alienation. Further, the U.S. forced Switzerland to disclose details of drug money being laundered through its banks.

III

This reverse capital flow represents the transfer of real resources from the south, which are often stagnant and shrinking economies, to the developed countries through the painful readjustment and other policies of the north. Today, overall the third world is said to be losing $500 billion to the first world. This is a continuation of the historical process of the last five centuries of imperialism ("expansion of the West"* as some westerners prefer to call it) which began with the discovery (conquest) of America by Columbus in 1492.** As Samir Amin observes :

> *If I were to pick a date to mark the modern world, I should choose 1492, the year in which Europeans began their conquest of the planet-military, economic, political and in certain sense, ethnic. But the world in question is also the world of capitalism, a new social and economic system qualitatively different from all previous systems in Europe and elsewhere.*[15]

This 500 years old process has undergone change in form but not in substance, namely, the extraction of surplus from the south. This process spans the settler colonialism in America involving the slaughter, rather, the outright genocide of American (Red) Indians and decimation of some of the superior civilizations like that of the Mayans and the Incas, plunder of gold and silver, piracy*** and loss in the guise of trade—all these constituted an essential part of the primitive accumulation in capital formation—down through colonialism to the present day market colonialism.

> *The discovery of gold and silver in America, the extirpation, enslavement and entombment in mines of the aboriginal*

---

* See, for example, **L. Blusse, H.L. Wasseling, G.D. Winius, eds.,** *History of underdevelopment: Essays on European Expansion in Asia and Africa* **(Leiden: Leiden University Press, 1980).**

** A few years ago, the fifth anniversary of the "discovery" of America was celebrated in the U.S. and other places where Columbus was hailed as a "courageous discoverer." Significantly, however, when the last Duvalior fled Haiti in 1980s, crowds pulled down the statue of Columbus and threw it into sea after denouncing him as a Satan perpetrated barbaric atrocities on their ancestors.

*** In 1761, Henry Morgan, who pirated Spanish colonies in Latin America, was appointed Governor of Jamaica by the British. This was in contravention to their public assurances to try him for piracy.

> *population, the beginning of the conquest and looting of the East Indies, the turning of Africa into a warren for the commercial hunting of black-skins signalized the raw dawn of the era of capitalist production.*[16]

Thus the glib talk about globalization and global village is a thinly veiled pillage of the underdeveloped countries under the leadership of the U.S. which in the post-Soviet world with impunity. Today, globally mobile capital is driving down the wages and intensely exploiting natural resources in its push for accumulation and expansion. Economic policies cannot be seen in isolation for it involves issues of conflict and power. The current changes are a re-definition of the place of the third world in the restructuring of the international economy. The world economy can no longer be understood merely through the terms of trade. There is a discernible trend towards location of non-material industries based on services and high technology communication in the north and the material production in the south. Income from the material production in the third world will be (re)invested in the non-material industries in the first world. It is not productivity, important as it is, but appropriation of the income from the material production in the south by the north through commodity pricing and patents and royalty charges. Trade Related Intellectual Property Rights (TRIPS) under the WTO will have sweeping and universal application. Technology (like internet, information super highway and the like) is going to further divide the super class (those who control it and who have access to it) from the under class.

In the absence of level playing field, the merger of the fragile economies with those of the first world leads to the former giving up nation's protectionism without their being able to compete. Globalization will deprive the UDCs of the capacity to manage their economies autonomously. It makes these economies increasingly vulnerable to external shocks. Loss of control over transnational movement of capital will exacerbate this. The trading in Western currency markets with an astronomical $1.4 trillion being switched across currency frontiers daily—for speculative reasons in "Las Vagas" style operations—threatens even the Exchange Rate Mechanism (ERM) of the European Union, necessitating occasional withdrawal from it by members as happened to Britain a few years ago. Its impact on southern economies will be destabilizing after they go in for free convertibility of their currencies in a world of border—less money markets where democratic institutions and democratic controls have been undermined. The August-Sept. 1997 turbulence in the Southeast Asian currency markets, engineered by the U.S. backed Hungarian born billionaire George Soros, was partly meant to punish the ASEAN for granting membership to Burma. The Malaysian Prime Minister, Mahater Mohamed, helplessly lamented that their decades of economic progress was grappling with economic war by currency speculators. The intervention by the Sultan of Brunei (world's richest man) did not help much. The basic fact remains that if a country accepts market mechanism for its upper-siders it has to live with its downside as well.

Ironically, globalization is based on water tight compartmentation between the national labour markets to, *inter-alia,* ensure competing low wages are pitted against each other for high corporate profitability. While international standards are being hammered out to protect the interests of the MNCs, all attempts to have an enforceable code of conduct for the latter have been thwarted by the north. There are increasing attacks on non-white workers in countries like Germany, France, Italy and some other western states. Germany is welcoming people of German extraction from the former socialist states but finds the presence of a lesser number of workers economically burdensome.

Globalization will catalyse and the dual process of homogenisation of the third world markets (and cultures) along with the fragmentation* of these countries. It will create unified and largely homogenized markets as, for example, by changing foods consumptions habits of communities which depend on local food resources, thereby destroying their food security. This is done through high pressure advertisements and activities of MNCs like sale promotion of baby food in violation of norms prescribed by the World Health Organiza–

* For a U.S. view of this, see **Leslie H. Gelb,** *"Quelling the Teacup Wars: The New World's Constant Challenge"*, **Foreign Affairs, Nov-Dec. 1994, pp. 2-6.** See also **Samuel P. Huntington,** *"The Clash of Civilisations and the Remaking of the World"* **(New Delhi: Viking, 1996).** Huntington believes that clash of civilizations will be the main conflict in future.

tion. But international economic integration will also promote the fragmentation of the countries in the periphery. The U.S. interest in ethnic and other conflicts and Pentagon's continued arms build-up (elusive "peace dividend") is part of U.S. post Cold War strategy for its domination of the south. The economic reforms will push the people further to the margins of the society. Poverty, unemployment, inequalities and unequal regional development will worsen. The UDCs are already fractured along multiple fault lines. The economic reforms will make them far too fractured and undergo implosion as is happening to former Yugoslavia and in many former republics of Soviet Union. In Italy, the 'Northern League" is clamouring for independent state in the developed northern part of Italy in order to get rid of the "deadweight" of the poor southern part of the country.

In the poor states, the backlash of the people who will take the hit of the reforms—growing unrest, protest, riots, and deprivation induced increase in crime rate—will be met with governmental repression. Even for the DCs. Paul Kennedy's prognosis is none too happy[17] as industries are relocated in low wage states and mounting (structural) unemployment because of continued corporate down sizing under pressure of competition. This may lead to the breakdown of the international trading system and trade conflicts. In some European democracies, post 1945 social compact will breakdown. Disillusioned population will swing to nationalism and fundamentalism. Extreme brands of political activities will rise in a bid for political control.

Thus "Globalization" is a smoke-screen for a world under the economic and political domination of the lone hegemon, the U.S., and also of other members of G-7. It seeks to camouflage the "Americanization of the world" and the fact that power is not de-centered but is much more concentrated today in the post cold war period than at any time in contemporary period.

The fundamental problem is that the development paradigm is inherently flawed as it is unsustainable both ecologically and in terms of its resource base. Western consumerism—unlimited production for un-ending consumption and rapid obsolescence—makes the very idea of the third world "catching up"* with the West self defeating. According to a 1992 World Watch Institute Study (*How Much is Enough: Consumerism and the Future of the Earth*) the post-1950 world has used as many resources as all pre-1950 generations put together. One fifth of humanity, mostly Northerners but also including the affluent minority of the peripherised South, indulge in consumerism which cannot be sustained by earth. With world's 5% population, the U.S. consumes about 40% of world's non-renewable resources which is why it is called the "waste economy". 15% of global population appropriates 80% of the resources. The existing development model is elitist and resource destructive and not people centered and resource regenerative.

Apart from the rapid depletion of non-renewable resources, this development model involves an unstoppable march towards ecological suicide through the destruction of life support systems.

The emission of green house gases will eventually cause flooding of low lying populated lands and islands. The chloro–fluro-carbon (CFC) are corroding earth's protective ozone layer, and toxic wastes are poisoning air, land, water and marine life. There has been no progress on Rio Earth Summit (1992) promise of cutting down green house gases, protecting tropical forests, and transferring eco-friendly technologies to the third world. North is keen on making profit on this score as TRIPS will make third world's access to such technologies

* Even otherwise, the thesis of 'catching up" with late capitalism is ahistorical. It ignores the differences in initial conditions in comparing today's UDCs with 18th and early 19th century Western states. Today's UDCs are not undeveloped but under-developed. Colonialism distorted their economic structures. When the West started development, the whole world was open to them. They had small populations, having shifted one fifth of their population (60 million) to America and Australia during 1860 to 1920. Colonialism gave them cheap raw materials and captive markets for selling manufactured goods. The West established international economic system which operates to their advantage and to the detriment of third world. For a detailed discussion, see **A.G. Frank,** *Latin America: Under-development or Revolution* **(New York, 1969).**

more difficult. With mere 1 percent of budget going to foreign aid, mostly to its strategic allies like Israel and Egypt, the U.S. is talking about its aid "weariness". Of course, the way Southern countries are organized, increased foreign aid will not reach their masses. Even the Rio plus 5 Conference (June, 1997) has failed. The U.S. refused to give any firm commitment on carbon gas emissions because powerful domestic political and industrial lobbies fear that drastic cut back in energy consumption will harm economy. The U.S. emits 20% green house gases.

The industrial world is trying to duck the issue by shifting to the third world such high pollution breeding plants such as Petro-chemicals and steel plants, and outright dumping of toxic wastes with the consent of self-serving third world elites. The WB is also used for this purpose. In a subsequently leaked memo to his superiors, the then Chief Economist of the World bank, Lawrence Summers, wrote ; "Between you and me should not the Bank be encouraging the migration of dirty industries to the LDCs on grounds that the LDCs are less polluted, life expectancy is low and infant mortality is high".[18] MNCs privatise profits (made in part by unsustainable exploitation of resources) and socialise the costs by passing on the burden of environmental destruction to the masses. The policy of "Rape and Leave" is best exemplified by export oriented shrimp farming in India's costal areas where the companies leave for new virgin sites after destroying the local eco-system.

Mega projects which are the hub of this development model annually displace 10 million people world wide. Even self-sufficient communities are driven away from livelihood on land to become poverty statistics in megalopolises. This overwhelmingly poor people ("Project Affected People") lose their ancestral dwellings and agricultural lands which has been the only source of subsistence for them for generations. In spite of promises of resettlement, these victims of development are often left to fend for themselves in a state of destitution as is happening in the case of Narmada project. Although such projects are sought to be justified in the name of development as an economic necessity, the beneficiaries are the elites—industrialists, rich farmers growing export crops, the well off urban dwellers—and vested interests like politicians, contractors, and suppliers involved in the project construction.

The development paradigm is thus anti-thetical to human welfare, environmentally destructive and unsustainable. However, the collapse of the bi-polar world has cleared the decks for the U.S. to roll the free market juggernaut over the third world in an uninhibited fashion.

The structural logic of capitalism—unemployment, intensive polarization between the top and the bottom of the social ladder, alienation and marginalisation of the underclass—is taken for granted as "natural" as are capitalist business cycles.* The post-depression Keynesian capitalist development has run out of steam.

The late capitalist societies are beset with intractable problem of growing unemployment which is compounded by determined steps to roll back the welfare state and workers rights which had been instituted in the first place after tortuous, bloody and costly struggles of workers stretching over decades. The U.S. is the only first war economy to have generated millions of jobs in the last few years but these jobs have severe limitations which have been described earlier. No wonder only one in seven U.S. workers is a member of a trade union. Unemployment benefits are being reduced and minimum wage regulations are being knocked out. This is happening at a time when the marginalisation of the minority of poor, blacks, Hispanics, and American Indians is increasing. Referring to the deprivation in many U.S. cities, Amartya Sen points out that survival chances in Harlem in New York are less than those in Bangladesh.[19] U.S. is a spectacle of liberalism in an illiberal state.

---

* There have been 40 recessions since the beginning of industrial revolution around 1800. Of these, four recessions have happened since the present economic crisis in mid 1960s. Between 1973 and 1983, almost entire first world experienced the worst recession in post-war II period. Then followed a seven year boom, trumpeted as a victory for Reagan and Thatcher, before the U.S., and U.K. slipped into a deep recession.

Reaganomics and Thatcherism swelled the numbers of their respective "card board" people, *i.e.*, homeless poor in the U.S. and Britain who sleep on streets in cardboard packing crates. According to President Clinton, 42 percent of people do not have access to health care in the U.S. Inequalities have intensified both in the U.S. and Britain. Ralph Nader of U.S. Green party says that one percent of population has wealth equal to bottom 90 percent of the population. According to Paris based OECD, bottom 10 percent of British population lost 50 percent of income while top 10 percent increased its by 60 percent as a result of Thatcherism during the 1980s. In France, Germany, Italy, and Belgium there have been public protests against cutbacks in social spending underway to qualify for the European Monetary Union through 3 percent deficit criterion by early 1998.

Historically, Adam Smith's invisible hand of the market was acceptable as long as the winners compensated the losers—the unemployed, the marginalised, the poor, the old. Their hardships were mitigated by measures such as unemployment allowance, old age pension, subsidized housing, health care, education. Thus a part of the social surplus is being used in late capitalist societies as a social safety. But this is not available in the third world and, even in the first world, it is sought to be rolled back.

The global Summit (4-11 March, 1995) in Copenhagen on social development and poverty eradication, full employment, and social integration drew a blank because of the lack of commitment of resources by both the developed and the developing world for realizing these goals. The first world and the ruling elites of the third world alike are unwilling to do anything substantive for eliminating deprivation and, thereby, ensuring social cohesion.

1.3 billion people out of world's 6 billion under privileged are so destitute as not to afford adequate food intake in a world where aggregate food production till a few years ago was 1 kg per capita per day.* Significantly, the U.S. opposed

* For a genesis of this aspect, see **Teressa Hayter,** *The Creation of World Poverty,* **(London: Pluto Press, 1981).**

right to food as a basic human right at the Nov.96 World Food Summit at Rome. 2 billion people use stiks and dung for their energy needs. 1 billion are without clean water while 1.7 billion are without sanitation. According to a World Bank report of August 1997, Asia alone has 900 million poor including those in the tiger economies of South Korea, Taiwan, and Singapore with yawning gap between rural-urban and skilled-unskilled people. Globally, very large number of people are without access to means of earning livelihood, housing, health care, education, water, sanitation and other such basic needs. The International Labour Organisation reports that the world is facing the worst unemployment crisis since the world econo–mic depression of 1929. Branding this as morally unacceptable, economically irrational, and socially catastrophic. It says that 30 percent of world's labour force is unemployed or under employed. This is all the more traumatic in the UDCs where, in the absence of social safety net, a job means difference between starvation and subsistence.

Each day, $1.4 trillion are switched across various currencies in money markets. Less than 10 percent of it is for productive economic activities, rest of this staggering sum is for speculative operations. But the proposed Tobin tax of 0.5 percent on this speculative capital, which would have generated about 1500 billion dollars annually for anti-poverty fund, was rejected by the North at the Copenhagen summit. Barring a few Nordic states and Netherlands, no first world country has raised its Official Development Assistance (ODA) to 0.7% of its GNP. Under the 20:20 proposal at the Copenhagen summit, the UDCs were to allocate 20 percent of their national budgets for social development and 20 percent of ODA was to be targeted at the same through small (not large) project assistance. But no such binding commitment was undertaken at the Summit. Neither did the governing groups in the UDCs accept suggestion for reduction in military spending to release resources for fighting poverty and unemployment. These states spend $125 billion annually on arms. During the last twenty years, India and Pakistan are reported to have spent more than $20 billion on arms which is higher than that of Saudi Aràbia. Yet India and Pakistan, with largest number of poverty stricken people, are reticent to cut down military expenditure for poverty alleviation. India spends $10 per capita on defence and Pakistan $26. On health and education, India spends $14 per person and Pakistan $10*. What is appalling is the cynical hypocracy of the U.S. and other permanent members of the Security Council in selling arms to the UDCs. In August 1997, President Clinton lifted the embargo on the U.S. arms sale to Latin America. U.S. "merchants of death" have fixed their sight on arms purchases by new members of NATO who are required to upgrade their armed forces in line with those of the military alliance.

It is futile to discuss elimination of poverty and provision for full employment without discussing who will pay for it in an unequal world. The financing of $237 billion needed to lift world's over 1 billion abysmally poor to a level where their basic needs can be met in the next five years, did not figure up in the final declaration, nor did the creation of jobs for world's grossly underestimated number of jobless.

Poverty cannot be alleviated, let alone eliminated, amidst growing inequalities in incomes and wealth. However, there was a determined silence on the causes of poverty at the Copenhagen Summit. Social development can not take place within the free play of market forces. It was left to Fidel Castro to point out that the savage and blind forces of market cannot eradicate poverty, provide full employment and combat social disintegration. He aptly remarked that there cannot be any human rights where there is no humanity.

The HDI report (1997) estimates the cost of eradicating poverty to be 1 percent of world economy of $25 trillion and no more than 2 to 3 percent of the national income of all but the poorest countries. There is room in most countries to restructure spending and reduce waste. The report says that the greatest potential in generating additional resources lies in generating pro-poor growth.

---

* For figures of social cost of military spending by Islamabad bases Human Development Centre, see **TOI, 10 April 1997.** Also see, **TOI, 28 March 1996.**

The additional cost of providing minimum basic services to all in developing countries is put at about $40 billion a year over 10 years to 2005. Less than 0.2 percent of World's income, this sum is about 1 percent of developing countries income—or half the GNP share that the United States transferred each year to Europe during the 1948-52 period as part of the Marshall plan for post-war reconstruction. Most of the resources can come from restructuring existing budgets. The report further says that for universal basic social services about 20 billion could come from national budgets and perhaps $10 billion from aid. The 20:20 guideline endorsed at Copenhagen and first proposed in the HDI report can achieve this.

But there is no political will to do this and predatory free market economic globalization is anti-thetical to poverty eradication.

IV

Such is the state of the international economy into which the Indian economy is being integrated through the reform process initiated in June 1991.

At the time of their independence, many third world states had declared that they would follow an independent path of development—"the third way"/"delinking from the north"—but failed to produce a real alternative and ended up following the dominant model of capitalist development. India, like some other third world countries, pursued an import-substituting industrialization within a highly regulated regime.

Ostensibly, state intervention in economy was justified for ensuring control of the "commanding heights of the economy" for realizing the objective of social justice. However, in reality, the rationale for it was to help the weak Indian bourgeoisie which had itself called for establishment of an interventionist state in the 1944 Bombay (Tata-Birla) plan. The State stepped in to provide core sector where investments are unprofitable or with long gestation period. State intervention was designed to provide the Indian bourgeoisie with highly subsidized infrastructural facilities, inputs, resources (cheap credit and subsidies), and an assured domestic market through protectionism.

Like other third world countries, the Indian political and economic elites were Janus-faced. Fearful of lower class insurgent movements, they cooperated with the anti-communist campaigns of Washington. But partly from a desire to gain popular legitimacy and outmanoeuvre the left, some southern elites took increasingly bold moves to gain more control over their economies and a greater share of the surplus being extracted therefrom in 1960s and 1970s. The state became a surrogate for private enterprise without challenging entrenched interest. Indeed, it protected them.

The plethora of regulations in India were said to be necessary for channelising investments into socially desirable areas. But the "license-permit-quota raj" turned out to be a source of distribution of patronage ("crony capitalism"/ "Statism") which yielded neither social justice nor economic growth. The elites used it to rake in huge unearned incomes which spawned massive corruption. According to Trans–parency International, India was nineth most corrupt country in 1996 but had deteriorated to the position of eighth most corrupt state by 1997. Foreign aid was used to cushion the life style of the top decile of population.

After four decades of planning, nearly half (officially 40 percent in 1997) the Indian population is below poverty line defined as food intake of less than 2400 calories per head per day in rural areas and 2100 calories in urban areas. The post liberalization steep hike in the prices of cereals has pushed many more millions into the ranks of semi-starving in world's largest democracy. Presently, those earning upto Rupees six per head per day are considered to be below poverty line. This is a cynical mockery of the tens of millions who, on paper, stand left out of the ranks of the destitutes. If these victims of economic genocide were to have purchasing power to afford adequate food, India's much publicized fraudulent "Buffer stocks of food" would disappear and India would emerge as food deficit. Around 5000 people in India die each day of malnutrition related diseases. In a report circulated at the 1995 social summit, the Indian External Affairs Ministry admits that for many Indians, employment does not mean much because the low wages do not ensure even a subsistence living.[20] In 1997, a report by WB has underlined India's poor record of poverty alleviation. With 52 percent literacy, India is not only way behind the dynamic economies of Southeast Asia, but is also trailing behind such disaster economies of Africa as Zambia, Uganda and Kenya. Malaysia spends 30 percent on education, but India spends about as much on defence and far too little on education. Only 30 percent Indians have access to modern medicine with these people vulnerable to death due to preventable diseases. If one were to take into account the availability of means to meet basic needs, the number of poor in India constitutes overwhelming majority—the economically disfranchised mass.

India has the largest child labour and bonded (slave) labour force who enter bondage to avoid starvation. Since, many of them work in the informal sector, their count is extremely difficult. India together with 100 countries has ratified the U.N. Convention on Rights of Child (1988) which bans child labour that violates right of child to education, or cause physical abuse. Article 24 of the Indian Constitution lays down that "no child below the age of 15 years shall be employed to work in any factory, mine, or engaged in any other hazardous employment". But like all other survival rights, Article 24, 39 and 45—which ban hazardous child labour and provide for free compulsory universal primary education—have been consigned to the dustbin of non-justiciable Directive Principles of the Constitution. In its report to the social development summit, the Indian government had given the number of child labourers in India as 10 million with two million in hazardous work like mine quarrying, match and fire works factories, carpet weaving and wool cleaning. According to an all India survey sponsored by the Union Labour Ministry in 1980s, there were 44 million child labourers out of an estimated 300 million in the world. According to some Non-Governmental Organizations (NGOs), the size of the child labour force is around 100 million depending on how one defines child labour. The NGOs put the figure of children in hazardous work at five million. Child labour engaged in cotton clothes industry in Tamil Nadu, which account for 80 percent of country's cotton garment exports, is made to work for 17 hours a day.

Child labour is docile and easy to abuse and exploit. They do not unionize, have no fixed working hours, are cheap and paid less than half the adult wages. Significantly, not even a single child labour employer has so far been jailed for any offense.

No wonder, the UNDP's Human Development Index (HDI), which takes into consideration purchasing power parity (PPP), adjusted GDP per capita, life expectancy at birth, and educational attainments, ranks India 134th among 173 countries. In its recent "World Development Indicators" report, the WB says that India has fared poorly as compared to several of its South Asian Counterparts judged by its performance in the social sector. Nearly 63 percent of Indian Children are malnourished and underweight.

A highly skewed income distribution has distorted the structure of production with resources being deployed primarily to cater to the wants of the elites* than for meeting even the basic needs of the vast majority. India's super class has adopted the life style of its Western counterparts, at the expense of the vast underclass through import of luxury consumer goods. They maintained their life style through long term and short term external borrowings. India's foreign debt soared from $16 billion to $64 billion while Rajiv Gandhi was in power. A disaggregation of its expenditure shows that a large part of it was spent on military (including the infamous Bofors deal) and luxury goods in semi-knocked down (SKD) and completely knocked down (CKD) condition. Ironically, it

* In a first study of its kind in India, the National Council of Applied Economic Research (NCAER) has exploded the myth of a large Indian middle class hungry for global brand name goods. It classifies the middle class into five categories in a highly price sensitive market. At the top are six million persons (one million households). Japanese electronic company, Sony sold 20,000 colour TVs in a market estimated at one million units. Forty million households buy such durable consumer goods as B & W TVs while 90 million households buy most consumer durables. **TOI, 30 May 1996.**

is the masses who have to bear the brunt of re-payment of $92 billion debt through the painful and costly SAP and export of those basic foods which are already in short supply domestically. Evidently, it is the elites who are living beyond means. The masses, in fact, are living below means, including the semi-starvation of half the population.

The economic crisis in India is the making of the elites. Day in day out since independence, the masses have been called upon to make sacrifices in the interest of national development. The elites are not only anti-national but out rightly criminal like crime syndicate/mafia group enjoying virtual legal immunity. As stated earlier, $100 billion—more than India's external debt—has been salted away from India. Further, Rs 1,50,000 crores is said to have been lost in tax revenue by the government since 1960s due to tax evasion on concealed income (black money). This is in spite of periodic governmental schemes for legalization of black money and hefty tax cuts for the super rich and steep decrease in direct taxes against swelling indirect taxes. Clearly the affluent minority has dealt a calamitous blow to economy and is holding the nation to ransom.

Thus the profligacy of the upper classes led to the balance of payment crisis by November 1991* which forced India to go in for IMF bail out in return for macro-economic and SAP which, as detailed out earlier, are restrictive and destructive of people earning a livelihood and access to basic entitlements though Western rhetoric on human rights excludes from its purview basic economic rights. Equally importantly, Indians will become retailers and sub-contractors concerns of Western multinationals. Indian economy will become a satellite economy and no such country can emerge as an autonomous power in international politics.

---

* On learning about an internal WB study underlining need for devaluation of Indian currency, NRIs withdrew about $ 1.8 billion from India between 1990-1991. GOI's current confidence about $22 billion in FOREX is misplaced for this "footloose" capital outside governmental control. This transient capital mostly of portfolio nature (in shares, debentures and the like) and can be withdrawn by NRIs and FFIs at any time.

"Freedom begins where necessity ends", wrote Karl Marx. An individual can devote himself to the full development of his potentialities only if he is freed from the struggle for meeting his basic needs which he shares in common with animals. Today, technological advance has given the possibility to human kind to graduate out of the "realm of necessity" into the "realm of freedom" for realizing the "essential humanity" of man. Given a humane social order, technology can give enough leisure to people for this.

The on-going economic restructuring in India presages a gathering storm which will stoke the fires of disintegration through the denial of even basic needs (which are the basis of human existence and dignity) and other disruptive social costs. When people feel overwhelmed by economic and social forces, they invoke their community, race or whatever.

Despite squabbles within the political class in most of the third world, there is an underlying consensus or at least a tacit acceptance of the current international economic orthodoxy. The political process has become irrelevant to the needs and concerns of masses. The theology of free market is a throwback to the philosophy of crass individualism of pre-welfare days which rationalizes the enrichment of a minority at the expense of deprived majority. This perspective is anchored in Social Darwinism which implies contempt for the poor, the deprived, and the disabled. It is based on the conviction that those who can not make it economically have no rights of any kind. Darwinism applied to human population raises profound ethical and moral issues.

The old basis of legitimacy—divine origin, religion, and the like—is no longer acceptable. New notions of legitimacy have to be forged in which each social group in society is part of social compact which ensures their participation in economic, political and social life. Until there is economic and political justice, there are going to be unhappy groups which feel left out. Democracy needs an economically empowered citizenry. But there are impoverished masses in the developing world which dampens enthusiasm for democracy and breeds public apathy. Democratic structures exist but there is precious little democracy. Mere ritual of periodic voting does not constitute a genuine functioning democracy. Political democracy has to be embedded in collective social security system which ensures economic enfranchisement and empowerment for all.

India is a land of continental diversity and is already faced with violence (*e.g.* private armies, "Senas", in Bihar), separatist movements, and insurgency in various parts of the land. Within India, the victims of "global pillage" will far outnumber its beneficiaries. The on-going economic liberalization will further widen the unequal regional development and intensify the divide between the super class and the under class. Social unrest will increase and implode the polity with ethno-nationalism and blood letting as is happening in some parts of the world. The mounting unrest will find variegated expression like chauvinism, fundamentalism* and crime. Hopefully, it will also find creative expression directed at systemic change for establishment of a humane society.

The growing unrest will be met with state repression with the full support of the media barons and of strategic constituencies like the FICCI, CII, and other segments of the power elite. Significantly, public posturing to the contrary not withstanding, there is an informal consensus across the entire spectrum of political parties on the acceptance of the on-going market reforms. Protests will get articulated outside the legislative forum and, indeed, outside the boundaries of

---

* Islamic fundamentalism is, to a large extent, the product of the failure of the product of development and neglect of the under priviledged majority even in such oil possessing states as Iran under the Shah and Algeria. The U.S. planted fundamentalism in Afghanistan has had a spill over effect on Egypt, Algeria, and elsewhere but the overflow is being exaggerated by these regimes to cover up their own failure. The phony U.S. concern for democracy is eloquently silent on Algerian military junta having pre-empted the electoral victory of the Islamic Salvation Front. The wide spread poverty and unemployment in Egypt provides a fertile ground for fundamentalism inspite of the Mubarak regime, a U.S. outpost in West Asia being the second largest recipient of U.S. foreign aid.

electoral politics.* The road—to human liberation, establishment of an alternate society, a humane society—is a long and bumpy one. It involves a long haul but there is no other way. As Eldredge Cleaver puts it, one is either part of the problem or part of the solution.[21]

Post colonial India's neglect of the northeast, a region with severe economic disabilities, further alienated the people of this area. Many parts of the northeast wrested statehood from a reluctant central government only after insurgencies, bloody struggles and agitations. Sino-Indian border dispute prodded the centre to pay attention to the region. This necessitated a large measure of direct governmental role in the economic development of this area and grant various concessions including special category status to ensure concessional transfer of resources from the centre to the northeast.

Despite the limitations of this strategy and notwithstanding the rampant corruption involving large scale loot of public funds by the elites, northeast did benefit as a result of this economic policy. India's march towards globalization and liberalization will shrink the role of the state in the development of the northeast while private capital is not likely to find this area attractive for investment. In all probability, this will further accentuate the economically disadvantageous position of this area while aggravating the unequal regional development across the country. This will add to the politically explosive situation in India's far east in the intensification of economic warfare within and between nations.

Notes and References

1. For details, see Stephen E. Ambrose, *ed., Rise to Globalism: American Foreign Policy Since 1938,* (London: VIKING, 1997).

---

* Ritualistic manifesto declarations apart, political parties have given up the agenda of economic justice in favour of the economic liberalization. It began from 1970s but became more pronounced around 1990. Political parties now drum up support on chauvinistic/parochial plank like religion and caste, *e.g.* all parties mobilise votes by stirring up communalism and in the name of caste, *e.g.* even the leftist parties whip up communalism to mobilise votes in the name of fighting communalism.

2. Daniel Bell, *The End of Ideology: On the Exhaustion of Political Ideas in the Fifties*, (London, 1965);

   S.M. Lipset, *The Political Man : The Social Basis of Politics*, (London, 1963).

   Raymond Aron, *The Industrial Society: Three Essays on Ideology and Development*, (London, 1967). Robert Dahl was another of its advocate.
3. Francis Fukuyama, *"The 'End of History' Debate"*, The American Review, March 1990. See also his earlier article in the summer 1989 issue of *the National Interest.* For a brilliant post-soviet exposition of the socialist alternative and demolation of the view that there is no alternative to the present system, see Istvan Meszaros, *Beyond Capital* (New York: Monthly Review Press, 1995).
4. The Times of India (New Delhi), 26 Feb 1996. Hereafter this newspaper is referred to as TOI.
5. *Ibid.*
6. Abdul A. Said & Luiz R. Simmons, eds,. *The New Sovereigns: Multinational Corporations as World Powers*, (Englewood Cliffs: Prentice-Hall, 1971).
7. Frederic F. Clairmont & John Cavangh, *"The Merchants of Drink"* (Goa: Third World Network, 1988), p. 39. See also, Clairmont's, *"The Transnational Gulag: Reflections on Power Inc.,"* Economic and Political Weekly, March 1-8, 1997, pp. 449-520. See also David C. Korten, *When Corporations Rule the Third World*, (Ithaca: Berrett-Koehler, 1995).
8. Mohsin Khan, *"The Macro-economic Effects of Fund Supported Adjustment Programmes,"* IMF Staff Papers, Vol. 37, No, 2, 1990, p. 196.
9. Sally A. Shelton Richard Nuccio in *International Herald Tribune, January 28-29, 1984.*
10. See Karl Levitt, *Reflections on Debt Crisis*, (McGill University Press, 1989).
11. TOI, 1 October 1996.
12. TOI, 30 January, 1997 & *"Capital Flight: Unstemmed Flow,"* Economic & Political Weekly, 4 Nov., 1995, p. 2774.
13. Meenakshi Rishi and James K. Boyce, *"The Hidden Balance of payments: Capital Flight and Trade Misinvoicing in India, 1971-86,"* Economic and Political Weekly, 28th July 1990, pp. 1645-48.

14. Rajeshwar Dayal, *"The Mobutu I Knew: CIA's Puppet in the Congo"*, TOI, 28th May 1997. Dayal was U.N. Secretary General, Dag Hamarskjold's special representative in that country.
15. Samir Amin, *Imperialism And Unequal Development* (New York: Monthly Review Press, 1977), p. 49.
16. Karl Marx, *Capital, vol. I.* (New York: International Publishers, 1954), p. 751.
17. Paul Kennedy, *"Globalisation: There May be Many Gales Ahead"* TOI, 17th June 1996. For a succinct analysis of the sweeping economic changes, see Frederic F. Clairmont, *The Rise and Fall of Economic Liberalism: The Making of the Economic Gulag* (Goa: Third World Network and Other India Press, 1996).
18. The Hindustan Times (New Delhi), 13 Sept., 1993.
19. TOI, 4 July 1993. The 1997 UNICEF report refers to the prevalence of child labour in the U.S. and some other parts of the developed world. U.S. is a deeply divided society with the blacks in ghetto, the Hispanics in inner cities, and native Americans in reservations. It was not any democratic institution—the Congress, the executive, or the judiciary—that gave civil rights to blacks in 1965 but the civil rights movement of Martin Luther King Jr.

    Voter apathy is reflected by the fact that only 30 percent voted in Nov. 1994 Congressional elections and only a record high of 50 percent voted in Clinton's first Presidential election, and nearly 30 percent of those eligible have not bothered to register to vote because, according to them, their conditions does not change with elections since the Republicans and Democrats are carbon copies of each other.
20. TOI, 10 March 1995.
21. Eldridge Cleaver, *Soul on Ice,* (New York, McGraw Hill, 1968, p. 9).

Chapter 2

GLOBALIZATION AND REGIONAL IMBALANCE : PROSPECTS OF NORTH-EAST INDIA IN A SUPER-COLONIAL WORLD ORDER?

—Apurbananda Mazumdar

Proponents of the globalization scheme often project before us the outlines of a new world order, where the participating nations would no longer occupy the space as colonizers or colonies, or as aid-donors or recipients, but would, instead, be the willing partners of progress. The roles of partners, meanwhile through GATT and other documents, have been made amply clear. With USA and other OECD countries already there as dominant partners, the gains via *unequal exchange* and numerous other *net transfers* shall continue to accrue to the OECD core; the less developed countries (LDCs), given their weak bargaining strengths, have to be content with their present peripheral status and, if the current trends are any indicator, shall progressively be marginalized in the sphere of global production and investment-decisions.

It seems worthwhile in this connection to look towards the respective positions of the countries participating in the deal and the pattern of their interdependence that is sought to be promoted.

First, one must have noticed, in the post cold war global economic scenario, market once again has come to occupy the central position informing every aspect of the economic life of the peoples and nations. It is the common thread passing through almost all the nations of the globe regardless of significant divergence in their size, economic structure and political regime. This implies that the integration of the economic structures of nations, as proposed through globalization, can only be on the basis of market decided terms. The said terms, that is, the relative gains accruing to the developed countries (or core) and their less developed counterparts (LDCs or Periphery) would have been just had the market performed perfectly, *i.e.*, had there been no market-imperfection or any Core-Periphery power imbalance. As we know, none of these possibilities are good. On one side, wide differential in economic strength persists between the core countries and the less-developed periphery; and on the other, with well entrenched monopoly, global markets, we shall show it later, are so imperfect today as had never been the case before. When, market, as a referee, is unable to act neutrally and remains heavily tilted towards the stronger, market decided terms in such a situation can only be the terms to be dictated by the stronger core. Given the centrality of the capitalist accumulation process in a market economy, these realities in turn suggest that the terms of the global economic integration must have been dictated in a way that allows core-capital to consolidate its control over the periphery and hence paves the way for speedier accumulation at the core.

We may address the point raised here from a somewhat different angle. The central dynamic force in the world capitalist system being the 'capital accumulation process in the developed countries' (Sweezy 1972:6) core-capital's prime concern always has been in the extension and activisation of the various circuits of capital: commodity, productive and finance (Harvey 1982,1985; O'Connor 1984). Had it been a competitive market situation, such a scheme, when successfully implemented, would have meant accelerated cross-border flows of *all* commodities and *all* factors. Marx himself had mentioned the possibilities of large scale migration of labourers from the countryside towards the favoured centers of capitalist accumulation (Marx 1954; Vol. I). Applied to the core-periphery context, large scale labour migration from the economically depressed national regions towards the global core could have generated for the former some positive impacts through reverse flow of factor incomes and associated equalization effects. However, it was not possible for Marx to forecast the magnitude of probable 'distortions' in the process. Such possibilities became strong in the later phases of advancement of capitalism with the emergence of monopoly market-structures (Emmanuel 1969; Sweezy 1972 b; Kalecki 1968). Giant trans-national corporations (TNCs) now not only enjoy enormous monopoly power to shape, re-shape or extend the various circuits of capital, but also to effectively distort, manipulate, contract or divert the circuits in a way that serves their basic interest of speedier accumulation (Prendergast and Stewart 1994; XIV).

Not surprisingly, therefore, while the on-going globalization programme lays stress on *liberal* cross-border flow of commodities, investment or finance, it ungrudgingly permits, at the same time, pervasive restrictions on labour-mobility, on entry of LDCs' products within the OECD territory and on LDCs' access to technology and new scientific knowledge (one may refer in this connection to the stringent provisions of TRIPS).

These contradictory positions in-built within the current phase of the globalization scheme at once brings to light the scheme's explicit bias against the interest of the less developed countries, which, handicapped by the limited access to modern technology and knowledge, have their only exchangeable surplus (or comparative advantage) in the nearly unlimited supply of cheap unskilled labour. The unequal and 'fundamentally exploitative' relation between the developed countries and the LDCs, that perpetuate and deepen the development-underdevelopment pattern (Sweezy 1972: 13) is also suggestive of the fact that there is, in fact, very little new in the offered new arrangement. As Paul M. Sweezy (1972: 5) reminds us in one of his essays on modern capitalism:

> *Capitalism as a world system had its origins in the late fifteenth and early sixteenth centuries when Europeans, mastering the art of long-distance navigation, broke out of their little corner of the globe and round the seven seas, conquering, plundering and trading. Ever since then capitalism has consisted of two sharply contrasting parts: on the one hand a handful of dominant exploiting countries and on the other hand a much larger number of dominated and exploited countries. The two are indissolubly linked together, and nothing that happens in either part can be understood if it is considered in abstraction from the system as a whole. It is important to stress that this is as true of "modern capitalism", meaning the global capitalist system of the last half of the twentieth century, as it was of the predominantly merchantile capitalism of the period before the Industrial Revolution.*

As might be understood, during the period following the Industrial Revolution, core-capital, driven by capital's in-built appetite of continuous self-expansion, had to repeatedly draw and re-draw its boundaries—technologically, organizationally and spatially. Global economic restructuring (popularly termed as 'globalization') has been therefore a natural and continuous process intrinsically linked to world capitalism's struggle for survival. It is possible to divide this prolonged course of history into three distinct phases of openness programmes :

(i) TRADE OPENNESS of the colonial era;

(ii) MANUFACTURING OPENNESS : 1949-1979, which created conditions for a 'new international division of labour' mediated by the transnational corporations; and

(iii) FINANCIAL OPENNESS forming the current thrust of the globalization programme.

Although these three types of openness have never been mutually exclusive and, depending on country specificities, have often overlapped one another at varying degrees, the central foci in the successive phases have nevertheless been clearly identifiable. Table 1 portrays, in a somewhat simplified manner, the successive phases of the globalization process and the associated paradigm shifts.

It may be seen from the table that the first phase of global economic restructuring (Trade Openness) triggered off the process of 'causation' around the then global core (*i.e.*, the colonialist countries in Western Europe) with strong backwash effects. This was done by linking even the remote inner regions within the colonies to the core-capital's spheres of circulation and realization. While such a scheme could facilitate fast accumulation at the core, by the same token it meant rapid impoverishment of the colonies and widening of inter-regional imbalance (Myrdal 1956 : 69-72). With the rise of the National model (1949-1979) during the subsequent phase of manufacturing openness (Schor, 1993 :4-5), there were some discrete attempts in several LDCs to soften the effects of causation. Such attempts, undertaken often at the initiative of the domestic capital in LDCs and their respective national governments, assumed the forms of centralized planning and an extensive import substitution strategy matched, in cases, by direct government intervention. However, the subsequent paradigm shift in favour of a TNC-dominated financial openness regime (cf. Column 4 in Table 1) is likely to reverse the entire process. Future of the economically depressed national regions not only in the periphery, but also within the core itself has once again become the central focus of the development debate.

Against the backdrop outlined above, the present paper attempts a review of the current phase of the globalization process from the view point of regional imbalance. The analysis is carried to the point of its enabling us to understand the implications of the ongoing programme for growth prospects of North-Eastern Region of India. The paper design is as follows: Section-I delineates some of the salient features of the contemporary global economic scene, Section-II makes a tentative assessment of the implications of these aspects for regional imbalance in a given context, Section-III concludes the paper with a brief note on the future prospects of North-East India.

The analysis, we admit, has remained sketchy. The issues raised through the paper indeed call for detailed analysis and empirical support.

Table 1

VARIOUS PHASES OF THE GLOBAL ECONOMIC RESTRUCTURING AND INTEGRATION PROGRAMME

Basis of difference	*Phase I*	*Phase II*	*Phase III*
1	2	3	4
1. Span	Roughly till the end of 2nd World War.	1949-1979	1980 onwards (gains momentum in the post Cold war era).
2. Events triggering off the transition to the given phase	Industrial Revolution in Europe	General Crisis of Capitalism as reflected by the World Wars, Depression and emergence of the Socialist Bloc	Recession in OECD countries in the 70s: BOP crisis in LDCs; and decline of the socialist system.
3. Prime focus	Trade Openness	Manufacturing openness	Financial Openness.
4. Theoretical Underpinning	Classical Comparative Advantage Model	Keyesian National Model	Neo-classical Model.
5. Suggested Basis of specialization	Sector specific	Labour-process specific	Firm-decided labour process specific.
6. Market Orientation	Outward looking	Generally inward looking	Orientation to be decided by firms (TNCs).
7. Maret Structure	Generally competitive	Oligopolistic (competition often regulated by state)	Monopolistic.
8. Allocative Machinery	Market	A combination of market and planning	TNCs' corporate strategy (under conditions of an imperfect market).

1	2	3	4
9. Principal mode (s) of interdependence among the countries	Trade	Loans and aids; technology transfer; Integration of labour processes along the manufacturing chain	Financial market integration; FDI inflow; intra—firm trade.
10. Role of the State in economic spheres	Dependent LDC States with limited regulatory role	Relatively autonomous State with strong power to intervene	States's role Shrinking; Balance of power shifts in favour of TNCs.
11. Core-Periphery relation (Mode of exploitation)	Colonial	Neo-colonial	Supercolonial (?).
12. Impact on regional imbalance	Disparity intensified due to backwash effects of circular causation	The polarization process is sought to be reversed by large scale State-intervention	The process of reversal is reversed. Hence, polarization likely to gain momentum, and proceed at an unprecendented speed (?)

Note: (?) indicates that the particular issues are under investigation in this paper.

I

Financial Openness *or* the Era of SUPER COLONIALISM?

The combination of conjunctural crisis in OECD countries and their less developed counterparts that propelled a general shift of focus of globalization towards financial openness has been documented by scholars in detail (Armstrong, Glyn and Harrison 1991 : 282-304; Ghai 1994: 16-22; Dasgupta 1997: 1093-8). Our endeavour in this section will be to identify some of the distinctive features of the current phase of financial openness campaign in as far as these are inexorably linked to the question of spatial distribution of the forthcoming pattern of global and national growth.

The most significant aspect of the current global economic situation is the rise of a given mode of finance capitalism which Sau (1997) has labeled in one of his recent essays as money-capitalism or 'dollar capitalism'. Uniqueness of the mode may be understood from the following contemporary trends:

(i) the emergence of giant institutional investors as the dominant player in global financial scene;

(ii) the diversion of lion's share of the investible funds by these institutional investors, and to a lesser extent by international banks, to financial market transactions across the globe primarily in search of hasty capital-gains (rather than normal dividend on shares, bonds, etc.);

(iii) the innovation of a wide range of new financial instruments to enable investors and corporate giants to diversify their risk portfolio and arrange 'securitisation' of their speculative dealings (Nayyar 1996: 9-10); and

(iv) accelerated cross border financial flows (made possible through international capital markets integration) and a concomitant rise of the number of cross border acquisitions and mergers.

The above trends, by now well-documented in literature (Cosh, Hughs and Singh, 1993: 19-42; Sau, 1997), signify that finance during the last two decades could free itself, to progressively larger degrees, from the interlockings that normally operate within and contribute to the process of 'circular causation' in given directions[1]. Thus, during the period following the oil shocks, while global economy in general and OECD industrial production in particular had been under the grip of a severe recession (Armstrong, Glyn and Harrison, 1991: 233-54; Glyn, 1992: 71-95), financial markets were practically booming with super bumper capital gains (Sau, 1997 : 837).

This increased ability of finance (or money in the truest sense of the term) to insulate itself from the general pattern of an upward or downward swing in given context means, in turn, that—

(i) finance (or money in the truest sense of the term) is now able to reproduce and multiply itself for its possessors and dealers without having been required to travel along the conventional chains of circulation or realization, and

(ii) for the sake of such *autonomous* reproduction at the fastest possible speed, it (*i.e.*, finance) is getting tied up, at an ever-increasing scale, to the global speculative circuit (*e.g.* the foreign exchange market, equities and bonds market, speculative dealings in land, etc.).

Diversion of investible funds from the spheres of circulation or production to the spheres of speculation are, of course, not entirely new to the world; these are reported to have existed in the seventeenth and eighteenth centuries (Nayyar, 1996: 9-10) and, as Lenin had noted in 1916, their magnitude was noticeably high even in the early years of the twentieth century imperial world order (Lenin, 1917). Yet the nature, volume and force that speculative financial dealings (as distinct from the purely financial dealings like the current international credit offensive) have come to acquire is clearly unprecedented. The figures cited by Sau (1997) from the World Bank, BIS and other sources provide a telling testimony to the events. To quote Sau (p. 834) :

> *Consider the foreign exchange market. The turnover is large in size and growing very fast; currently it is of the order of 300 trillion dollars a day...The enormity of it can be appreciated against the following figures: the world GDP is worth some 25 trillion dollars, savings and investment 5 trillion dollars, and international trade in goods and non-factor services 5 trillion dollars... Foreign direct investment is comparatively small, being 234 billion dollars in 1994.....The total stock of financial assets traded in the global capital market increased from 5 trillion dollars in 1980 to 35 trillion dollars in 1992, equivalent to twice the GDP of OECD countries. In the coming three years it will become three times the OECD economies' GDP.*

What follows from the above is that, in the first place, in the sphere of circulation and production, commodity had already receded in the background leaving the center of the stage to derivative commodities (stocks, bonds, futures, options and the like); secondly, a formidable rentier class with vested interests in strengthening and perpetuating the new arrangement has emerged and it now serves as the architect as well as the support-base of the on-going financial openness programme. This rentier class, spatially widely dispersed among practically all the nations of the globe, consists of a cross section of social groups belonging to the upper income strata: the financial capitalists, the DC-based corporate magnets and their local collaborators in LDCs and the very long chain of stake-holders and other beneficiaries, including of the political elites ,the bureaucrats, the technocrats and finally, the privileged sections among the labouring classes in core countries and in LDCs. Not only this class is politically and economically most active, capable of providing the new arrangement legitimacy and life, even its size is considerably large now to resist any attempt to overthrow the regime coming, if any, from the unprivileged sections (for instance, in India, an estimate from some optimistic quarter projects the size of the support-base at more than 30 percent of the total population in the near future. (cf. BM 1997: 1304).

The impact of the given flow of events on global and national growth can easily be assessed.

As mentioned earlier, the *rent-seekers' boom* propelled by the financial openness campaign has meant large scale diversion of investible funds towards the speculative sectors. Such diversions, by putting effective drag on the supply side, blocks the possibilities of probable production expansion; given their low levels of capital formation and low consumption per capita, LDCs in all likelihood are affected more by diversions than the developed countries in terms of the growth foregone. Worse still is the fact that the two phenomenon (a booming financial market vis-a-vis the relatively stagnant productive sectors) once set in motion, often get interlocked and operate, thereafter, in a mutually re-enforcing way: speculation via its generation of huge capital gains means capital's increased ability to expand, while the slow-moving or stagnant productive sectors offers little incentive for expansion (incentives further dry up as the 'net transfer' effects of speculation narrows down the market base and creates drag on the demand side as well); the unspent incremental income generated by speculation, hence find their way back to the speculative circuit.

The above line of analysis, although oversimplified and partial, must be able to provide a good part of the explanation for the contemporary huge mismatch between the pace of volume-growth of the global financial market transactions and that of the growth of the global industrial sector. Extending the same logic, it may also be argued that the spatial dispersal of growth under the given situation is likely to be uneven. Because to contain the inflationary tendencies generated by the speculative boom, governments normally take recourse to tight monetary policies, thereby hiking both the nominal and real interest rates (Armstrong, Glyn and Harrison 1991: 307-10). High interest rates, combined with the near-impossibility for new entrepreneurs to raise funds out of the capital markets (cf. Table 2.9 in Cosh, Hughes and Singh, 1993: 34), discourages new initiatives and enterprise; the limited investment initiatives which are actually undertaken normally come from giant corporate houses and are channelised towards established locations with well-developed infrastructure (for their offering external economies). These tendencies, in turn, suggest acceleration of the process of concentration and the widening of regional disparities.

Indeed, the most noticeable aspect of the contemporary global scene is the TNC-centric market concentration. To a certain extent, this is a natural by-product of the financial openness programme. As capital markets have become the major source of business capital in recent years (Cosh, Hughes and Singh, 1991) and as only the bigger and more successful ones among the companies (TNCs, in particular) can effectively exploit this source to the near-total exclusion of others, the operation of the capital market system is increasingly becoming TNC-centric; for smaller firms as well as for the new entrepreneurs, road-blocks are really formidable.

Yet the major factor contributing to market concentration is the compulsions of the TNCs themselves. Despite their being the major beneficiary in the system, the giant corporations can not ignore the threats constantly originating from their dynamic external environment. Responding rightly to the market-signals and retaining investors' confidence are considered, in the given context, the sine-qua-non for successful corporate strategy. The problem is compounded by the fact that giant institutional investors, who now are the major stake holders for most transnational corporations, simultaneously invest in the shares of numerous companies across the globe to diversify risks of investments and to maximize both normal and capital gains. These stakes are continuously re-shuffled (through buying and selling of shares) depending on investor's own calculation of relative profitability and risk-contents of different sets of investment. Any sudden change in the external environment or a minor lapse on the part of a given company to respond rightly to the market-signals may prompt stake-holders to dispose of their entire stake in the company thereby generating instant flush in the market of the said company's shares and a consequent collapse of the prices of scrips. The giant TNCs with billions of dollars of investments around the globe often feel more insecure than smaller firms, as they have to confront diverse sets of external environments related to widely differing country-specificities. The mad rush for mergers reflects, among other things, this insecurity in-built within bigness and the TNCs' desperate drive to arrange the necessary defense for their own survival and growth. While commenting on the merger waves in USA, an observer noted as follows (Fortune, Feb 17, 1997: 55):

> *...companies are merging like never before for a surprisingly sensible reason. They have no choice. Thousands of companies today of every shape and size are facing the business climate equivalent of 100 year storms. Deregulation has turned entire industries completely upside down... Companies are ... aspiring to shape their own destiny in an era when no one knows what will happen next, and anything seems possible.*

David Whitford, the observer, reported further in the context of USA (*Ibid.* : 54) :

> *(in 1996 alone) More than 10,000 mergers have taken place, with more than $660 billion changing hands. In dollar terms, 1996 beat the old record, set just the year before, by an amazing $140 billion. And in terms of the sheer volume of activity, 1996 thumped 1989, the peak year for mergers during the 1980s, by a factor of two.*

The focus of corporate restructuring programmes, it is worthwhile to note, is no longer confined to mergers among national firms. The liberalization of financial markets has opened up the gates for cross-border mergers and take-over activity on a far larger scale. Cosh, Hughes and Singh (1991) have shown refering to the 1980s that the role of institutional investors in this growth has been substantial and that large corporations are now massively engaged in restructuring their global operation via the linked phenomenon of international take overs.

Takeovers of outright purchase of firms are preferred and, sometimes even dictated, by financing institutions; these are treated as secure investment proposals with guaranteed returns. Takeovers, for the same reason, also boost investors expectations and interest in the acquiring company's shares leading to rise in the prices of the scrips and, therefore, paves the way for windfall capital gains by institutional investors. At the same time, takeovers, when implemented lead to further market concentration and, hence, strengthens the monopoly-power of TNCs. The on-going waves of national and cross-border mergers exemplify how the interests of finance capital and monopoly capital collude and work together to give shape to a new world order, where neither the nation states nor the market, but the autonomous TNCs, informed by their capital market considerations, would act as the driving force of the capitalist accumulation machine.

Not surprisingly, if the recent phase of financial openness records phenomenal growth of the income and wealth of the biggest sized TNCs with concomitant rise in their global monopoly power (Ghai, 1994: 28), by the same token it also offers evidences of gradual marginalization of LDC firms and systematic 'crowding' out of local enterprise and initiative (cf. Lewis, 1994; Hamilton and Thompson, 1994; Anand, 1997; Lee, 1997). The methods used by TNCs for monopolization of the LDC markets (*e.g.* subordination, enslavement, capturing or killing of local firms) are diverse and cruel (see Chaudhury, 1995) and would remind us of the ferocity of settler colonialism in its early merchantile era.

Closer scrutiny, however, would reveal that the current scheme (we think fit to term it as *super colonialism*) is not only more ferocious, but also is far more deep rooted; because it aims towards enslavement of *mind*, uses the power of *technology* and *organization*, hence, makes *lesser use of force*, consolidates itself by creating a *vast army of collaborators, allies and stakeholder across the globe*, perpetuates itself via liberalization through *autonomous transnational corporations* and *subservient states*.

II

FUTURE OF THE REGIONS

Discussion in the preceding two sections is suggestive of the following :

> *First, the current phase of global economic restructuring, being a reflection and also an inseparable part of capitalism's constantly evolving pattern, is logically expected to reproduce the same contradictions and unevenness of growth as had always been the case with capitalism;*

Secondly, given the strongly regressive and exploitative profile of the current super-colonial mode of exploitation, it seems very much possible that the unevenness of growth in this phase would be far more intense than what has been experienced so far.

In the present section, the above probabilities are weighed against the general dynamics of core-periphery relation in both the global and national contexts and keeping, particularly, in view the direction of the current scenario.

As noted earlier in Section I, from the very beginning, capitalism had advanced by subjugating, plundering and exploiting foreign countries and territories. The continued transfer of wealth from the periphery to the core, while paving the way for fast impoverishment of the former, led to enormous concentration of wealth (primary accumulation) in core countries and 'by the end of the nineteenth century, the whole world had been polarized into a handful of wealthy capitalist countries and a host of colonies and semi-colonies' (Sweezy, 1972: 19). The continued drain of resources from periphery to the core was operative at the national level as well (*Ibid.* : 20-21).

The era of Trade Openness in the late nineteenth and early twentieth century (Nayyar, 1996) accelerated the process of polarization. Roads, railways and communication links were built to connect the remote primary producing and labour-surplus inner regions in core countries as well as in colonies to the colonizers' global trading networks. Extraction and continued drainage of surplus (absolute surplus value) from all the peripheral regions to the centers of capitalist accumulation was the central theme of the colonial scheme of exploitation and added momentum to the polarization process (Myrdal, 1956: 67-72).

The process did not subside much even during the subsequent phase (Baran, 1973; Amin, 1977; Frank 1980, 1981). Yet this second phase of *manufacturing openness* significantly deviated from the earlier pattern in terms of the channels and mode of the centripetal flow of resources (as well as surplus value). The first noticeable feature of this phase was the co-option of a number of newer areas (national regions in particular) within the web of global industrial production system. The co-option was not natural, but resulted from 'active intervention' by endogenous forces in major part of the newly independent third world (See, for example, Cuyvers and Bulcke, 1992; Singh, 1994; Page, 1994; Amsden, 1994; Kwon, 1994). However, as most of these newly independent nations did not severe the links altogether with the global core (Armstrong, Glyn and Harrison, 1991: 284) and as transfer via trade and other routes continued, all these newly industrializing countries in the so-called free world could conveniently be accommodated as satellite sub-systems within the overall global accumulation process. That means, in the altered context, the circuits were effectively redrawn so as to permit accumulation on a two-tier basis: at the grass root, it operated around each sub-system's cores, thereby, sharpening the core-periphery dichotomy at the level of each individual nation; these sub-systems' core were then linked, via TNCs and other routes, to the global core for continued net transfer of surplus.

This latter phenomenon, that is, the emergence of relatively advanced regions (nations as well as territories within nations) within the periphery itself, prompted the introduction of the concept of semi-peripheries in contemporary attempts to theorize global uneven development (cf. Wallerstein 1979). The concept, seemingly applicable, at least to a limited extent, to the intra-national contexts as well, "not only does... express the possibility for capital accumulation in certain parts of the periphery, but it accepts that some of that capital is able to be retained (in the semi-periphery) rather than necessarily being transferred to the core" (Henderson, 1989: 14).

While the entire arrangement, designed as above, worked persistently towards widening of inter-regional economic disparities at the national level, the significance of certain counterveiling forces operating in the reverse direction was nonetheless undeniable. For example, with improved transport and communication linkage with the relatively more advanced national regions and a certain degree of political influence over the national governments, it now appeared feasible for the economically backward regions to hasten realization of potential spread effects[2]. Arranging reverse transfers (*e.g.* the relatively large central government assistance and transfers to special category states in North-East India and elsewhere) on a regular basis has been an important attempt in the given direction.

In fact, during the phase of manufacturing openness, LDC governments generally could wrest for themselves a considerable degree of operational autonomy when metropolitan governments' influence on LDCs' state-policies became indirect and thin. This enabled many LDC states to emerge as active counterveiling force vis-a-vis the process of polarization. By setting up public sector units in backward regions, developing industrial infrastructure, arranging incentives for agricultural and industrial investments and through a variety of other measures, LDC states (India, for instance) could neutralize to a certain extent the backwash effects of circular causation.

The era of manufacturing openness did not last long. With gradual decline of the national model and consequent ascendance of neo-classicism during the current phase of financial openness, the entire set of policies followed so far have been reversed. Impact of such policy-reversal in the spatial distribution of global economic growth may be understood from Table 2. It is evident from the Table that during the period 1948-1980 approximately coinciding the manufacturing openness phase, inter-regional disparities at the global level (in terms of per capita GNP) has marginally narrowed down. The entire span of manufacturing openness can be conveniently broken down into two sub-periods: the first one was 1948-1970 when the OECD economies (or global core) were experiencing fast post-war recovery and unprecedented economic growth; during the second sub-period (1970-1980), the OECD economies hit by successive oil-shocks were all subject to a severe recession and, for most of them, a massive slow down of economic growth became inescapable. Despite the wide divergence between the growth-experience of the two sub-periods, the other regions of the globe with the exception of South Asia could significantly improve their position *vis-a-vis* the OECD economies and the trend reflecting a slow but gradual decline of economic disparities remained unaltered throughout the manufacturing openness phase. However, a dramatic reversal on the trend can be noticed during the period following 1980 which suggests existence of a strong positive correlation between the greater degree of financial openness and widening of inter-regional economic disparities.

On the question of inter-regional disparities at the national level, it seems that experiences would widely differ among countries depending on individual country specificities. Nevertheless, as is generally known, very few countries in the global periphery today have the necessary strength in their economic or policy-making structure to insulate themselves *vis-a-vis* the general global trends. The Indian experience in this regard during the financial openness phase (as presented through Table 3) is a pointer in the given direction.

Table 2

COMPARATIVE ECONOMIC PERFORMANCE OF THE LDCS *VIS-A-VIS* THE OECD CORE

	1948	*1960*	*1970*	*1980*	*1988*
I. OECD Core	100.0	100.0	100.0	100.0	100.0
II. Latin America	14.4	16.7	15.5	19.8	10.6
III. Middle East and North Africa	-	11.5	8.1	11.1	7.1
IV. Subsaharan Africa					
(a) Western & Eastern	-	3.6	3.4	4.7	1.6
(b) Southern & Central	-	10.5	11.3	-	6.1
V. South Asia	7.5	3.6	2.8	2.0	1.8
VI. Southeast Asia	-	6.6	3.8	5.7	3.7

Notes:

1. The figures represent GNP per capita of the region divided by the GNP per capita of the OECD core countries times 100.
2. Southeast Asia consists of Indonesia, Malaysia, Philippines, Thailand and Singapore.
3. OECD core countries consist of Benelux and Scandinavian countries, (West) Germany, Austria, Switzerland, France, United Kingdom, the US, Canada, Australia and New Zealand.

Source: Arrighi (1991 : 49).

Table 3
COMPARATIVE ECONOMIC PERFORMANCE OF THE STATES IN INDIA

	1980-81	*1990-91*	*1993-94*
GROUP A: top 10 Indian States	100.0	100.0	100.0
GROUP B: 7 States in NER	70.0	68.0	61.0
GROUP C: Remaining 9 Indian States	67.0	61.0	54.3

Notes:

1. The figures represent average per capita Net State Domestic Product at current prices (PC NSDP) of the group divided by the PC NSDP of Group A (top 10 Indian States) times 100.
2. Group A consists of Delhi, Punjab, Goa, Maharashtra, Haryana, Gujrat, Tamilnadu, Karnataka, Andhra Pradesh and Himachal Pradesh.

   Group B consists of seven states in NER, *i.e.*, Assam, Manipur, Tripura, Meghalaya, Mizoram, Nagaland and Arunachal Pradesh.

   Group C consists of West Bengal, Uttar Pradesh, Madhya Pradesh, Bihar, Rajasthan, Kerala, Orissa, Jammu and Kashmir and Sikkim.

Source : The PC NSDP of the groups have been calculated on the basis of data provided in Government of India, *Economic Survey : 1995-96 & 1996-97*.

Part of the explanation for the growing inter-regional economic disparities has already been provided in Section II. It has been noticed that there are three inter-related trends drawing sustenance from and, at the same time, giving shape and direction to the current focus of the globalization scheme: *(i)* rise of finance capital as an autonomous player, rather, as the super-guardian of the global economic system; *(ii)* collusion between industrial capital and finance capital achieved often at the latter's initiative; and *(iii)* consequent monopolization of the global spheres of circulation and production by giant transnational corporations who now act as the chief mediator of the global economic restructuring and integration programme. The interplay of these three trends has successfully transformed North-South relation into a super-colonial frame, which despite the sophisticated and stable appearances, can not but lead to intense unevenness in growth patterns. In what follows we present some additional logic and evidences in support of our contention.

For most of the less-developed countries in today's world, colonial experiences are not new. What matters, however, is that the current phase of super-colonialism is likely to be worse in terms of its disequalizing effects than any of the earlier periods of the colonial regime. Whereas during the colonial regime, for instance, machine-made industrial goods coming from Western Europe replaced oriental hand-made fabrics and other industrial products in LDCs (in many cases these were replacement of relatively coarse and costlier varieties by finer and/or less costly ones) and, via the creation of a national market and exposure to newer possibilities, paved the way for subsequent industrialization initiatives in these countries (Myrdal, 1956: 58-59), the dislocation of domestic manufacturing efforts in LDCs in the current phase is not being compensated by any visible beneficial impact. Rather, as noticed earlier in Section II, the aggressive monopolization of the spheres of circulation and production by autonomous transnational corporation (through mergers, takeovers and the like) means, on the one hand, a tendency towards gradual de-enterprising of the nations, and, on the other, reducing the scope for probable expansion of production bases, particularly, to economically backward regions or sub-regions.

The immediate implication of the rapid monopolization of the market can be understood from the fact that for most of the biggest sizes TNCs income growth has been much faster than the growth of their product volume. Such a mismatch between income and production might occur in two situations: *(i)* out of an inflationary rise in price, when the incremental income represents a nominal gain, and not gain in real terms; or *(ii)* as a result of incremental net transfers, when income is pooled in a few hands through impoverishment of others. Scrutiny would reveal that the present global as well as the national scene in India and elsewhere conforms to this second trend: concentration of income and wealth in a few hands (the mega business houses including TNCs) and, hence, in a few advanced regions, implying thereby rise in income disparity and regional imbalance.

Given the fact that large scale industrialization, irrespective of the degree of monopolization of the market, have a natural tendency towards concentration, two suggestions are commonly forwarded to counteract this trend: *(i)* promoting the growth of small scale industry (SSI) sector; and *(ii)* arranging active intervention by the state to foster industrialization in the backward areas. However, in view of the close linkage that conventionally exists between the growth of agriculture and SSI growth in a given region, it may safely be postulated that areas underdeveloped in terms of agricultural growth (North-East India, for example) are likely to offer little possibilities of success in a state-sponsored SSI-promotion programme.

Apart from the above, one has also to bear in mind the emerging pattern of global industrialization. The global manufacturing space now stands clearly divided between two interdependent sectors : organized and unorganized. Whereas the organized sector is relatively stagnant in terms of output-growth, the unorganized sector, in contrast, is fast growing in terms of output and number of operating firms (Bose, 1996: 151). However, a substantial part of the new entrepreneurial ventures in the unorganized sector has been in response to the growing tendency among the large firms to farm out labour-intensive operations and the consequent massive rise in ancillarisation and sub-contracting in recent years.

In the context of the aforesaid linkage between the two sectors, growth of SSI sector in a given area is to be seen largely as a function of the status of growth of the large scale industrial sector. Factors like geographical proximity to one or more developed industrial base, strength of the available infrastructure, particularly, the transport and communication linkage, availability of skilled manpower, and/or access to a relatively large market base, *inter-alia*, have been found so far as playing decisive role in fostering SSI growth along the lines of national or international subcontracting.

It seems logical to postulate then, that those areas or regions in a nation which have not seen large scale industrialization of even a modest scale offer little chances for an SSI-led industrialization.

The other option, *i.e.*, directing States to operate as effective counterveiling force *vis-a-vis* the polarization process at national or global level also seems, at the moment, an unreal proposition. Assignment of such a role to the States would go against the neo-classical frame underlying the current phase of global economic restructuring. In an era of extensive deregulation and liberalization, the power and reach of the State have considerably declined. There has been, in fact, a significant shift of power in favour of metropolitan capital, the reflection of which in third world may be found in an effective transfer of decision making in vital areas of economic and social policy to an alliance of international lending organizations, institutional investors and transnational corporations (Ghai, 1994: 35).

III

CONCLUSION : PROSPECTS OF NORTH-EAST INDIA

The current phase of the global economic restructuring and integration has been closely associated with the emergence of a formidable rentier class. Spatially this class is now widely dispersed among all the nations of the globe and consists of the industrial as well as financial capitalists at the core countries, their collaborators in LDCs, corporate stake holders, political elites, the bureaucracy, technocrats and also the privileged sections among the labouring class. Being the chief architects and support-base of the on-going globalization programme, all these groups have successfully secured their respective places in the different layers within a composite global ruling hierarchy.

To the mass of underprivileged of the globe, of course, the future at the moment looks grim. Country studies across the third world provide evidences of increased impoverishment, unemployment, marginalization and casualisation of labour, income as well as regional disparity and, also, evidences of growing malnutrition and hunger (see, for example, Maoyo and Amin, 1992; Hamilton and Thompson, 1994; Wood, 1997).

In the so-called 'one-world' of the dominant rentier coalition of the globe, political boundaries are fast becoming irrelevant. This does not, of course, mean that boundaries will disappear. To perpetuate the labour-rate differentials now forming the basis of unequal exchange between the developed countries and the LDCs (cf. Emmanuel A., 1969) and also to keep the rising voice of dissent compartmentalized and wherever necessary, misdirected, boundary restrictions are likely to be enforced even more rigorously in future. The current *super-colonial* scheme of exploitation would, to the contrary, require local state-apparatus to brutally suppress the rights of the labouring class and, hence, to silence their dissent. The trends are fairly clear; indeed, as Harris (1994: 8) has noted "governments appear now less as representing a people to the world at large and rather more as representing a world system to the people".

Among the aforesaid two worlds—one resided, nurtured and protected by the globalized 'haves' and the other, which is actually divided into many and many others, being the abode of impoverishment, marginalized and compartmentalized millions of 'have nots'—where can the people of North-East India find their rightful place? The answer probably is obvious. The locational disadvantage of the States in North-Eastern Region (NER) combined with their infrastructural and other shortcomings make difficult their placement anywhere along the global highways of capital and finance. This remains true even if due consideration is given to the fact that, NER, endowed with abundance of cheap unskilled labour, has the ability to provide to transnational corporations low-cost production sites. We have shown elsewhere, although in a different context, that the "availability of cheap labour of any description can no longer be seen as the prime source of comparative advantage of LDCs" (Mazumdar, 1996). The present pattern of global relocation of production by TNCs is reflective of the extremely cautious approach followed by these corporations in the matter of selection of sites which leave almost no scope for areas like NER to be coopted within the said TNCs' global production chain.

Therefore, away from the cross-border movement of finance and stock market glitterati of the hour, the people in the North-Eastern Region of India continue to languish. A glance over the data relating to the Net State Domestic Product

(NSDP) of states (cf. Table 3 in Section II) confirms the tendency towards increasing divergence of NER from the nation's core. The table reveals that NER is continually sliding in terms of the per capita NSDP relative to the top ten Indian states.

How should we conclude then? The discussion in the paper is suggestive of the numerous contradictions that the scheme of globalization has already promoted and are nurturing. These contradictions, in all likelihood, will disallow the present order to survive for long. Yet, the transition may not be evolutionary and surely would call for active peoples' intervention. Seeking long-term solution to NER's problems within the framework of an exploitative world order carries, at the moment, little practical meaning.

Notes

1. Gunner Myrdal developed the methodology of circular and cumulative causation in sociological analysis of the racial problem in the United States [cf. Myrdal, G. (1944) *An American Dilemma*, New York, Harper & Row]. Later, he applied the methodology, rather forcefully, to explain intra and international economic disparities (cf. Myrdal, 1958). While challenging the popular assumption of *stable equilibrium* underlying the traditional economic theories, Myrdal wrote:

   ... in the normal case there is no such tendency towards automatic self-stabilization in the social system. The system is not by itself moving towards any sort of balance between forces, but is constantly on the move away from such a situation. In the normal case a change does not call forth countervailing changes but, instead, supporting changes, which move the system in the same direction as the first change but much further. Because of such circular causation a social process tends to become cumulative and often to gather speed at an accelerating rate (Myrdal, 1958: 25).

   He also clarifies that, often " the variables are so interlocked in circular causation that a change in any one induces the others to change in such a way that these secondary changes support the first change, with similar tertiary effects upon the variable first affected, and so on" (*Ibid.*, 29-30).

2. Myrdal (1958) emphasizes that the process of circular causation will have certain positive *spread* effects, whereby the expan-

sionary momentum of the growth area is spread centrifugally on other areas. However, as per Myrdal, unless intervened, the *backwash effects* of circular causation process are likely to be much stronger than its spread effects in as much as the growing centers would attract factors of production away from other areas and regions, leaving them 'more or less in a backwater' (Myrdal, 1958 : 38).

References

Amin, S. (1997), *Imperialism and Unequal Development*, Hassocks, Harvesters.

Amsden, A.H. (1994), 'Why Isn't the Whole World Experimenting with the East Asian Model to Develop? : Review of the East Asian Miracle', *World Development*, Vol.22, No.4, 627-33.

Anand, M.R. (1997), 'Private Corporate Investment and Deployment of Funds: Some Recent Trends', *Journal of Indian School of Political Economy*, Jan-March, Vol. 9, No. 1, 37-64.

Armstrong, P. , Glyn, A. and Harrison, J. (1991), *Capitalism since 1945*, Oxford, Basil Blackwell.

Arrighi, G. (1991), 'World Income Inequalities and the Future of Socialism', *New Left Review*, No. 189, Sept-October, 39-65.

Baran, P. (1973), *The Political Economy of Growth*, Harmonds–worth, Penguin.

B.M. (1997), 'Falling in Line, Smartly', *Economic and Political Weekly*, Vol. XXXII, No. 23, June 7-13, 1304-5.

Bose, A.J.C. (1996), 'Subcontracting, Industrialization and Labouring Conditions in India : An Appraisal', *Indian Journal of Labour Economics*, Vol. 39, No.1, Jan-March, 145-62.

Chaudhury, S. (1995), 'Government and Transnationals : New Economic Policies since 1991', *Economic and Political Weekly*, Vol. XXX, Nos. 18-19, May 6-13, 999-1011.

Cosh, A.D., Hughes, A. and Singh, A. (1993), 'Openness, Financial Innovation, Changing Patterns of Ownership, and the Structure of Financial Markets', in T. Banuri and J.B. Schor, (eds), *Financial Openness and National Autonomy*, Delhi, Oxford University Press, 19-42.

Cuyvers, L. and Bulcke, D.V.D. (1992), 'Some Reflections on the 'Outward-Oriented' Development Strategy of the Far Eastern Newly Industrializing Countries', in W.L.M. Adriaansen and J.G. Waardenburg, (eds), *A Dual World Economy : Forty Years of*

Development Experience, Bombay, Oxford University Press, 169-193.

Dasgupta, B. (1997), 'SAP : Issues and Conditionalities', *Economic and Political Weekly*, Vol. XXXII, Nos. 20 & 21, 1091-1104.

Emmanuel, A. (1969), *Unequal Exchange*, New York, Monthly Review Press (Eng. Trans., 1972).

Frank, A.G. (1980), *Crisis in the World Economy*, London, Heinemann Educational Books.

Frank, A.G. (1980), Crisis in the Third World, London, Heinemann Educational books.

GOI (1996, 1997), *Economic Survey 1995-96, & 1996-97*, Ministry of Finance, Government of India, New Delhi.

Ghai, D. (1994), 'Structural Adjustment, Global Integration and Social Democracy' in R. Prendergast and F. Stewart, (eds), *Market Forces and World Development*, Houndmills, The Macmillan Press Ltd., 15-44.

Glyn, A. (1992), 'The Costs of Stability : The Advanced Capitalist Countries in the 1980s', *New Left Review*, No. 195, Sept-Oct, 71-95.

Hamilton, N. and Thompson, C. (1994), 'Export Promotion in a Regional Context : Central America and Southern Africa', *World Development*, Vol. 22, No. 9, 1379-92.

Harris, N. (1994), 'Nationalism and Development', in R. Prendergast and F. Stewart, (eds), *Market Forces and World Development*, Houndmills, The Macmillan Press Ltd., 1-14.

Harvey, D. (1982), *The Limits to Capital*, Oxford, Basil Blackwell.

Harvey, D. (1985), *The Urbanization of Capital*, Oxford, Basil Blackwell.

Henderson, J. (1989), *The Globalization of High Technology Production*, London, Routledge.

Kalecki, M. (1968), *Theory of Economic Dynamics*, New York, Monthly Review Press.

Kwon, J. (1994), 'The East Asia Challenge to Neoclassical Orthodoxy', *World Development*, Vol. 22, No. 4, 635-44.

Lee, W.K.M. (1997), 'Foreign Investment, Industrial Restructuring and Dependent Development in Singapore', *Journal of Contemporary Asia*, Vol. 27, No. 1, 58-70.

Lenin, V.I. (1917), *Imperialism : the Highest Stage of Capitalism*, Moscow, Progress Publishers.

Lewis, P.M. (1994), 'Economic Statism, Private Capital, and the Dilemmas of Accumulation in Nigeria', *World Development*, Vol. 22, No. 3, 437-51.

Mazumdar, A. (1996), 'Globalization, Transnationals and India's Exports : Reflections in the light of the SEEPZ Experience', *The Indian Economic Association, Seventy Nineth Annual Conference Volume, Gwalior*, IEA, Calcutta, 63-71.

Marx, K. (1954), *Capital*, Vol. 1, Moscow, Progress Publishers.

Moyo, N.P. and Amin, N. (1992), 'The Development Experience of Post-Colonial Sub-Saharan Africa', in W.L.M. Adriaansen and J.G. Waardenburg, (eds), *A Dual Word Economy : Forty Years of Development Experience*, Bombay, Oxford University Press, 209-50.

Myrdal, G. (1958), *Economic Theory and Underdeveloped Regions*, Bombay, Vora & Co. Publishers Private Ltd. (published originally in London in 1957 by Duckworth).

Nayyar, D. (1996), 'Globalization : The Past in Our Present', *The Indian Economic Journal*, Vol. 43, No. 3, January-March, 1-18.

O'Connor, J. (1984), *Accumulation Crisis*, Oxford : Basil Blackwell.

Prendergast, R. and Stewart, F. (eds), (1994), 'Introduction', in *Market Forces and World Development*, Houndmills, The Macmillan Press Ltd., xiii-xix.

Sau, R. (1997), 'Dollar Capitalism : Reconstruction of Keynesian Economics for the Long Run', *Economic and Political Weekly*, Vol. XXXII, No. 16, April 19-25, 833-8.

Schor, J.B. (1993), 'Introduction' in T. Banuri and J.B. Schor, (eds), *Financial Openness and National Autonomy*, Delhi, Oxford University Press, 1-14.

Singh, A. (1994), 'Openness and the Market Friendly Approach to Development : Learning the Right Lessons from Development Experience', *World Development*, Vol. 22, No. 12, 1811-23.

Sweezy, P.M. (1972), 'Modern Capitalism' in author's *Modern Capitalism and Other Essays*, New York, Monthly Review Press, 3-24.

Sweezy, P.M. (1972b), 'On the Theory of Monopoly Capitalism' in author's *Modern Capitalism and Other Essays*, New York, Monthly Review Press, 25-50.

Wallerstein, I. (1979), *The Capitalist World Economy*, Cambridge : Cambridge University Press.

Whitford, D. (1997), 'Sale of the Century', *Fortune*, February 17, 52-60.

Wood, A. (1997), 'Openness and Wage Inequality in Developing Countries : The Latin American Challenge to East Asian Conventional Wisdom', *The World Bank Economic Review*, Vol. 11, No. 1, January, 33-57.

Chapter 3

Structural Adjustment and the Politics of Recognition and Redistribution in the North-Eastern Region of India

—B.S. Butola

Structural Adjustment or Developmental Entropy?

The spectre is alive once again. The spectre of communism[1] that haunted the capitalist world for over one hundred and fifty years (from the year of publication of communist manifesto till the dismantling of Soviet Block) is increasingly becoming a thing of the past. But, the spectre is not dead. It is here and every where. The new spectre has not only replaced the old one but its victims are also different. The spectre of Structural Adjustment (S.A.)/Globalization/Liberalization is haunting the workers, the subaltern, the marginalised and the dispossessed of the world alike. It is history repeating itself. But, this time (second time) as a farce.[2] Today, Structural Adjustment has been accepted almost like the law of gravity.[3] It has become so pervasive that it is steam rolling one and all without discrimination. However, the success of its campaign is anything but due to its positive achievements and liberating potentials. In fact, it is mainly due to the logic of moribund capitalism after loosing all of its transcendental potentials that it has become incapable of throwing up any alternative. More–

over, the crisis are so deep that it finds itself in no position to resolve its own internal contradictions. As a result it is not only strangulating that forces which could create the conditions of its structural transformation but also promoting counter liberationalist forces world over. Moreover, apart from being a parasitic system it continues to survive without any creative and transcendental potentials. Thus, degeneration and existence sans development have become its important characteristic feature.

Today, the sustenance of world capitalist system along with the world ruling classes lie musty in their diabolic activities particularly in their abilities to destroy, frustrate, suffocate, corrupt and discredit any constructive alternative to itself. In the absence of an alternative along with lack of its own transcendental potentials the world capitalist system along with its twin the liberal democratic system (Liberalism) stand for developmental entropy rather than development itself. Since, at present there is no alternative to capitalism then the crises it has created and got accumulated over the past three hundred years of its life have proved insurmountable to itself and the world capitalism finds itself completely bewildered in facing these crises. Thus, the only thing that remains possible for maintaining its survival is to paralyze and discredit one and all the up coming alternatives with its entire might and force. Lack of alternative over a long time does not only make the system to stagnant and decay but it also causes erosion as well as degeneration of all the creative and humanizing elements in the representative system. In other words continuation sans transcendental potentials asks for Structural Adjustment instead of structural transformation. Since, there in no alternative then everything tends to continue in the same manner irrespective of their merit whether good or bad. Therefore, persistence of the structural crises instead of leading to its collapse or structural overthrow are causing its gradual degeneration without replacement (structural transformation). A situation of real crises. End of imagination and end of History. The crises have got enhanced importance because, the world elites are neither capable nor willing to solve these. On the contrary, they are only capable of and also active in paralyzing any attempt to solve these. Structural adjustment or globalization is thus, deeply rooted in their attempts to create a system without any transcendental potentials where development has its entropic value only.

Capitalism has always relied on its own innovative potential for its growth as well as in the management of crises. Technological innovations and their absorption in the production process have always had a ontological significance in the capitalist modes of production. The logic continues to work even now though, in a distorted form. Today, technological innovations are no more hindered or paralyzed by social structure or more precisely by the relation of production. Contrarily, technological development continues unhindered but it ceases to improve the life of the masses. With the graduation of capitalist relations of production over these centuries technology has progressively lost its organic links with the mass human experience. On the contrary with every new innovation new social contradictions and disproportionate accumulation of social wealth is taking place. Technology, that once stood for the extension of humankind over temporal and extra-temporal dimensions and contributed in the better and emphatic realization on human creative potentials has become as instrument of coercion and human enslavement. For Habermas the success of technological rationality build around successful implementation of new production techniques for the technical control of nature has blocked the possibility of achieving practical reason (emancipatory rationality) for the liberation of human kinds from externally imposed compulsions both private and collective, individual as well as citizens.[4] Supremacy of instrumentality in our life has given rise to the culture of dominance or a sense of cynicism. Today, Technology has become inimical to freedom as it contributes in the diffusion of power located throughout uncountable capillaries yet, exercising it more subtly and intensely throughout the system with the help of instrument like the optical gaze or panopticon and other devices of surveillance. In a nutshell the lord of the world has become the slave of technology. Under the prevailing entropic nature of technology its Frankensteinian role has left it with anything but the possibilities of limited structural adjustment.

On its way to maturity from mercantilism, industrialism and Imperialism capitalism has been as annihilating, alienating and appropriating force to both society and nature. The uninterrupted exploitation of natural environment leading to ecological crises and environmental degradation have become so alarming that it is increasingly being realized that in the absence of an alternative to the going "development" if remained unhindered then exterminism will be the inevitable last stage of human civilization. A crisis which is not only gigantic ensambling the entire globe and unprecedented but also beyond the scope and power of all the existing institutions particularly the nation state and the world bodies like the UNO and its sister organizations. On its part, in the post Soviet era (though temporary) the triumphant world capitalism and its political replica, *i.e.*, liberal capitalism has succeeded in presenting itself as the only and eternal alternative available before the humankind. Though, this has been possible by destroying, suffocating, corrupting and discrediting all the up coming alternatives to itself. Thus, it has emerged as the guardian and the custodian of the entire unipolar world. Thus, it has become imperative to the world elites to take limited measures of structural adjustment for the postponement of impending disaster caused by ecological crises such as depletion of the life saving ozone layer due to emission of CFC gases, global warming due to trapping of incoming solar radiation by lead, carbon and carbon monoxide coming mainly from the automobile and industries etc. leading to green house effects and melting of Ice caps and ultimately submergence of important centres of modernity along with poisoning of water, air and soil by chemical and nuclear wastes etc.

Structural Adjustment an Interrogation : A Paradigmatic Shift

Ever since the great depression of 1920's and the Keynesian revolution of 1930's the sphere of capitalist economy was enriched and enhanced by the capitalist political system mostly by the liberal democracies. The role of state as an investor and entrepreneur particularly in the sector of social overhead capital, an agent of bringing about social equality through eradication of poverty, generating employment leading to increase in the purchasing power of the people and creation of internal market by establishing an army of bureaucrats and white collar workers and ultimately by providing market for and acting as the sole protector of indigenous capitalist class had been the characteristic feature of development world over. In short states in their limited role had been the agents for carrying out the tasks of social distribution justice (limited). In India the state and government did not only accept the state regulated Five Year Planning as the sole option for the development as well as carrying out redistributive justice both on social and spatial scales but, exercised effective control and provided guidance in bringing about balanced regional development and social equality. Moreover, state also provided the leadership in the diffusion of industries in the backward areas and carried various welfare and poverty elevation and employment generation programmes. Such steps on the part of the state and the government had the underpinning in their theoretical and ideological commitment towards the people whereby the roots of regional disparities were attributed to the national political economy particularly the nature of class relations. Therefore, it was thought to be amenable to the measures of redressal and ratifications. Which was in its essence people centered though in a limited sense. Today, under the structural adjustment approach the emphases has shifted from the Nehruvian concept of social bases of inequality to that of natural bases of inequality. Under the liberal regimes the most common view held responsible for all the economic and social inequalities are the differences in the peoples capacity and motivation or some other natural advantages/disadvantages. Previously it was thought to be rooted in the social relations hence could be redressed through concerted human efforts in which planning was considered vital. Now these are thought to have natural or extra-human causes. Hence, precious little could be possible to change the state of affairs. An interesting point to note here is the shift in the approach. There exists a total unanimity about the nature of social inequality at the social, cultural and legal points but it is being withdrawn from the economic fronts and economic remedies. Bringing about the social equality through progressive reduction in the social distribution of wealth and opportunities etc. through leading role played by the state etc. that constituted base of Indian path of democratic socialism for all these days since independence have suddenly relegated to the background of the state policy and planning. Moreover, the shift does not only involve the process of displacement of human/social causes by the natural ones but it has also called for a shift in the entire development ethos. Under the changed circumstances the project of economic development has culminated in making wealth an end in itself and not as a means to an end. Thus, the Gandhian ideals of a meaningful life with minimum wants through moral and spiritual restraints on our greed have been replaced by a new consumerist philosophy and ethos of unlimited wants which is increasingly cutting down the human inner strength needed for minimizing the wants and self restraints and making these dependent upon the market. Spuriously enhanced consumerism, exhibitionist affluence have become the culture of new development project. Economic efficiency as indicated by higher rate of profit leading to higher rate of accumulation is justified and is in vogue and often at a very high socio-environmental costs. As a result of this development has become menacing to both environment and society. In its turn the ethics of our development planning has also shifted from maximum equalitarianism to minimum entitlement egalitarianism. Meaning thereby masses are allowed to persist at a bare minimum level of their subsistence so that they remain always vulnerable to all types of disempowerment. And ultimately, generation and accumulation of physical assets and material wealth have marginalised and pushed the interests of the people to the periphery of new development ethos.

True to the logic of a growth oriented development approach based on ever increasing technocratisation, and automatisation the role of bureaucracy is becoming increasingly indispensable. In its turn this leading to the concentration, and centralization of power, opportunity and assets along with the displacement of people including their withdrawal from active participants in the development to that of passivity. Once again true to the structural logic of bureau–

cratic path of development the people has a significance only to the extent they become consumer in the market, and remain contented with their status of becoming the goal of development rather than partner of development. Therefore, according to bureaucratic logic development centering around the social well being focusing on the social problems like poverty, unemployment, landlessness and disempowerment etc. are giving place to higher rates of growth and higher rates of accumulation of capital. Therefore, development of social and economic infrastructure that was considered essential means for attaining real development once have lost their significance. In the new capital centered, growth oriented approach of development people have become means for achieving certain ends. It is undeniably true that efficient and modernized physical infrastructure constitutes the basis of development, but greater emphasis on growth of these tends to relegates the concepts like social redistribution justice etc. to marginal importance.

Social well beings of people presupposes the availability of means with the people for satisfying their basic necessities. Once it is ensured that people are free from the limitations for maintaining their biological survival then only a true and humanistic aspect of development will ask for the empowerment of people along with their endowment. It is so because conditions of social well being requires both, i.e., physical assets as well as empowerment. This very concept of development is antithetical to the Structural Adjustment approach that creates and survives on the conditions of disempowerment. Thus, people will always remain mere objects of development instead of its active agent. In the former case development acquires a participatory nature on the part of the people while in case of the latter they get alienated and marginalised with every additional steps of development. A situation of paradigmatic shift.

The Metamorphosis of the State

The other significant component of the shift is the changing position and role of the state. As mentioned earlier state has emerged as the most potent force for bringing about development particularly after the October Revolution of 1917 in the socialist countries and also after the Keynesian Revolution of 1930's in the capitalist world. By virtue of being a giant force it had also dominated the space, and wherever it was possible the state also played significant role in demarcating and defining all other spaces including the economic space and the space of the market (local, regional, and global). In fact the state has emerged as the "other" to all the other spaces. It did not only demarcate and qualify the other spaces but also became fundamental in creating, recreating, and appropriating various other spaces. It was able to do so because of its position in the entire socio-economic structure. Thus, while emanating from the specific nature of class relations it could enjoy the benefits of relative autonomy from the basic socio-economic structure on the one hand and from the direct control of any particular class on the other. In fact state became the sole legalizing and legitimizing power for the entire society. For doing so the state evolved the Repressive State Apparatuses and Ideological State Apparatuses for the reproduction of specific social relations in relation to economic space and the market. Moreover, the state was not only a regulatory and legalizing force in the market but it was also the market in itself. Market remained one of the many spaces that were created by the state for the reproduction of these social relations. In the changed circumstances, *i.e.,* under the agenda of Structural Adjustment the aims of the so-called "liberating the economy" is nothing but liberating the economy from the control of the state and its interferences. However, it would be incorrect to say that it asks for complete withdrawal of the state from the market. On the contrary, it asks for the control of economy particularly its market over the state. It asks not only for the reversal of the relative autonomy status of the state but also to become an instrument in the hands of market forces or forces that control the market. In other words liberalization asks for instrumentalisation of the state in its totality. State as a mere player in the game whose rules have been set by the market. The metamorphosis of the state is to take place in definite phases. In the initial stage the existing apparatuses of the state will be used to buttress the interests of the economy and the power of the state will be used against other economic competitors. In the later phases state will support the economic interests and transfer its power to the private entrepreneurs. Thus, the Leviathan will be tamed and the Promatheuses will be metamorphosed in to Gin.

In the Foucauldian paradigm of epistemology all social relations are power relations and power is both the end as well as the measure of all social relations including the relations of production. Therefore, the age old concept of power something descending from the above and bestowed on certain individuals/institutions on permanent basis has given way to a new concept of power. The new concept of power stands for more diffused and ubiquitous in nature yet operative through various perceptive and imperceptive channels/capillaries. It is under only certain special circumstances that it gets articulated in the form of multiple centres of power.

Such a shift in the nature of power is another aspect of structural adjustment. World capitalism in its latest phase has been resorting to a new power game. The repressive tolerance of 1960's has given way to repressive or coercive hegemony from above and evolution of capillary power from below. Power under feudalism was more imprecise and haphazard yet it was mostly articulated through natural body representations concentrated on one or a few persons. Power was always associated with some thing corporal occupying specific space/s. In this respect modern times are different because in society the effects of power circulate through progressively finer channels (capillary power) thus gaining access to the inner self of the individuals. In material terms most often it represents vacant spaces therefore, providing temptations at least at the theoretical levels to be occupied by any one on non-permanent basis. In doing so the devices of super-surveillance such as an optical gaze or panopticon etc. contribute in radicalizing the effectiveness of power without any physical constraints other than the geometry and the architecture. Moreover, today under liberal regime the nature of power control from above incorporates the power that has got accumulated in the hands of the World Bodies like U.N.O.

and its other bodies along with world marketing institutions like the GATT, WTO, MTO, TRIPS, TRIMS, IPRS etc. The diffusion of power into finer channels for disempowering the dispossessed, the displaced, the marginalised on the one hand and yet taking about human rights, civil liberties, rights of the minorities, the marginalised and the unrecognized etc. on the other. These all form part of a broader game plan of structural adjustment. Empowering (recognizing) the dispossessed without exception is the most progressive and objective aim of the redistribution politics but, it has its own limitations too. The bogy of empowerment is not for the self recognition of these minorities but it is more to liberate them from the dominance of the universalist discourse of modernity and its universalizing entity, *i.e.*, nationalism, culture, polity etc. thereafter absorb them into global entity on a permanent basis. It envisages the end of the rights of the state particularly its right of ownership, right to control and right to manage and subsequently transfer of these powers from the state to the hands of the private. Therefore, state which has been so far an important force in the regulation of the markets are likely to act as the proponent of the so called free market in which the economic progress becomes possible by progressive dissolution of multiple cultural identities into an over lording and supra universal global entity. Thus, the so-called empowerment of the people is in no way means making them partners of equal in the distribution of power but, on the contrary it means dismantling the power that prevents the free access of the market forces to these and then subsequently cannibalising on them with least resistance.

The weakening of the state has numerous greater and far reaching repercussions particularly on its citizens and theirs rights. The rights of the citizens those have been bestowed upon them by the state after a series of prolonged struggles and sacrifices world over particularly for meeting their basic necessities and minimum level of subsistence including right to maintain minimum human dignity will now stand withdrawn as far as state citizenship is concerned and in their turn these will pass over to the omnipotent forces of globalization. Thereafter, the state will progressively disown its basic responsibilities like providing security, empowerment, opportunities and other freedoms towards citizens.

In the midst of growing withdrawal of the state from its responsibilities and indifference towards its own citizens the climate thus created will suit to the interest of the elite classes of the society more favourable that of the subaltern. This will provide the much desired climate and social conditioning for the unhindered growth of these interests groups which will thus logically force the other sections of society towards their partial to total exclusion, marginalisation in terms of their resource endowments, economic life and political identity. The material conditions of the marginalised will become subservient to the interest of the rich and the needs of the poor masses will get relegated to the periphery of the growing global needs of the rich. The planned or the semi planned economy of India will experience disorientation from its people centre goals to market centre goals.

It was mentioned earlier that the primary objectives of The Structural Adjustment is the opening up of the National economy towards world market. The logic of market being the rate of growth and rate of return this compels the mode of the economy to shift towards the market principle which thrives at the cost of sustainability. Meaning thereby, aspects like resource conservation, sustainable development, environ–mental degradation, pollution, culture of recognition, identity and difference etc. will relegate to the background. The penetration and flow of foreign exchange into the national economy will take place mainly for accelerating the process of extraction of resources and depletion of environment. Evidences show that areas where the foreign interests are being attracted and foreign capital is flowing in a large way includes the marine and mineral resources, areas rich in bio-diversity, organism (agriculture, forest and animal lives) for creating gene banks and gene pools and ultimately monopoly control in the hands of the MNC'S through TRIPS and APRS. The most important and equally disturbing aspects of it is related to the transfer of resource ownership as well as indigenous knowledge and traditional cultural and social rights from the individuals and community to the corporate bodies like the MNC'S which will exploit it to their maximum advantages after establishing patentship through the TRIPS. The promotion and subsequently production of a few products and varieties based on the market logic will prove detrimental to both, *i.e.*, the bio-diversity as well as rights of the technologically less developed traditional communities. It is an undeniable yet true fact that the diversity of environment that have been preserved by various indigenous and ethnic communities over the generations is so closely related to their life style, social ethos and economy that any loss of it is bound to have wider and disastrous consequences for them. Apart from their alienation from their hereditary and traditional rights that will be annihilated by the forces of market, it will also facilitate their quick and speedy integration in a much higher and larger whole, *i.e.*, the world market but this will also put an end to their traditional skill, techniques and identity etc. that they have preserved over the generations.

Loss of bio-diversity along with the social and cultural rights of the people is though significant yet, only a partial repercussion of it. The other significant and in some respect most detrimental aspect of it is related to the threat of mass annihilation that is implicit in the development and stock piling of the nuclear and chemical weapons of mass destruction along with the export of the industrial and nuclear waste from the developed countries to the developing countries. Today, the third world countries do not only supply raw materials and provide market to the developed countries but these are also the proletarian reserves and also the waste dumping grounds for the developed countries. Most often it is noticed that accumulation of such waste in the developing countries had proved menacing to the environment in the post colonial countries. As a consequence, the threat of annihilation to these countries is also coming from the accumulation of industrial and nuclear wastes in the third world countries.

Structural Adjustment : The Wuthering Heights of Recognition and Redistribution in North-Eastern India

Nearly over one hundred and fifty years ago Karl Marx wrote that the history of all the hitherto existing society is the history of class struggles.[5] The causes of struggles in history therefore the march of history has been possible because "no regime-no socio-economic system is able to satisfy all men all places.[6]" Therefore, "those who remain dissatisfied will always have the potential to restart the history.[7]" For a long time the cause of the dissatisfaction of the people was thought to be rooted in their inability to meet the necessities of their life particularly in a class relations (which basically mean class struggle). But, certain sea changes are taking place in the recent historical past that have compelled historians and other scholars to re-look at the inadequacies of materialist conceptions of human history. To name only a few of such events like the resurgence of world capitalism from its grave crises of 1920's and 1940's and ultimately culminating into Two World Wars and success of the national movements in the post war periods, rise of exacerbated material inequalities, loss of identities, and also the dissolution of the soviet block etc., the world history stands confronted with new problems. In the backdrop of these the struggle for recognition has not only become intense but it also joined its other twin and natural ally the fight for redistribution. Thus the fight for recognition and redistribution form the basis of new form and orientation of class struggle.

In the changed circumstances startling inequalities in terms of income and property ownership, in access to paid work, education, health care and leisure times, along with caloric intake, exposure to environmental toxicity, low life expectancy and high rates of morbidity and mortality along with struggle for women's rights, rights of the minorities, ethnic, cultural and national identities etc., have become important bases of the class struggle. Today, the entire globe is infested with the wider and sustained protests and social movements interrogating and questioning the very existence of such a system that has placed the future of mankind at such an impasse and moribund stage. The first and the foremost aspect of it relates to the nature of socio-economic injustice emanating from exploitation, marginalisation, alienation, appropriation and deprivation of large masses on the name of development and modernization. Secondly the socio-cultural injustices rooted in denial of opportunities of social and interpretation to various cultural groups subjugated under a universalizing and over arching entity like the nation, state etc., under the modernity discourses. The intrinsic relationship between these two types of injustices though, look apparently separate yet, these are the two consequences of the same process because the claims of redistribution presupposes the claims of recognition and similarly recognition presupposes the injustices of redistribution. Since, the injustice of redistribution is rooted in the economic exploitation therefore, an economically exploited class is also the one that is culturally dominated. Thus, the struggle for both and not for one at a time will also ensemble the totality of liberation. For example the working classes are both economically and culturally dominated. The hidden injuries of classes are rooted in their economic exploitation. The exploitation of the oppressed classes by the ruling classes also perpetrates a sense of cultural inferiority among the exploited classes. At the other side of this lies the recognition dilemma. In this case misrecognition of their culture also leads to their economic exploitation or subjects them to distributional injustices. For example the discrimination of female with respect to their work and pay is done because they are also subjected to recognition injustices. Similarly, the gayist and the lesbians are economically victimised because they are also subjected to misrecognition.

The situation is more complex in societies and cultural groups that had experienced lackadaisical exposure to the impact of modernity. India, a land of numerous cultures and cultural identities had always been an intriguing issue to the thinkers. Today, when it is exposed to the forces of liberalization and world market the issue have become more important. Opening up of the Indian economy to the forces of globalization has exposed the nation and its people to the enactment of these dilemmas. The North-Eastern Region of India is facing the major brunt due to the close intermingling of the two.

The North-Eastern Region does not only lie at the geographical periphery of India but the ongoing national mainstream discourses are also less popular among the people of this region. It is largely due to these reasons that the nation state that followed after the independence of India was bestowed with the tasks of maintaining its integrity, defending political sovereignty and economic development based on the principle of democratic socialism for the purpose of bringing about economic equality within and without the region. This also constitutes the core of Nehruvian path of development popularly known as a mixed path of economic development in India. The principal aim of this path was to bring about equality in terms of economic development among the regions of the country and minimized the levels of social disparities. The North-Eastern Region of India was better placed and stood firmly gaining in this process. It was mentioned earlier that according to the Nehruvian model the root cause of social inequality was considered to be socio-historical in nature. Therefore, concerted efforts were made on the part of the state in bringing about development through people's active participation. It was thought that peoples participation is mandatory for development, social justice and regional balance. With the enunciation of the measures of structural adjustment the socio-historic causes of inequalities have been replaced by the natural factor. According to the inverted logic of development the differences in the economic status of people is largely the result of people's (in) capabilities and (lack of) motivation. It is however, interesting to notice that under the new cause-consequence relationship too inequality continues to be the theme of discussions at the socio-cultural and politico-legal fronts but it is conspicuous by its absence in the realms of economic decision making or measures of the distributive justice. Once, the role of the state is curtailed in bringing about development in these backward areas then the upliftment of the poorer sections of our society will receive a great setback, along with this the objectives of social distributive justice of the Gandhian and Nehruvian philosophy with the ideal life of minimum wants will be replaced by consumerist philosophy of unlimited wants and desires. This will not only undermine the tribal solidarity and co-operation but it will also accentuate the process of social differentiation in these relatively less differentiated culture groups/communities. In place of the communal ownership of means of production and resources, individual and private property will come into existence. Classes and class struggle will become the dominant mode of social interaction.

The exposure of the North-Eastern Region of India to the forces of market after the withdrawal of state from economic spheres the people of this region with their large resource base but low levels of economic development are likely to be subjected to unprecedented level and intensity of exploitation including depletion of their resources. Loss of their hereditary rights over their natural environment and in matters of their economic and socio-political activities etc. will lead to the disempowerment of these people. In its turn disempowerment of the people has its own socio-economic ramifications. It has been proved beyond doubt that under such circumstances manipulations and manipulative consciousness takes the place other dominant social and personal ethos. The fear of disempowerment among the people is so frightening that not only the loss of power but even any temporal detachment from it amounts to loss of ones beings. Thus, power creates the 'being' and 'being' such created retains it through manipulation and ultimately generalized alienation breeds social tension and political unrest.[8]

Disempowerment in case of this region particularly in the areas inhabited by the tribals will mean loss of their right over the use and preservation of their environment in its complete biodiversity. Once, the tribal are alienated from their natural environment then the objective bases of their social activity, art, culture and popular science etc. too will loose its significance and meaning. The displacement of the tribals from their land (mostly under community ownership) and emergence of private property relationships in land will not only create classes and social tensions among the relatively less differentiated tribals of the region but it will also transform their self sustaining economy into a dependent one.

Though, the loss of biodiversity and alienation from the traditional resource base will adversely affect all members of the community alike. However, the loss for the females in the region is more traumatic than that for the men folks. It is so because, in a traditional society the division of labour is such that most of items of the female is confined to the collection and gathering of items like fodder, fuel, fruits, nuts, leaves, roots, etc. from their immediate environment particularly land and forest. Once, their traditional rights over the use of the forest resources are forfeited then the females will suffer more than the men. Secondly, in these societies women have very small personal or private property worth naming. As a result of this large part of the realization of this particular right among the females come from their free access to the environment and natural resource base. Therefore, after the implementation of the measures of structural adjustment women will suffer more. Thirdly, the direct and free access of the tribals to their environment is both a basis of their subsistence economy as well as treasure of their immense knowledge and craftsmanship. Once, the natural environment is destroyed this will also complete the loss of their own identity.

Structural Adjustment and the Politics of Difference in the North-Eastern Region

The fall of socialism and the triumph of liberalism accompanied by exacerbated material inequality, alarming environmental toxicity and degradation, spread of cultural imperialism, loss of identity and finally subjection of mankind under twin injustices of non-recognition and ill-redistribution have become inseparable part of structural adjustment. The North-Eastern region of India stands out as an example here because, the various cultural groups inhabiting this region for many centuries have not only been able to maintain their socio-cultural and politico-economic identities for a long time but, they have also been the repository of indigenous knowledge, peoples technology and organic relations with their environment against all odds. It is not that the isolation of those communities that remained impervious to outside influences in the past was responsible for their seclusion. In fact, interaction of the people of this region with that of other region had been in existence for a long time but, it is only now, particularly after the introduction of the measures for structural adjustment that they are being completely engulfed and ultimately facing the threat of their total submergence into the global identity. This particularl fear had come to them more like a shock. The exposure of these people to the forces of globalization have not only shattered the basis of their identity but it has also placed them to fight against the twin injustices of recognition and redistribution.

The nature of the struggle in the region is centering around the demand for cultural identity and economic opportunities (or recognition and redistribution). They are afraid of both because globalization will lead to their economic marginalisation and cultural extinction including patterns of representation, interpretation and communication along with their cultural symbols and signs.

It is widely accepted that in these relatively less differentiated societies the underprivileged sections mostly earning their livelihood by using the resources owned by the community through community labour etc. have been the specific characteristics of most of the culture groups in the region. But, now on the name of modernization, globalization and liberalization private property has not only come into existence and class differentiation. Community labour is increasingly becoming a thing of the past and it has been replaced by contractual relations. Moreover, the organic links of the people with their environment and their knowledge about the environment (both plants and animals) have always been the intrinsic part of their social existence. Any effort to alienate these communities from their immediate environment and its bio-diversity will not only rob them off their heritage and identity but will also lead to their biological extinction. Imposition of any economic, social, and cultural standard on the name of economic efficiency, functional feasibility and national culture, rules, and legislation will also prove detrimental to their identity. It has become all the more important because the path opened by the forces of liberalization has everywhere proved antithetical to people specific recognition. Finally, in the case of this region the recognition and redistribution issue can be solved only by greater empowerment of people and not by their disempowerment. Liberalization does talk of dismantling the power of the state but it does not talk about the empowerment of the people. Thus, by implication it means empowerment of market forces and disrecognition and maldistribution among the people.

References

1. K. Mark and F. Engels, *The Manifesto of the Communist Party*, Selected Works, Vol. 1, Progress Publishers, Moscow, 1977, p. 108.
2. Karl Mark and F. Engels, "The Eighteenth Brumaire of Lois Bonapart", Selected Works, Vol. 1, Progress Publishers, Moscow, 1977, p. 398.
3. Dave Broad, "Globalization v/s labour, "Monthly Review", Vol. 47, No. 7, Dec. 1995.
4. Paul Connerton, (ed), *Critical Sociology, Selected Readings*, Penguin Books, Harmondsworth, 1976, p. 27.
5. K. Marx and F. Engels, *op. cit.*, p. 45.
6. F. Fukuyama, "The End of History", The National Interest, No.16, Summer, Washington D.C., 1989, pp. 3-18.
7. F. Fukuyama, *The End of History And the Last Man*, Free Press, New York, 1992.
8. P. G. Vijaya, Sherry Chand and Anil K. Gupta, "A River Without Tributaries—Liberating the Mind Through Harnessing Grass–roots Creativity", The Indian Journal of Public Administration, Vol. XLII, No. 3, 1996, pp. 98-301.

Chapter 4

Economic Reforms, Patent Regime and Economic Development of the North-East India

—*Mahesh Lalwani*

1. Economic Reforms and Balance of Payments

Authors of Economic Reforms, Jagdish Bhagwati and TN Srinivasan, have opined that initiation of reforms in 1991 was essential to correct macro imbalances in India's Balance of Payments (BOP) and Union Budget. They argued that India then was faced with unsustainable deficit in her BOP and internal budget leading to macro economic inefficiencies. And this they argued could be remedied only through (micro economic) structural reforms resting on the tripod of liberalization, privatization and globalization. In general terms, the structural reforms have to be pushed forward in critical micro economic areas such as industrial and trade licensing policies, increased privatization of the economy by lifting physical controls and providing incentives for fresh direct investments (both domestic and foreign); disinvestment in public sector; and finally the acceptance of the Dunkel Draft Text. The structural reforms have also been justified in terms of sustainable growth and the twin objectives of fighting the menace of poverty and unemployment. The structural reforms were believed to bring forth *sustained economic growth.* This was their basic hypothesis. Content of growth, the process of growth and the distributive aspects of growth are equally important issues that they ignored. There is a conjecture in circulation that benefits of growth will percolate automatically to the lowest cross sections of society through employment. Let us take empirical data. With the advancement in GDP (Table 1) in India, for instance, growth in employment has sizably lagged behind the growth in Gross Domestic Product. Growth in annual employment slowed down from 2.4% (1971-76) to 0.70% (1981-86). It rose by little in subsequent decade to touch 1.3% during 1992-97. Compare these growth rates with the average growth rate in Gross Domestic product of 5.6%. In fact, the 1993 Human Development Report of the UNO described this phenomenon as the period of jobless growth. And surely with the growing monopoly power of TNCs, employment growth would slacken even more in the coming years in the sectors where they are likely to enter.

Table 1

GROWTH RATES OF GDP, EMPLOYMENT AND SHARE OF SAVINGS, INVESTMENTS AND ICOR

	*GDP** %	*Employment*	*Savings*	*Investment*	*ICOR % of GDP+*
1951-56	3.61	NA	10.28	10.66	2.95
1956-61	4.27	NA	11.73	14.52	3.40
1961-66	2.84	NA	13.21	15.45	5.44
1966-71	4.66	NA	14.35	15.99	3.43
1971-76	3.08	2.4	17.27	17.87	5.80
1976-81	3.24	2.6	21.65	21.47	6.63
1981-86	5.06	0.7	19.36	20.98	4.15
1985-90	5.81	1.5	20.37	22.70	3.91
1985-92	5.31	1.2	20.70	23.17	4.36
1992-97#	5.60	1.3	21.60	23.20	4.10

* at factor cost, % p.a.

+ at market price.

projected in the Eighth Plan.

Source : Tata Economic and Technical Sciences, India in Brief, Mumbai, 1997.

In this paper, economic reforms are evaluated against the backdrop of empirical data related to India's BOP and

GDP; and India's share in new patent and trade mark regime. The impact of economic reforms on the North-East India is examined separately.

We recall that balance of trade showed a deficit of 6 billion dollars in March 1991 with barely 1 billion dollars as foreign exchange reserves. Inflation had soared to 17 percent with slackening industrial production and a low growth rate in Gross Domestic Product (GDP) of barely 1.1 percent that year. Economic reforms have indeed stabilized the economy to register over 6% growth rate in Gross Domestic Product in both 1995 and 1996; have brought down the annual inflation rate below 10%, have raised the foreign exchange reserves to 25 billion dollars. The EPW Research Foundation has put India's foreign exchange reserves excluding gold reserves to 21 billion dollars as on March 21, 1997. Exports at current prices have grown from Rs. 44 thousand crores in 1991-92 to Rs.96 thousand crores in 1996-97, thereby registering trend growth of 13% per annum with mean export level of Rs. 77 thousand crores. When expressed in dollar terms, India's exports have registered lower trend growth rate of 8% because of dollar's appreciation *vis-a-vis* Rupee (IR). India's imports in rupee and dollar terms have respectively registered trend growth rates of 14% and 9% per annum for the same period with a mean import bill of 87 thousand crores. Thus, import bill has outpaced India's export earnings for the entire considered period (Table 2). India's Balance of Trade (BOT) has registered phenomenal increase in volume indeed! One must remember that the recent upsurge in India's net foreign exchange reserves is fickle-natured. The equity participation can come and go as may please the investor. That is why we notice that foreign exchange reserves in 1995-96 are lower than what they were in 1994-95 by 4 billion dollars. In the current financial year of 1996-97, foreign exchange reserves have risen over 1995-96 level by 3.5 billion dollars but are still lower than what they were in 1994-95.

Balance of trade continues to be negative but now with a difference. The deficit of 6 billion dollars at the fiscal end of 1991 has never been seen again. In fact, it reached a low of 1.5 billion dollars the next year in March 1992 and barely 1 billion

Table 2

INDIA'S BALANCE OF TRADE

(Units : Rupees in Crores and Dollars in Millions)

Year	*Exports*		*Imports*		*Balance of Trade*	
	Rupees	*Dollars*	*Rupees*	*Dollars*	*Rupees*	*Dollars*
1991-92	44042	17866	47851	19411	-3809	-1545
1992-93	53688	18537	63375	21882	-9686	-3345
1993-94	69751	22238	72101	23306	-3350	-1068
1994-95	82674	26331	89971	28654	-7297	-2324
1995-96	106465	31831	121647	36370	-15182	-4539
1996-97	95876	27074	111069	31365	-15193	-4290

Source : E.P.W., March 22, 1997.

Table 3

SELECTED EXPORT RATIOS

Year	*India's exports as % of*			*Value terms of trade (1978-79)=100*
	*World exports**	*India's imports*	*India's National Income+*	
1960-61	1.05	57.8	4.2	na
1970-71	0.65	91.0	3.8	127.4
1980-81	0.42	52.4	5.4	80.8
1985-86	0.45	54.7	4.7	107.6
1989-90	0.53	69.5	6.9	121.1
1990-91	0.58	66.2	6.9	109.3
1991-92	0.55	86.7	8.1	119.5
1992-93	0.56	81.2	8.7	127.3
1993-94	0.58	94.6	10.0	136.9
1994-95	[0.64]	92.8	[10.2]	n.a.

* calendar years, *e.g.* 1960-61 for 1960 etc.

+ National Income at market price.

Bracketed figures as the estimates.

Source : Tata Economic and Technical Sciences, India in Brief, Mumbai, 1977.

dollars in March 1994. It is about 4 billion dollars in March, 1997. Indirectly, it is to suggest that exports as proportion to India's imports have risen (Table 3). India's exports could barely meet 55% of her import bill in 1985-86 but could meet 93% of her imports in 1994-95. This is a phenomenal change in India's foreign trade. The difference on two sides is met through external borrowings and shown in capital account of Balance of payments. Since India's exports could never pay for her imports, external borrowings have shown an increase from year to year. And since such borrowings don't come free, debt servicing has posed a serious threat to external value of Rupee. India's cumulative external debt in fiscal end of 1995 stood at 95 billion dollars of which 13 billion dollars was debt servicing forming 14% (10% in 1992) of the total (Table 4). A bulk of this debt has been raised at high rates of interest particularly that from NRI's and commercial markets. This is not a healthy trend.

Table 4

INDIA'S OVERALL EXTERNAL DEBT OUTSTANDING

End March	*1995*	*1994*	*1993*	*1992*
		U.S. $ Mn.		
Total external debt	95,301	91,074	90,023	85,285
Multilateral	28,400	26,258	25,008	23,090
of which concessional	17,819	16,044	15,503	14,320
Bilateral	19,641	17,122	16,154	15,466
of which concessional	17,578	14,984	13,978	13,447
IMF	4,300	5,040	4,799	3,451
Export credit	4,342	4,399	4,322	3,990
Commercial Borrowings	12,364	11,876	11,643	11,715
NRI deposits	12,422	12,665	11,141	10,420
Rupee debt (owed to Russia)	9,588	10,088	10,616	10,420
of which defense	8,763	9,159	9,661	9,222
Total Long-term debt	91,057	87,448	83,683	78,215
Short-term debt	4,264	3,626	6,340	7,070
Debt servicing+				
Debt-Service payment (US$ bn)	13.0@	10.5@	8.4	8.1
Debt service as % of current receipts	n.a.	27.1	25.3	30.3

@ provisional.

Source : E.P.W., March 22, 1997.

The growing debt servicing ratio in total indebtedness may weaken our BOP situation. This surely does not augur well for the reformists. Another notable observation worth mentioning here is that composition of India's imports has favoured in that order capital goods, petroleum and petroleum products, chemical elements, fertilizers and non-ferrous metals. All looks well except the excessive import of petroleum and petroleum products. (Table 5). This group of imports has formed 25% and 21% of total import bill in fiscal end of 1994 and 1995, respectively. It has besides grown in absolute and relative terms over the years. Its share in total imports was barely 8% in 1971 but was a high of 42% in 1981. These shares are volatile and would continue to haunt us for long unless India practices prudent energy policy. Truth is that we have no energy policy in operation today. This group of imports

Table 5

PRINCIPAL IMPORTS

Rs. Crores

	*1994-95**	*1993-94*	*1992-93*	*1980-81*	*1970-71*
Cereals and preparations	108	290	966	100	213
Petroleum Products	18,470	18,046	17,142	5,264	136
Edible oils	610	167	167	677	23
Chemical elements and compounds	6,838	4,299	4,134	358	68
Drugs and pharmaceutical products	859	809	813	85	24
Fertilizers	3,246	2,631	2,832	818	86
Paper	776	696	514	205	37
Iron and Steel	3,815	2,494	2,255	852	147
Non-ferrous metals	2,689	1,503	1,144	477	119
Capital goods	23,177	19,581	13,123	1,910	404
Pearls, precious stones	5,019	8,263	7,072	417	25
Total imports (incl. others)	88,705	73,101	63,375	12,549	1,634

Note : * Provisional.

Source : Tata Economic and Technical Sciences, India in Brief, Mumbai, 1997.

would throw all our planning effort out of gear if global oil prices start rising. So far, India has seen lucky years of stable global oil prices for almost five to six years. Indications are to the contrary now. If that persists, oil imports would eat away the largest share of our export earnings. So our present BOP stability rests on the volatile assumption of constant global prices of oil. Declining home output of oil have made things worse for us.

Exports, on the other hand, have shown maturity of exhibiting a shift from primary commodities to manufactured goods. Share of this group of commodities has constantly increased from 45% in 1960-61 to 76% in 1994 (Table 6).

Table 6

EXPORTS BY COMMODITY GROUPS

Rs. Crores

	1993-94	*1990-91*	*1980-81*	*1970-71*	*1960-61*
Agriculture and	13,021	6,317	2,057	487	284
Allied products	(1[illegible].7)	(19.4)	(30.7)	(31.7)	(44.2)
Ores and Minerals	2,371	1,497	814	164	52
(excl. coal)	(3.4)	(4.6)	(6.2)	(10.7)	(8.1)
Iron ore	1,374	1,049	303	117	17
	(1.97)	(3.2)	(4.5)	(7.6)	(2.6)
Manufactured	52,702	23,736	3,747	772	291
products	(75.6)	(72.9)	(55.8)	(50.3)	(45.3)
Mineral fuels and	1,554	948	28	13	7
lubricants (incl. coal)	(2.2)	(2.9)	(0.4)	(0.8)	(1.1)
Total (incl. others)	69,751	32,553	6,711	1,535	642

Note : Figures in brackets indicate percentage share to total exports.

Source : Tata Economic and Technical Sciences, India in Brief, Mumbai, 1997.

This entire discussion has relevance to India's North East Region. In this group of rising export of manufactured goods, share of the seven NE states is almost nil. Since reforms would touch this sector the most, it is most likely that this region would be left out in receiving gains of reforms. Looked differently, India's four principal group of imports namely the capital goods, petroleum and petroleum products, fertilizers, and chemical elements and compounds account for 58% of the total in 1995. But there are hardly any industrial

Table 7

INDIA'S SHARE IN WORLD EXPORTS OF PRINCIPAL COMMODITIES

	World exports (US$ Bn)		*India's share in world exports (%)*	
	1992	*1980*	*1992*	*1980*
Meat and preparations	39.25	17.83	0.2	0.4
Fish etc. and preparations	37.22	12.26	1.8	2.0
Rice	3.93	4.36	3.4	3.7
Vegetables and fruits	56.65	24.02	0.7	1.1
Sugar and preps. and honey	14.23	16.18	0.6	0.3
Tea and mate	2.13	1.63	10.5	27.7
Coffee and substitutes	7.87	12.98	1.2	2.1
Spices	0.17	1.07	64.1	14.5
Animal feed	17.98	10.32	2.5	1.6
Tobacco and manufactures	21.10	3.42	0.4	4.4
Oilseeds & oleaginous fruits	10.17	9.49	0.2	0.3
Leather	9.86	3.42	3.4	10.0
Iron ore and concentrates	7.88	6.52	9.4	6.3
Textiles	118.33	48.88	2.0	2.3
Apparel & clothing accessories	133.82	32.37	2.4	1.8
Pearls, precious stones etc.	27.87	18.56	10.1	3.1
Organic chemicals	75.77	31.84	0.5	0.1
Inorganic chemicals	25.64	15.49	0.2	0.2
Medicinal and pharmaceutical preparations	49.10	13.92	0.3	0.8
Iron and steel	102.98	68.23	0.4	0.1
Metal manufactures	74.46	36.84	0.6	0.6
Machinery	865.78	281.83	0.1	0.1
Road vehicles	349.48	127.35	0.1	0.2
Total (incl. others)	3,218.91	1,997.67	0.6	0.4

Note : Totals may not tally with those shown in other tables.

Source : Tata Economic and Technical Sciences, India in Brief, Mumbai, 1997.

units in the North East that may utilize such imports. So North-East has lost the race here, as well. Yet look at the things differently. Export strength of North-East particularly that of Assam is found in Tea. It is precisely here, Indian tea has seen a dwindling share in world exports of tea from 28% in 1980 to barely 11% in 1992 and less than 10% in 1995 (Table 7). To top it, world market for tea has grown only marginally from 1.63 billion dollars in 1980 to 2.13 billion dollars in 1992 for being an item with low income elasticity and high price elasticity. Cheap Sri Lankan and Kenyan Tea have grown their respective share in world tea markets.

2. Shift Away from Poor to Rich

Liberalization has affected fiscal policy, as well. The 1997 budget, for instance, has announced sizable cuts in tax rates both direct and indirect. But most forget that a country's budget has equally important expenditure side. In fact, Government outlays can change course of economic events in a country. Coming back to tax cuts, these have been offered on board despite having huge fiscal deficits, leading to rapid rise in prices of rice, wheat and sugar. The procurement of wheat by the FCI even at the enhanced price of Rs. 450 per ton is abysmal in the entire wheat growing region where free market wholesale price has touched Rs. 600 per ton. It is likely to touch Rs. 900/- per ton soon according to trade circles (see Economic Times of recent dates). Indications therefore are clear that the coming days would see rapid rise in food prices. In fact in a pre-budget scoop, the Government of India picked the pockets of the poor by increasing the issue prices of all essential PDS commodities like wheat, sugar, rice, despite having huge oil pool deficit of Rs. 12,000 crores. On the other hand, government has refused to raise prices of petrol and petroleum products on the grounds that it would lead to inflationary trends. What an argument! The same argument did not hold when food prices were raised under PDS by the same government. Reduction in excise and income tax rates may shift aggregate demand upwards besides, which will have its own dynamics leading to price rise unless supplies in the real commodity sector increases by matching magnitudes and same mix.

The recent upsurge in cost of living index for agricultural labourers and industrial workers has surely eroded the real wages of the poor, whose money wages are not compensated by the revision of pay scales and disbursement of periodic instalments of dearness allowance. Do such reforms then convey any meaning for the poor? It is a well known fact that the landless farmers seek employment in crop and livestock activities which are capital and land intensive. Agriculture and exploitation of India's inland and oceanic economic zone for marine products are other capital intensive activities which by their intrinsic nature cannot be the avocation of the poor. Besides, there is found crowding of animals in marginal and small farm sizes (expressed in landholding), resulting in low capital and land availability per animal. The only redeeming factor is more labour use per animal in these farm sizes. These are precisely the activities where North-East India may have some potential. But all these are high technology fields plagued by patents and trade marks. Discussion in this direction therefore would not be out of place here.

3. Patents and Intellectual Property Rights

The UN convention in 1967 establishing the World Intellectual Property Organization provided that intellectual property shall include rights relating to :

(a) literary, artistic and scientific works;
(b) performance of performing artists, phonograms and broadcast;
(c) inventions in all fields of human endeavour;
(d) scientific discoveries;
(e) industrial designs;
(f) trademarks, service marks and commercial names and designations;
(g) protection against unfair competition and all other rights resulting from intellectual activity in the industrial, scientific, literary, or artistic fields.

The intellectual property is protected and governed by appropriate national legislations under the forms of patents, copyrights, trademarks, designs and knowhow. Patents are the most important form of protection, although in computer software copyright protection is most effective. Indian legislation in this direction includes *(i)* Indian Patents Act, 1970 (amended in 1994); *(ii)* The Designs Act (1911); *(iii)* The Trade and Merchandise Act, (1958); and *(iv)* The Copyright Act. Besides, India is signatory to two international treaties namely *(i)* Agreement on Trade Related Aspects of Intellectual Property Rights (TRIPS); and *(ii)* Berne Convention for the Protection of Literary and Artistic Works.

A *patent* is a legal monopoly right granted by the state for a specified time to owner of an invention for its commercial exploitation. Each patent right is further subjected to scrutiny based on considerations related to military and health aspects. Like all economic rights, a patent can be given away, inherited, sold, bought, licensed and may even be abandoned. State can, besides, revoke patents in the general interest of the public. An invention is patentable only if it involves an inventive step and commercially exploitable to achieve a practical result. Publicly known cumulative technical experience and knowledge does not qualify for patent rights. So patentable invention need to be different from "prior art". There is no such thing as world patent (see GOI, TIFAC publication: DOC 020).

Copyright protects only the form of expression of ideas and not the ideas themselves. The creativity protected by copyright law is creativity in the choice and arrangement of words, musical notes, colours, shapes and so on. Works of drawings, painting, architecture, photographic works, works of applied art, the map, plans, sketches, three dimensional works relating to geography, topography, architecture or science may all receive copyrights irrespective of the mode of expression.

Trademark is an identification symbol used in the course of trade enabling seller to distinguish his product from similar products of other sellers. Servicemarks are used in the tertiary sector like those of hotels, airlines, tour operators, boutiques, etc.

The expression *"Design"* refers to the feature of shape, configuration, pattern or ornament applied to any article by any industrial process or means whether manual, mechanical or chemical, separate or combined, which in the finished article appeal to an end are judged solely by the eye. The features are conceived in the author's intellect and given material shape as pictorial illustration, or as a specimen, prototype, or model. Under registration act, the features are protected as design (thums up bottle, for instance).

Know-how could be in the form of an aggregation of known processes/procedures, and accumulation of data, a secret formulation, or a combination of any of these. Know-how is not patentable and is often transferred together with licensing of patents and transfer of technology transfer.

4. Grant of Patents, Industrial Designs and Trade Marks in India

Number of applications for patent rights in India has been in the region of 3000 to 3500 per year (Table 8). Not all applications are favoured with a grant. In fact, in the recent years between 1980-81 to 1994-95, it has been in the region of 1000 to 1750. The cumulative patents in force has, however declined from a high of 30,726 in 1971 to 10,031 in 1992-93. One reason could be the expiry of earlier patents.

Table 8
PATENTS IN INDIA

	1992-93	*1991-92*	*1985-86*	*1980-81*	*1971*
	Number of patents				
Applications filed	3,467*	3,552	3,526	2,954	4,345
Patents granted	1,272+	1,676	1,951	1,019	3,923
Patents in force	10,031	10,299	13,393	17,205	30,726

* in 1994-95 and 1993-94; 5,228 and 3,868 respectively.

\+ in 1994-95 and 1993-94; 1,759 and 1,716 respectively.

Source : Tata Economic and Technical Sciences, India in Brief, Mumbai, 1997.

What is of more interest to us is Table 9 in which position with regards to designs and trade marks has been discussed for the post reform period of 1991 to 1995. Over the years, designs and trade marks rights granted in India have grown. Foreign institutions have raised their share faster. From a low of 5% in 1991-92 (38 out of 675) in favour of foreign entities, their share has gone up to 14% in 1994-95 (210 out of 1453). USA, Japan and UK are the largest beneficiaries in that order. But the scenario is quite different in the Electronics Industry where from February 1996 to June 1996 only 6 applications were filed by Indians/Indian companies. In contrast there were 286 applications from foreign companies and 8 among these filed 5 or more applications. No Indian/Indian company filed 5 or more applications (IPR, 1996, p. 1). Daewoo Electronics put up 93 applications in this industry alone followed by Motorola Inc. (22), Siemens (24), Aktiengesellschaft (24), Sony Corporation (13), Qualcomm (7), Philips (11), LG Electronics

Table 9

DESIGNS AND TRADE MARKS

	1994-95	*1993-94* *Number*	*1991-92*
Design registered			
Total :	1,453	816	675
Domestic	1,243	735	637
Foreign+	210	81	38
of which			
USA	58	20	14
Japan	36	8	3
UK	22	6	4
Switzerland	17	-	4
Sweden	15	-	-
Germany	13	1	-
France	12	1	4
Netherlands	8	10	-
Others	29	35	9
Trade marks			
Total Applications filed	29,252	16,968	13,107

Note : All figures are provisional.

+ According to country of origin.

Source : E.P.W., March 22, 1977.

(5) and Wavelink communications (5). Within Electronics, applications filed in the field of telecommunications (111 out of 286) have constituted 39% for the same period. Only a single application is there from an Indian/Indian company, the rest 110 filed by foreign companies. Out of total applications filed in telecommunication field, 16 applications have been filed in the area of cellular telephone and related technology. The major players are Motorola, Daewoo, Qual–comm, Philips, Siemens, Aktiengesellschaft and Ionica.

Receiving patent rights, trade marks and registered designs is an expensive proposition in India and prohibitively expensive in the West. For this reasons, patents may increasingly go in favour of foreign entities in India and Indian's chances of receiving patents in the west getting remote. Scrutiny of government records by this author in the Department of Science and Technology gives the impression that not a single product patent has been received by a firm having operations in North-East India. A few are found in Calcutta.

5. Effects of New Patent Laws

Recently concluded GATT to which India now is signatory (15th April, 1994) has certain clauses related to patent rights that may jeopardize the interests of farmers directly. We recall that both production and distribution of foundation and certified seeds in India has never been patented. In fact Indian Agricultural Universities have disseminated their innovations free of cost to both progressive farmers and laggards. As a result, adoption of HYV seeds by our farmers has been so easy at a nominal cost. In contrast, in Europe and North America, seed production and distribution has always been in the commercial sector. The *sui generis* system commonly refers to the system of Plant Breeder's Rights (PBRs) under which the patentee breeder has the exclusive right for 16 years to produce and market the patented seed. Such rights are extendable by another 10 years if the commercial exploitation of the patent had not sufficiently paid back the patentee (section 14 and 15 of the Patents and Design Act, 1911). Codified in the Union for the Protection of New Plant Varieties

(UPOV), seed patentees have enjoyed monopoly rights on the sale of variety but not on the variety itself or its genes. Thus other breeders could use any patented variety for further breeding work under the Breeder's Exemption clause. Besides, farmers could also use such a variety for production and recycling it indefinitely in the subsequent seasons under the Farmer's Exemption. This is what existed till 1994. **The recently signed Dunkel Draft Text does retain the farmer's clause but has dispensed with the breeder's exemption**. This would have serious implications for both livestock and crop husbandry activities in India's agriculture. India's self sufficiency in foodgrains was largely a result of her sound plant breeding programmes in public sector ensuring dissemination of new knowledge to small and large farmers in every nook and corner of the country. Under the proposed farmer's exemption clause, our farmers lawfully cannot retain sizeable quantities of patented seeds and surely cannot market such seeds to other farmers. In this direction, it is relevant to note here that the bulk of the basic genetic resources are actually found in the tropics and sub-tropics. The USA forgets that her status as the largest exporter and producer of rice is due to her stealing away of Indica and Japonica rice germplasm from India and Japan in the past without paying a single pice to India and a single Yen to Japan.

With the advent of recombinant DNA technology, today's biotechnologist may be able to manufacture 'Transgenic Plants" through the modern molecular biological methods. His greatest advantage lies in his ability to shift genes across the species barrier, thereby making possible migration of disease resistance attributes from one crop to the other. The new variety of disease resistant crop therefore would qualify for product patent rights under the new scheme of things. It is pertinent here to distinguish between the process patenting and product patenting. Under the former, the process by which a new drug or plant seed is manufactured is patented and not the product itself. This left adequate room for others to produce the same product through an alternative process or improve upon the existing process to get the same product. Under the product patenting now implemented under WTO, it would not be possible any more to do so since the product itself is patented. Many would be wondering if such patent rights could practically be practiced across the globe. The answer unfortunately is yes. The world's biggest bully, the USA under the Special 301 intellectual property provisions of the Omnibus Trade and Competitive Act of 1988 (commonly known as 1988 US Trade Act) is empowered to take retaliatory action against any country which deny adequate and effective intellectual property protection. After making enquiries, an accused country is promoted from the watch list to priority foreign country status as a prelude to trade sanctions (USIS, 1993). In April 1992, imports from India to USA of pharmaceuticals were denied duty free benefits on the ground that India had failed to provide effective protection to American intellectual property. What had happened was that many Indian drug companies (Dr. Reddy's Laboratory, Cheminor Drugs, Shasun Chemicals, etc.) had produced some patented drugs through alternative routes at sizably lower costs for the export markets in USA, thereby inviting wrath. When implemented, the Dunkel Draft provisions on patents would prove worse than the 1911 patent act. Firstly, it would immediately take away the right of a country to have her own patent laws. India's 1970 patent act would soon look defunct. Secondly, patenting of both the process and the product looks unjust since the bulk of the patents are already in the hands of capital rich countries. This bulk would bloat further with the upcoming rat race for acquisition of fresh patent rights among these countries. India could also join it provided man and material are found and deployed in this direction. Thirdly, with the sacrifice of breeder's and farmer's exemption clauses, interests of both farmers and researchers are going to be affected seriously. Fourthly, the net result of this would be the rising prices of drugs, medicines, pesticides, insecticides, seeds, fungicides, etc. which would make adoption of new technology by poor animal and crop husbandsmen even more difficult. For them much of scientific advancements will have little relevance. How sad for millions of them! One can imagine the fate of India's Integrated Rural Development Programme in which livestock rearing is an important activity. Fifthly, patenting of all life forms would make our crossbreeding programme infeasible for the want of patents locally and financial muscle in the hands of farmers as well as research institutions. Sixthly, India's drug exports may diminish sizeably and drug imports may rise in value terms creating macro imbalances in her balance of payments. Seventhly, there could be genetic erosion of all life forms under the new scheme of things. Green revolution has already lent disservice to conservation of biodiversity. And now the increasing influence of TNCs in the world movement of trade in all life forms would further lessen the chances of biodiversity found on the multitude of farms and cattle yards across the globe. Plant varieties or animal semen carrying economic traits of high yield or high profitability or disease resistance would get marketed more aggressively by the patentee TNCs. This would lead to fewer seed varieties or bovine strains being adopted by farmers. "This would have very unfortunate consequences for the viability of livestock and their ability to survive biotic and abiotic stresses" (Sahai, 1993). And, although under new patent laws research exemption clause has been retained, the results of such research cannot be commercially exploited. Indian agricultural scientists would thereby be constrained to use domestically found plant and animal germplasm (if patented) to breed improved species. Profitability would be the hallmark of all scientific research and acquisitiion of more and more patents would become an end in itself. What looks sure is that India's endorsement of new patent laws surely would harm her thousands of farmers in the North East. Forthcoming process and product patent rights mostly in the hands of TNCs, having headquarters in the North are going to make livestock and crop activities capital intensive. Globalization of India's agriculture may bring direct foreign investments in food processing industry including dairy, agriculture and meat industries. Those who have the land and capital resources may stand to benefit. How many in the NEI would benefit is a matter of further empirical research.

References

Bhagwati, J. and Srinivasan, T.N., *India's Economic Reforms*, Ministry of Finance, New Delhi, 1993.

Chaudhuri, Sudip, *"Dunkel Draft on Drug Patents—Background and Implications"*, Economic and Political Weekly, September 04, 1993.

Government of India, *Economic Reforms, Discussion Paper*, Ministry of Finance, New Delhi, 1993.

Government of India, *Patenting in Electronics, Intellectual Property Rights*, D.S.T., Technology Bhavan, New Delhi, Vol. 2, No. 9, September, 1996.

Government of India, TIFAC, *Some Questions and Answers on Patents and Copyrights*, D.S.T., Technology Bhavan, New Delhi, Vol 2, No 9, September (year not mentioned).

Jain, L.C., Economic Times, March 25, 1994.

Omen, M.A., *"Bhagawati-Srinivasan Report on Economic Reforms"*, Economic and Political Weekly, October 02, 1993.

Sahai, Suman, *"Intellectual Property Rights for Life Forms—What Should Guide India's Position"*, Economic and Political Weekly, January 15, 1994.

UN, Human Development Report, 1993.

USIS, *US Acts to Protect Intellectual Property*, USIS, New Delhi, 1993.

Chapter 5

Future of the Present of a Frontier : India's North-East in the Age of Libertarian Market

—Abhijit Choudhury

This seminar on Liberalization, Ethnic Identity and Economic Development in India's North-East has set its definitional approach to the concept of liberalization as follows : "The term `Liberalization' is *generally* used to mean transition from a controlled to a more open and market-driven economy....". Integrated to this is the general meaning ascribed to `globalization' that the latter is cosmopolitan aspect of world capitalism which combines the home market with the global. One cannot go without the other. Because, the globe has shrunk further with virtual retreat of the socialist mode of production from the erstwhile socialist systems of Europe, making the *second* world redundant.[1] With the decline of apparently self-sufficient mode of socialist production, the remaining vestiges of it in the Europeanized socialist system like Cuba and in the non-European models of such systems as in China, Vietnam and North Korea are proceeding towards a critical point in terms of survival, no matter how they may try to adjust themselves to a changing scenario when the capitalist system of the West is establishing its hegemony over the world. The crux of the matter is, we like it or not, the current trend in the world is compelling us to give in to the market forces. I think, it would be a half truth to say that injustice is, thereby, done to us the children of the lesser gods! We need not blame the rich states in an altruistic manner. Rather it represents a situational exigency. My contention has two grounds behind it. In the first place, the First World—which built up its financial and commercial hegemony through the instruments of colonialism and later-day high imperialism—is now feeling insecure as the rich states have already reached the saturation point in terms of growth. This is after all, an historical process which saw a series of struggles among them culminating in the two World Wars. The cold war era saw these states reformulating their policies and practices *vis-a-vis* the challenges from the Second World.

The experiences of the second world clearly suggests that, historically speaking, the ultimate key to success of a system rests with the *human* factor. It is not merely the over centralized structure of command economy, with large scale party and bureaucratic control that imposed a *mechanical* face on the human operators; but also the individual and collective follies which have been equally responsible for the failure.[2] The question of general human development in all aspects of life, therefore, continues to be treated in a *vacuum* in the absence of an alternative system of political philosophy. Herein lies the sense of insecurity of the First World. I believe, to the extent of conviction, that more than the fear of Communism, the retreat of socialism has made the West feel insecure as the latent antagonism among them are resurfacing. The emergence of the apparently unbridled market powers of the United States of America and Japan relegated the three or four rich West European states to the third spot on the global market hierarchy. So, the latter are in a hurry to combine.

An interesting contradiction is manifested in their attitude, however. On the one hand the European Union represent an attempt to safeguard European financial and commercial interests in a highly competitive world market which demands viable pricing and quality products. But, on the other, the internal squabbles among the member states on the question of Europarliament, Eurocurrency, and Euro Bank since the Treaty of Maastricht reflect the continuing dominance of the theme of *national* interest.[3] The term 'trade war' has entered with full vigour into our vocabulary of international relations. Though various types of manipulations are resorted to in order to adjust the problems of mutual gains, another front is fast emerging. This is the Islamic Economic Union involving Kazakhstan, Iran and etcetera. It reflects both cultural and economic resistance to the American dream of *unipolarity*.

Speaking of the adjustment of commercial antagonism among the rich states one can observe its immediate manifestation in the formation of the multi/transnational corporations through *tie-ups* and business/manufacturing *alliances* of giant companies. At times this may take place through "gobbling up" of losing concerns by the bigger ones.[4] In any case, the parties, when they cut across national borders hope to minimize `national' conflicts through joint inter–national efforts at market domination. Such domination, as our experiences would show, is actually exercised by the rich states who bless the lesser states with `collaborations' which is, of course, a symbiotic process. True, it would generate employment in the less developed parts of the world and expand the scope of diversification of their economies. But one cannot ignore the potentials of *gluts* in the global market irrespective of this silver-lining. The recent massive protest of the workers of the Paris-based automobile giant, the Renault, with multinational collaboration with Spain and Belgium against the proposed closure of its plant in Belgium is a case in point.[5] The strains in the Sino-US and US-Japanese commercial ties are linked to the trade surplus of China and Japan. The USA have also accused Japan of not giving access to the US firms in the Japanese market while enjoying itself generous conditions in the US market,[6] on the other hand, the return of the erstwhile communists as important political weights in Russia, Poland, and Hungary reflects further that the Western `doles' did not help their transition. Recently, therefore, Boris Yeltsin resolved to fight against corruption and crimes in the Russian polity.[7]

Years ago, delivering a talk on *economic darwinism* before the Study Circle, Shillong and later at the Post Graduate Training College, Shillong, I pointed out that the future of international relations would depend on how the multi/transnationals adjust the world market amongst themselves. The main theme of their mutual relationship would be a sophisticated form of 'survival of the fittest'. The subtleties of diplomacy would involve the back-stage manipulations by them in deciding the nature of government in various states. International agencies would provide a forum for this purpose. This point is clearly visible today.[8] This perspective of economic darwinism, I think, cannot be ignored in our analysis of the corporate *fears*.

The second reason for my aforesaid argument is provided by the happenings in the Afro-Asian and Latin-American countries. After independence of these countries, their governing elites took half-hearted measures towards economic emancipation. The politico-economic structures they tried to build up ranged from purely populist (as in some Latin American countries like Peru) to welfare state models (as in Nehruvian India). In all such states the *vicious triangle* of political leadership/bureaucratic/military/business nexus operated in nullifying even the positive consequences of planned economy wherever they attempted its practice. One major instance is the Nehruvian model of coordinated development of 'public' and 'private' sectors.[9] In India, the entrenchment of the vicious triangle has been completed by the electoral game plans of those concerned. The populist slogans like 'Garibi Hatao' were floated to keep alive the illusion of welfare state. The result was two-fold : while the concept of welfare state metamorphosed into populism, a parallel 'black money' economy emerged.

Meanwhile, India achieved, painfully, an average four percent growth in GDP in forty-seven years of independence (1947-1994). Compare this to China's more than nine percent almost within a comparable period! The recent observation of Montek Singh Ahluwalia, Finance Secretary to the Central Government, that our economy can sustain seven to eight percent growth seems to be a highly optimistic dose of confidence.[10] For, if we look at some of our other achievements on the eve of the golden jubilee of independence, the following picture emerges :

(i) More than forty percent of our population still live below poverty line necessitating a redefining of poverty level by our Planning Commission in 1996.

(ii) Forty-eight percent people are still illiterate.

(iii) Sixty-three percent villages go without basic sanitation and health facilities.

(iv) Twenty percent of our legislators have behind them criminal records (both at Central and State levels).[11]

These facts clearly indicate that India, like many other 'developing' countries, will find it difficult to reach the status of the 'developed'.

While developmental programmes have been under–taken, their adverse effects on the ecosystems are being justified officially in the name of sustenance of growth. Interestingly enough, a few years ago, a Malayasian minister rebuffed a Western suggestion at controlled exploitation of forest resources, during an international ecoconference (Rio Summit) by saying that the West had already degraded the eco-system in the Third World during their colonial hegemony; and that therefore they had forfeited moral claims of advising the Third World on this issue. In speaking their minds out through one of their representatives, the Malayasian governing elites rightly aired the sentiments of the Third World. How–ever, the concerned elites forgot/suppressed the fact that their own vested interest was thereby defended. I seek to place the point straight that the manipulations of the emerging governing elites in the Third World have had their share of the loot and in the resultant avarices in public life. Once again, the *negative* role of the 'human' factor compelled them to surrender, say, the Nehruvian model to the Open Market Economy (OME). So, why blame the vulgar Western model of OME alone? Greed and avarice are part of the game of economic darwinism to which we have surrendered of our own will! The 'Fabian' illustrations of Nehru have therefore passed into history as a phase of unfulfilled dreams.[12]

Looking at the problem from this angle, I am compelled to observe that 'liberalization' and 'globalization', which ultimately involve restructuring of our political economy, are dictated by the situational exigency which were largely self-created and threw us into the waiting laps of the rich states who are bound to guide us in our new found openness. But this contemporary historical process, which cannot by neutral to the 'human' factor, actually will give rise to a system of *libertarian* market in which very concept of economic sovereignty is risked. Even the equality of opportunity might be sacrificed at the alter of the "struggle for survival". *Libertarian* market may be defined as a system in which transactions would be controlled by the unrestrained market forces generated by the cartels of multi/transnationals and through the mechanism of 'go as you will' in which the cardinal principle would be either *proceed along or perish.* The age that has dawned since the late 1970s is an age of libertarian market. Mankind will find it difficult to reverse this process.

Situating the problem of ethnicity and ethnic identity in this context, one has to remember two things. Firstly, the North-Eastern region of India primarily represents an *international* frontier zone in the sense that it is the *meeting point* of the three civilizational systems—the Indic, Sinid and the South East Asiatic with especially the Indic and South East Asiatic playing a key role in the evolution of culture patterns here. The history of migrants and cross migration over and through this region is too well-known to be treated in details in context. Therefore, I shall avoid it. But this point is raised to hint at the patterns of the civilizational influences in every aspect of life of the various *ethnoses*[13] living here. It is especially visible, through such patterns, that this region served not merely as a transit route for cultural and commercial exchanges particularly between the Indic and the South East Asiatic systems; but also as a *meeting ground* of the two. Seen from this perspective, the present proposal of opening India's trade with South-East Asia through this region assumes significance. The priority is our joining the ASEAN.

In the second place, precisely for this reason of its being a meeting point for exchanges, I do not subscribe to the "melting pot" theory in context of the North-Eastern region. Had it been so, the ethnic assertions of the small ethnoses here *vis-a-vis* the larger ones in the Pan-Indian situation would not have been so exacerbated since the second decade of this century. For various historical reasons the distinctiveness of this region was juxtaposed to what is described as the Indian "mainstream". Though I consider the concept of this main–stream as a `created' *myth*,[14] I have to concede that it has come to stay thanks to the myth-makers manipulating our polity.

One form of the ethnic assertions has been manifested in the emergence of the so-called "insurgent" movements epitomed by the NSCN, ULFA, PLA etcetera; and the other was the hill state movement in Assam during the post-1947 period. While the former were chiefly directed against the Indian State, the latter represented the aspiring local elites' grievances *vis-a-vis* the State of Assam. That insurgency was given expression to a sense of deprivation on the part of this region cannot be escaped. I had an opportunity of going through the various pamphlets issued during the Assam Movement in the 1980s, including the one published by a late Chief Secretary of Assam, who happened to be a local. These pamphlets clearly reflects the agony of deprivation apparently caused by a discriminating Indian State. Much earlier, in 1918, the Naga Club articulated its fear of future dominance by the `Hindu' majority state of Assam. Thereby, ethno-cultural interpretation was given to the question of resource control. This apart, the recent and current ethnic assertions and animosities such as happening in Nagaland, Manipur, Tripura, Meghalaya and Assam are primarily centered around this question.[15] General apprehensions in respect of the `others', in all these cases, are percolated down to the popular level through the elites, who partake of lion's share in the benefits of developmental processes.

Now, I may raise two questions in view of our current policy of liberalization: *(i)* Should this region participate in the on-going processes of restructuring etcetera? and *(ii)* What will be the future of this region, especially in the light of its recurrent theme of ethnic assertions, in the new situation?

Exercising my mind over these issues, I may take a stand that there is no question of "should" participate. Rather, the logic of the contemporary historical compulsions emanating from the frame of *economic darwinism* will force this region into the orbits of both domestic and global market systems. One such compulsion is public corruption in all the states of this region, which is carried to the level of an industry.[16] I doubt, if the practice of sustaining the state-initiated and subsidized developmental efforts in this region could remain viable any more. This doubt comes from the fact that the pressures from the international funding agencies to justify the outputs in terms of developmental investments would make the Indian state rethink the structural aspects of its developmental/welfare functions. Already hints are coming as the states are being asked to generate their own resources. The strings attached to the aids from the international agencies have the basic aim of opening up of the protectionist economies of the beneficiaries.

The rise of public corruption centered around our developmental efforts are clear for all to see. The World Bank had already stated that such efforts in the developing countries are not working due to the appropriation of a large percentage of aids by a few. Certain States in the North-Eastern region which can generate internally less than five percent of resources required to sustain their budgetary proposals are becoming a liability to the overall process of development due to the reason just cited. The irony is that such states talk of more financial and administrative autonomy in a federal structure of governance without considering that such autonomy also demand capability of self-sustenance. The governing elites concerned, may even oppose an expansion of the scope of public income from direct taxes in their own financial and political interests. Looking from a holistic perspective, the present situation does not augur well for the future unless they themselves see the urgent necessity of change in attitude and approach as well.

Before taking up the second poser, I may consider the question of the need of a philosophical basis that can provide a humane face to the emerging libertarian market, I have tried to visualize. Without being a professional economist, I can only think of an economist who is trying hard to provide a philosophical basis to our economic practices. He is Professor

Amartya Sen. In other words, he is trying to develop an alternative philosophical system to regulate unrestrained practices associated with what I call *economic darwinism* of the emerging face of Capitalism. In contrast to Fukuyama's glorification of the apparent triumph of Capitalism, Sen, it appears, is yet to be convinced of a full-proof system of liberal democratic governance. Otherwise, unlike Fukuyama, he would not have appealed to a conscientious system of economic practices. Sen wants a uniformly developed global economy to avoid regional disparities by safeguarding right to food, to work, and to education. His emphasis on freedom of expression is to be seen in this context. He believes that only an humanized economy can ensure human rights. An healthy economy is dependent on democratic state structure and protection of freedom. However, I may caution those concerned on this last aspect of Sen's thought. Though here he apparently seems to be nearer Fukuyama, the latter has never emphasized this point in his abstractions in clear terms.[17]

Sen's thesis is pertinent for a world where the principles of the state as an agency of public welfare and security continue to be valid more than before. The state requires to resolve the contradictory pulls of liberal democracy and libertarian market forces. The emerging state-global business *nexus*, therefore, has immense responsibility to implement Sen's suggestion. Because, social justice is the basic foundation for an equitable world. Without it violent upheavals would continue to be the main theme of political economy. The system has to devise mechanism to minimize it if not completely neutralize. If we cannot achieve this end, then the *libertarian market* will find it difficult to uphold the liberal system. In such an eventuality, the present would be *frozen* in the North-Eastern region exacerbating further the inter-ethnic and intra-ethnic suspicion, fear, and conflict. I fully agree with Montek Singh Ahluwalia that government alone can deliver the goods like social infrastructure, infrastructures in rural areas, basic education, and health and therefore Government's energy should be directed to these problems.[18] I suggest that in the transition of this region into the yet uncertain future, three agencies can play their roles as the soothing healers on the line suggested by Sen. These are the

States regulating the process, the Religious institutions, and the NGOs. The two last mentioned agencies can act in mobilizing popular awareness and pressures where necessary. The first requirement is the sincerity of purpose in the part of our policy makers and the executive. That this is wanting is currently manifested in the compulsions of judicial activism.[19]

SUMMARY REVIEW

In a Braudelian sense this paper attempts a short-term analysis, in 'historical time', of contemporary trends in North-East India within the larger Global and Indian frames in view of the on-going processes of liberalization. Braudel's perspective of 'historical time' as the "the only language" that binds history to the present "creating one indivisible whole", I think is applicable to our understanding of the current state of affairs in the light of immediate past ! Though such an exercise cannot strictly have a predictive function, it may at least indicate some possibilities in future on a short-term basis. Keeping this point in mind, I have tried to hint at one/two possibilities which may occur within the next ten/twenty years. I have tried to relate some of the world-wide developments since the late-1970s, which served as historical compulsions leading to 'Liberalization'; to the future of ethnic assertions in India's North-East.

The first part of this paper deals with our experience in the World context to show three dimensions of the problem that *(i)* the human factor is the most important aspect of any given political economy; *(ii)* the theme of 'national' interests still dominates our diplomatic discourses; and *(iii)* the 'cut-throat' competition for market domination necessitated adjustments between the States and the MNCs/TNCs, on the one hand; and, on the other, tie-ups and alliances are arranged between the MNCs/TNCs themselves. Corporate fear of survival actually motivates such moves.

In the process economic darwinism would ultimately decide the nature of the coming World order. The juxtaposition of the US-Japan or the EU-Japan, and the formation of the Islamic Economic Union in recent past indicate that the World cannot be Unipolar.

The second part of this paper argues that in context of the Third World, India included, the failure of the 'human element' has largely contributed to the compulsions of giving-up our past professions and taking to 'liberalization'. I made this point in reply to Dr. H. Srikant's question. He was told that I would be for liberalization but only with State control and supervision. Locating the foci of the problem, I have tried to define the process of liberalization, in the light of economic darwinism, as the 'emergence' of libertarian market where competence would be the last word.

In the third part, situating the North-East in the above context, it is shown that this region too, could not escape the baneful influence of public corruption although huge resources have been invested in the name of development. The elites have appropriated ninety percent of the resources so employed. The creation of smaller States did not actually lead to the desired level of progress. This however, does not go to say that their emergence have never represented popular movements like the Hill States Movement. It is also argued that as this region has to participate in the liberalization process, the problem of ethnic assertions, in different forms, would take shape depending on the nature of the emerging political economy. In reply to a question from Prof. B.P. Mishra as to whether the existing elites of this region would be effected by liberalization, I said that they would participate in the process of realignment in order to retain their control over resources and power. In doing so, they might take compromising positions. I have taken a stand that the humanizing aspects of politico-economic programmes as envisaged in the alternative philosophical basis, Prof. Amartya Sen is trying to provide to the entire process, must be addressed by our policy makers; and in doing so they should take into confidence the religious institutions and the NGOs. To me the thesis of Francis Fukuyama, that the collapse of the Socialist Systems confirms the final acceptability of Liberal Democratic form, is suspect ! Because, the question remains as to how it is going to tackle the problem of economic darwinism.

References

1. The *second* world, here, is used to categorize the socialist systems for our purpose of analysis. First World means the technologically highly developed countries like Japan, and some rich countries of the West (G-7).
2. A vast literature is already available on these issues. I shall cite two recent instances. The North Korean President, Kim Jong II, had declared that the anarchic situation due to food crisis in his country was the creation of the apathetic attitudes of "administrative officials and party cadres" (see *The Asian Age*, March 20, 1997). The Vietnamese President Le Duc Anh told the National Assembly: "Individualism is tending to develop in various forms in state enterprises and offices causing damage to solidarity, state property and is a hurdle to national development. The Vietnamese Prime Minister told the reporters: "We are sick of talking about corruption, now is the time to take action" (see *The Asian Age*, April 3, 1997).
3. See *The Asian Age (Business Age)*, March 26, 1997. The European Union has asked Japan to ease market rules to open its market to European products. It will also bring South Korea's discriminative tax on liquor to the WTO panel on trade dispute.

   See the report in *The Asian Age (Business Age)*, March 4 and 5, 1997. The European Monetary Union (EMU) is struggling to fuse the national interests into a system of consensus. While Germany and Austria reiterate that they would stick to the Maastricht criteria for EMU norms, Britain insists that a *referendum* is a must on its interests alone before it joins the single currency on January 1, 1999.

   See also *The Asian Age (Business Age)*, February 13, 1997. Germany is facing a very high unemployment level of 4.66 million, not seen since the depressions of the 1930s. The current Neo-Nazi upsurge has to be seen in this light. The author adds: Just as this paper was being finished, Russia and China had signed treaty declaring that they would uphold 'multipolarity.'
4. One recent instance is the case of the Boeing Company trying to gobble up McDonnell Douglas Corporation which could sell only three percent of its commercial planes compared to fifty percent of the former in 1996-97. The European airlines, too, are trying to neutralize the domination of Boeing Co., by assisting in the market for its European rival, The Airbus. See *The Asian Age (Business Age)*, March 18, 1997.

5. See *The Asian Age (Business Age)*, March 6, 12 and 13, 1997. Posting a huge $1.2 billion loss, the Renault blamed "cut-throat" competition in the European market. The Renault's work force in its French and foreign factories, put together, declined from 169,500 in 1989 to 139,500 in 1995. The recent decision to close down its plant at Vilvorde outside Brussels brought its 3,500 workers there and 10,000 in Paris on the streets. The Belgian Government, meanwhile, decided to sue the Renault accusing it of violating the Belgian and European Union legislations which require the companies to consult workers representatives about possible lay-offs. The Belgian Prime Minister, Jean Luc Dehaene called for new European regulations stopping multinationals from shifting plants and jobs across national borders. Emmanuel Couvreur of the Socialist-led CFDT Union of this company stated: "The Unions are taking the initiative to create a Europe of social standards... Europe's politicians cannot be relied upon to move things forward socially. Only the European Unions can provide a counter-weight to free marketing excesses." This point, in a different context, is equally pertinent for India. The recent experiences in a local jute mill in Calcutta, The Kanoria, or in the organized peasant protests in Karnataka against a multinational, the Cargil prove our point.
6. See *The Asian Age (Business Age)*, March 5, 1997. While the USA says China maintains a trade surplus of $40 billion, China refutes this claim by stating that its trade surplus is $10 billion. The USA is eager that a "fair share" of contracts in China's ambitious infrastructural development project be given to the American firms to close this gap. The USA has said: "The trade deficit with China is not politically sustainable." With Regard to Japan, the US position is that money exchange rates rather than market barriers is the main obstacle. In fact, the American Chamber of Commerce has asked Japan to strengthen its economy by fostering domestic demand instead of weakening the Yen vis-a-vis the Dollar to favour export. The US trade deficit for 1996 ran to the level of nearly $48 billion. This tussle is particularly visible in the automobile sector. The interstate relations are determined by MNC/TNC needs. An example is the US-brokered accords between China and the Boeing C. and the General Motors to the tune of $2 billion (*The Asian Age*, March 26, 1997).

   See also *The Asian Age (Business Age)*, March 12, 1997. This controversy overshadowed the recently held dialogue of top financial and Central Bank officials from the Asia-Pacific zone.

State intervention is a necessary outflow of the multi/transnational vs. State equations.

7. See *The Asian Age,* March 7, 1997.
8. My readings for the past ten years, centred on the Reports of the activities of the International financial institutions like the World Bank and the IMF, confirms this contention.
9. Seen in its historical context, the Nehruvian model was an urgent requirement for India in a particular historical moment. One may disagree with Professor Stanley Wolpart, author of a recent biography, *Nehru: A Tryst with Destiny* that Nehru's "economic belief that planning was the solution proved to be simplistic." See also *The Sunday Observer,* March 16-22, 1997. After a long colonial drain, there was no other alternative for India than to adopt it for a build up to begin. The experiences of many Afro-Asian countries which did not adopt this model justify my stand. I am not speaking of the Asian Tigers whose future status in the global market hierarchy is yet to be decided. The bubble may burst unless immediate structural reforms are undertaken by them (see *The Statement,* March 2, 1997), "Asia's precarious miracle). But a question mark hangs on the Nehruvian experiment! Have the accounts of Rs. 800 plus crores, spent to prop up the 'private sector' after 1947, ever been made public?
10. See his interview to *The Sunday Observer,* March 23-29, 1997. This is a long-term objective as he has defined it. The two fold approach involves economic liberalization and deregulation, and giving a greater role to the private sector and foreign investment "in those parts of the economy where market forces will lead to a much better results." Thus Government would be let free to direct its energy in upgrading services in the social sector. He visualizes foreign investment to the tune of $5 to 6 billion. The Finance Minister, P. Chidambaram, also corroborates this stand by saying that seven percent GDP growth is possible keeping the target at eight percent *(The Statement,* March 8, 1997). The World Bank lauds India and Pakistan as among the ten potential "economic giants", in its *World Development Indicator 1997,* sharing fifty-nine percent of the developing world's GDP and eleven percent of the World's as a whole *(The Asian Age Business Age,* March 13, 1997). However, the UN *1997 Report on the World Social Situation* states that inspite of "marked progress in lifting the levels of income", 1.3 billion people out of 5.7 billion are now living below the poverty-line. This population, constituting one-quarter of the

World population, come from South-Asia, Sub-Saharan Africa, Latin America and Eastern Europe. In South Asia alone, population living in abject poverty (one Dollar a day) has registered an increase from 480 million in 1987 to 515 million in 1993 (UN Department of Economic and Social Information and Policy Analysis). As regards the Foreign Direct Investment (FDI), while Myanmar could attract $4 billion worth of inflow, India could boast of only $2 billion. We are not talking of China which is already emerging as economic superpower! What could be the reason (s)? If we compare our situation with those of East Asian countries, we shall see that like some of them as South Korea, Indian economy is also a byword for *state intervention.* Coupled with that, protection to domestic industry (as in some such countries), and inefficient financial systems controlled through tight regulations (as in some of them) have so far acted as a deterrent. Add to this, the fiscal mismanagement through the erstwhile loan melas organized earlier with overt political motive. Add further to this, the exasperation caused by a lackadaisical bureaucracy. The other day, the former Prime Minister, H.D. Devegowda has bitterly stated in the Rajya Sabha that he was disgusted with the non-compliance of the bureaucracy to even the cabinet decisions (*The Asian Age,* March 21, 1997). The author adds: The present Prime Minister, Mr. I.K. Gujral, appears to be determined to initiate a struggle against corruption. Our Supreme Court has, of late, Advised the setting up of an independent commission not controlled by senior bureaucrats, to act on the findings of the Vohra Committee Report on criminalization of politics since the present nodal agency set up for this purpose by the Government cannot act without interference from the top *(The Asian Age, ibid.).* Considering these types of practical problems, therefore, I call Ahluwalia's an highly optimistic dose of confidence, which runs the risk of being rendered meaningless.

However, state regulation must be maintained on the financial sectors including the insurance. Otherwise, an Albania-like situation may occur in India too. See *The Asian Age,* February 12, March 2 and 4, 1997; and *The Frontline,* March 21, 1997, which reported on Albania. India has already experienced as Harshad Mehta—political beneficiaries nexus!

11. These estimates are prepared on the basis of reports in the dailies and periodicals since 1987.

12. I call Nehru's "socialist pattern" as Fabian illustration, because influenced more by Social Democracy than the more forthright

Marxist doctrines, Nehru, like the Fabians, saw the State as an instrument foe assuring social betterment and security to the citizens. But the State that evolved in India under the Nehruvian regime could not carry the Fabian ideals much farther. For instance, the regime and its successors could not incorporate free *compulsory* primary education and Old Age Pension, among others, as part of a welfare state system. This, however, does not go to say that the Nehruvian State did not serve some purpose within these limitations, for some decades after independence.

13. See my paper, "Ethnogenesis and Ethnic Consciousness: The Mythic Horizon", in Agrawal, M.M., ed., *Ethnicity, Culture and Nationalism in North-East India*, New Delhi: Indus Publishing Co., 1996: 134-157. I prefer the use of this term in place of 'Nationality', as the latter can be subsumed in the 'Ethnos.'
14. See my paper, "National Mainstream Syndrome and the North-East: A Note", in Bhuyan, B.C., ed., *Political Development in the North East*, Vol. II, New Delhi: Omsons, 1992.
15. The Naga-Kuki clashes is one of the many instances as one may cite. The hill states movement of the 1960s had its base in economic grievances besides the language policy of Assam Government. Similar roots may be traced in the Karbi demands as well as the Bodoland movement. Land question is an important issue in the Bodo-Adivasi and Bodo-immigrant Bengali conflicts-situation. Recently, the NSCN (Khaplang faction) has accused the NSCN (Issas-Muivah faction) for the latter's designs of expanding its resource base and of the hegemony of the Thangkul tribe over the others (see *The Statement*, April 16, 1997).
16. For an example, see Sanchet Barua, Springboard of insurgency" in *The Meghalaya Guardian*, March 7, 1997. Since 1947, total plan assistance to Nagaland (from pre-1963 days), amounted to Rs. 163,534 crore with no significant progress towards poverty alleviation. The life styles of the Naga politicians and bureaucrats have already earned the envy of the average Naga. Many roads exist only on paper. There are 12,000 schools, existing on paper, which regularly draw the salary of teachers. When I joined the State Civil Service in Arunachal Pradesh in 1978, a joke used to circulate among the officials that the total land developed since 1947 under various schemes were double the actual geographical area of Arunachal Pradesh. The author adds: The very recent abduction and murder of Mr. Sanjoy Ghosh by the ULFA at Majuli has exposed the fact of their 'unholy' nexus with the local contractors.

17. (a) My observations on the thoughts of Professor Amartya Sen are based on some of his stray articles and interviews published in some dailies and periodicals between 1985 and 1996. Apart from this, the professional economists would surely agree with me on the significance on his work on the problem of inequality from which emanate his attempts at an alternative system of philosophy to provide a frame for action.

(b) See Fukuyama, Francis, *End of History and the Last Man*, Harmondsworth: Penguin Books, 1992. Herein, he proposed his basic thesis that in the ultimate analysis of forms of government, liberal democracy represented end-point of our ideological evolution with a final form of government it would provide. The incomplete implementation of the liberal democratic principles did not essentially negate its utility. In this sense, history has reached its final stage as a "single, coherent, evolutionary process." Societies have become "increasingly linked with one-another through global markets and the spread of a universal consumer culture." The logic of modern natural science "would seem to dictate a universal evolution in the direction of capitalism." He equated the World's most developed countries with the most successful democracies. However, liberal democracy has to continuously balance two mutually contradictory manifestations of the urge for recognition on the part of man—"megalothymia", that is, the desire to be recognized as "superior" to the others; and "isothymia", or the desire to be recognized as the "equal" to other people. The movement of history is often characterized by the struggle between the two. The publicly stated goals on modern democracy usually do not encourage 'megalothymia.' However, I think, collectively speaking, the USA which considers itself as the epitome of modern democracy exhibits megalothymic approach to the world at large. In its own federal affairs the treatment meted out to the American natives is a case in point. At the same time, in its foreign policy, its *official* 'megalothymia' is betrayed when the Economic Espionage Act-1996 stated: "There can be no question that the developments of proprietary economic information is an integral part of America's economic well being. Moreover, the nation's economic interests are a part of its national security interest. Thus threats to the nation's economic interest are threats to the nation's vital security interests." Described by the media as a "new vision of gun-boat diplomacy', this statement has two important dimensions about it. Firstly, it confirms that "national interests" are not waning. Secondly, if it wished a powerful

State may/can force the issue. Apart from this, the fear of economic survival coming from a feeling of insecurity could goad a State to adopt aggressive posture. Given this type of paranoia, the question remains: would liberal democracy be the final "language" for an equitable world! Prof. Sen does not indulge in Fukuyamian style of polemic. There is no indication that he subscribes to the concept of history as having ended. Rather, unlike Fukuyama, he suggests some remedy to counter hegemonic discourses. It is, of course, true that Fukuyama is perturbed with magalothymia "all around us" (see Fukuyama, "The End of History, Five Years Later, in *History and Theory*, 34, 1995: 27-43). One cannot agree with his Straussian stand that history cannot show a way out.

18. See the aforesaid interview. However, the apathetic attitude of the officials concerned have already led to almost breakdown of the structures wherever these were built up. Attitude is an important dimension of the problem. Proceeding from Ahluwalia's *ideal type* (in Weberian sense) one may find, the problem lies in the *real type* as one encounters in life.
19. Take the instances if the Supreme Court's ruling on the polluting industrial units in West Bengal or on tree felling elsewhere which have effected the political clouts.

Chapter 6

Cry, My Beloved Motherland Cry : A Review of Economic Policy 1991-1996

—B. Datta Ray

India adopted the policies of globalization, liberalization and market economy in the wake of economic crisis of 1991 which arose due to collapse of the Soviet Union and East European socialist economy and the Gulf war which resulted in global economic power imbalance. The immediate cause is the serious balance of payment crisis, fall in exports and in the decline in domestic production of crude oil, agriculture and industrial outputs. The new economic philosophy was a desperate response to the crisis of confidence. The authorities adopted an adjustment programme that was directed towards stabilization and structural reforms to dilute the philosophy of planned development prospect of modified socialistic pattern so far followed since 1950 modeled on Mahalanobis formula of economic development in India. Stabilization efforts brought some kind of restoration of foreign confidence and improved foreign exchange reserve following the devaluation of rupee and the tightening of fiscal management such as cutting down of much of public expenditure particularly non-planned ones.

Industrial and trade liberalization was targeted to attract foreign investment. Slowly the flood gate was opened. Some foreign capital inflow surged in demanding immediate deregularisation of industry and trade, liberal exchange rate regime and reduction of state economic activities by privatising public enterprises. The conditionalities directed and guided by International Monetary Fund and World Bank asked for free flow of foreign investment in all sectors including service sectors, reduction and removal of controls, low involvement of the state in production and servicing, privatization of public sector units. Without much thinking of the effects and ramification in the economy, the authorities opted for this soft way of survival. The argument is that this would expand production, increase employment and export and there will be prosperity in the country.

The results achieved so far is not much encouraging. So Far, it has failed to make a viable economy where the benefits, if any, of economic globalization percolates down to the small person in the village and of the town. The 8th Five Year Plan period (1991-1996) coincided with the first five year of the post economic liberalization. The result achieved so far is not much encouraging. Industrial growth rate never exceeded 7 percent. The agricultural growth rate is dismal. The national income increase is marginal. The employment growth rate is nearly stagnant. Exports are not encouraging. The foreign investment flow is hardly Rs. 1500 crores annually. The growth in industrial sector (not exceeding 7 percent) has been at the cost of social sector like health, education, shelter, food and medical care.

The Planning Commission's latest revelation that 37 percent of India's population is below the poverty line. The result of liberalization presents a picture of dismal poverty for about 350 million people of the country. Between 1987-88 and 1993-94, the rural income went up by 2.7 percent. But rural poverty hardly moved due to rise in food prices. The rich farmers benefited. Between 1987- 88 and 1993-94, urban poverty fell from 40 percent to 33.4 percent. There is no decline in the proportion of the poor since the mid 80s. Liberalization has not led to any improvement in the life style of the masses. Poverty line is fixed at Rs. 264.00 per capita per month for urban areas and Rs. 228.00 per capita per month for rural areas (in 1992-93 prices poverty estimates are bared on figures of household consumption expenditure). Planning Commission based its findings accepting Professor Lakdawala methodology. This is near to ground realities.

China's experience may here be mentioned as a contrast. There was a steady decline of absolute poverty from one third to less than ten percent of the total population following liberalization up to 1985. Much of this poverty is rural in areas where there is low level of infrastructure resulting in low level of yield. The experience show's that the radical reduction in rural poverty has been due to radical land reforms and increasing technology mostly in resource deficient remote upland areas. In the post liberalization period in China, the role of state remain to pursue poverty removal efforts.

India has major constraints like low capital, low level of technology, millions of small and marginal farmers alienated from land, widespread rural unemployment. There should have been genuine radical land reforms in rural India pursued prior to present day globalization and economic liberalization providing infrastructure and human resource development. Without this precondition, the present day policy of liberalization and globalization might reduce India to a stunted growth of Argentina, Brazil and Peru variety. In these countries, liberalization and globalization have created the worst form of concentration of national wealth in the hands of few and poverty is widespread in severe form for the majority of the people. It seems that trans Atlantic countries are trying to find outlets in South Asian and in Latin American countries to compensate their declining global competitive positions in other regions, using the World Bank and the International Monetary Fund as their tools imposing certain conditionalities on the developing countries.

Against this background since the onset of the Eight Five Year Plan period (1991-96) in the name of globalization we are allowing foreign capital in labour intensive industrial areas like small sectors and consumer goods. In the name of liberalization, we are allowing developed countries to enter our market without even promising ecofriendly technology transfer. It is true we need foreign capital and import of ecofriendly technology in infrastructure building sectors. But it cannot be an unrestricted entry of outdated technology discarded elsewhere.

The process of liberalization has not helped the social development in India. The gains of economic development are concentrated in few hands who have very little concern for the advancement of the poor people. The economy has to take care of poverty removal measures. But the private sectors are seldom anxious in investing in social obligation fields like education and health care. In a country like India there is wide economic disparity. The ratio between the lowest and the highest is about 1:300 against 1:4 in Scandinavian Countries like Sweden and Norway. With globalization, the farming sector will be thrown open to multinationals and agri big business.

The entry of big business houses into farming sector will change the farming profile of India. Seven out of every ten people live in the village of which majority are marginal farmers producing barely enough for themselves. The food economy of the country bases on millions of farmers will be changed drastically. The big business will control both the inputs and the output. The big business are not interested in providing food security but in switching to profitable cash crops. This will result in the fall in cereal production threatening the public distribution system. Food prices will rise up, farming profile will change and India will resort to food imports. Millions of marginal farmers will be uprooted from their lands. The corporate farming will push us to costly food imports. We had a buffer stock of 35 million tons of foodgrains in 1995 and it is now reduced to 15 million tons or so. There is now a steady decline in foodgrains growth and some increase of cash crops. To quote an observation of Dr. Amartya Sen in another context that with massive illiteracy and lack of health care, India might one day go to the way of Brazil.

Between 1960 and 1975 the number of public or state owned enterprises grew fast. But after initial years, the loss in public sector units in the country was heavy which became perpetual. This is primarily due to poor management by the bureaucrats who had very marginal faith in public enterprises and in the lack of modern management knowledge and experience. There was slow down of economic growth, resulting into depressed commodity prices and heavy debt burden. The total investment in 240 major public sector units reached Rs. 159,307 crores in 1993 and the average return was a little over 2 per cent.

Following the collapse of a Soviet Union and other socialist countries in Europe by 1990, there has been a growing demand for privatization. But privatization is not an answer to India's economic problems. The primary objectives of the new terms like privatization, globalization and liberalization is to reorient the social productive forces towards the market principles of economic return. One has to remember that the economy of the country has to take care of the poverty eradication measures. The private sector has always been reluctant in investing in areas of social concern. Social sectors like education and health care require continued higher outlay by the state. There are needs for infrastructure development demanding heavy social investment. In a poor country like India, privatization would cause hardship to the poor people who constitute the bulk of the majority. Privatization of health care and education is being considered in the name of quality improvement by adopting the market principle for making the user pay and denying the services to those who cannot pay. This is unfair.

Like every denationalisation move since 1991 reforms in the field of bank, power, telecom, oil, there is now a decision on coal. Multinationals have called for deregulation of the coal mining sector. The present constraints on majority foreign equity to be removed by amending coal mining Nationalization Act. The supply-demand equation is particularly relevant since denationalisation is accompanied by some price deregulation. Prices will rise. Price deregulation and static supply benefits only the incumbent quasi-monopolists. This is not a happy start for denationalisation.

The fact remains that the constitution of India tried to set up a welfare state which in 1977 was redefined as a socialist state. The founders of the Constitution wanted an activist state to promote the welfare for the vulnerable section of the people of India now numbering about 400 million. The new vocabulary of globalization and liberalization—the new policy since 1991 run counter to the basic principles of the Constitution of India.

The policy of globalization and liberalization so far has very little impact on the people of North-East India and likely to remain so in foreseeable future. This is due to economic backwardness of the region with its semi-feudal anarchy in land relation which is basic anchor of the economy of the region.

The policy of globalization might have some adverse effect on region's tea export to the world market as the compe–titiveness of India's tea industry is marginal. What is worse, the North-East tea may face stiff challenge in its home market from Sri Lanka and East Africa. They may market quality processed tea in India's vast market in a big way.

The possibility of foreign investment in a big way for the region's economic development is not bright. Even N.R.I. investment, if any, would be limited to service sector. The sociological constrains are deep rooted deterring even big investment from outside the region. Major industrial houses are unlikely to invest in a significant way in the region. Rather it is alleged that there has been flight of capital from this region during the last fifteen years.

The credit deposit ratio which is usually indicative of the state of industrialization is dismal in North-East India. In the hill states, there is a concentration of bank loan in the service sector, with the declining credit to the primary sector. There is also shifting of credit to non-industrial areas. The recovery of bank credit is poor indicative of lack of industrial productivity initiative. Even Assam is no better in this. Under these circumstances, the present stagnant socio-economic status is likely to continue which is inconsistent with the philosophy of economic liberalization which is the cry of global capitalism in search of fresh pasture in India.

In a semi-feudal social set up even capitalism is a distant dream in North-East India. A social welfare state has still an important role to play to lift the masses from the semi-feudal anarchy. Here the states have a commanding place and economic initiative for social development in North-East India for decades to come.

PART TWO

LIBERALIZATION : ECONOMIC IMPLICATIONS FOR INDIA'S NORTH-EAST

Chapter 7

The Theory of Competitive Advantage : Its Implications for the North-Eastern Region

—P.R. Bhattacharjee

The national option for globalization of the Indian economy is bound to pose a difficult challenge to the backward regions like the North-East. For, the opening-up process associated with globalization will entail a switch-over from the protective ethos to the competitive ethos in policy formulation. In the emerging scenario, the North-Eastern States can no longer take concessional treatment and special advantages for granted and industries located in this part of the country have to stand on their own feet. Even if globalization is achieved in phases with some measures of restriction, the pangs of competition cannot be avoided in the long run and one has to live up to the norms of efficiency which has no substitute.

In this connection it is highly useful to have a look at the contents of the theory of competitive advantage which has important implications for policy formulation in the context of globalization. The present paper is a humble exercise in examining the applicability of the theory of competitive advantage in the subnational inter-regional context although international perspective is not to be forgotten in the process.

Michael E. Porter[1] is the main exponent of the theory of Competitive Advantage. By Competitive Advantage, Porter means the ability of the enterprises (Porter uses the term 'companies') to sell their products profitably in and outside the country of their origin. Along with this notion of competitive advantage, Porter enunciates the concept of national competitiveness. He says that the only meaningful concept of competitiveness at the national level is productivity. The principal goal of a nation is to ensure a high and rising standard of living for its citizens; and the ability to do so depends on the productivity of the nation's labour and capital. Again, productivity depends on both quality and the features of the product (that determine the prices they can command) and the efficiency with which they are produced. Thus productivity is the essence of competitive advantage that a nation's enterprises enjoy in the world economy.

Porter is of the firm view that national prosperity is created and not inherited and therefore, he rejects the classical view of comparative advantage which lays stress on natural endowments, labour pool, economics of scale etc. The most important factor determining competitiveness to him is the capacity of a nation's enterprises to innovate and upgrade. Innovation in the form of new product design, a new production process, a new marketing approach or a new way of conducting a training is almost always the product of an unusual effort and it involves investments in skill and knowledge as well as in physical assets. But the fruit of innovation, *i.e.*, competitive advantage can be sustained only through relentless improvement. Otherwise, imitation will erode the advantage.

Porter identifies four broad attributes of a nation that as a system determine the nature and extent of competitive advantage. He calls the set of these attributes the *diamond of national advantage*. These are : (1) factor conditions, (2) demand conditions, (3) related and supporting industries, and (4) firm strategy, structure and rivalry. These elements are discussed below in short.

Factor conditions refer to a nation's position in factors of production such as skilled labour or infrastructure. But this advantage is not inherited, but created through sustained and heavy investment and are specialized. Basic factors, such as a pool of labour or a local raw material source do not constitute an advantage in knowledge-intensive industries. Enterprises can access them easily through global strategy or circumvent them through technology. Only highly specialized factors like a scientific institute or a pool of venture capital ready to explore new areas of production constitute the diamond. Greater the scarcity of these factors and less the scope of imitation, stronger will be the competitive advantage. Even a disadvantage like labour scarcity in static terms may become a source of advantage if it prods the enterprises to innovate in order to overcome it.

Demand conditions refer to the nature of home-market demand for the industry's product or service. Home demand must send the right signals to the enterprises in order to inspire them to innovate. Demanding buyers pressure the companies to improve and change and also provide emerging picture of buyer needs. If the culture and tests of a society shape those of other societies, its enterprises can easily attain competitive advantage in respect of demand in the global market.

Related and supporting industries constitute the third element in Porter's diamond of competitive advantage. Internationally competitive home-based suppliers create advantages in downstream industries by delivering cost-effective inputs and by aiding innovation and upgrading.

Suppliers and end-users can mutually help one another by exchange of information and ideas. Of course, such interaction does not take place automatically although it is helped by proximity.

Firm strategy, structure and rivalry also profoundly influence a nation's competitive ability according to Porter's view. National circumstances and context create tendencies in how enterprises are created, organized and managed. They also determine the nature of domestic rivalry. Although no one managerial system is universally appropriate, firm strategy must be farsighted, pragmatic and global in outlook. The presence of strong local rivals is a powerful stimulus for attaining dynamic efficiency.

Porter emphasizes the fact that the elements of the diamond do not act in isolation but reinforce each other as they constitute a system. Naturally, nations are not home to just one competitive industry, the diamond promotes industry clusters.

Porter's theory does not ignore the role of the government in promoting competitive advantage, although it mostly lays stress on the indirect role of providing incentives to the industries and creating proper environment for them. According to Porter, government should focus on specialized factor creation, enforce strict product and environment standards and promote competition. Tax incentives should promote goals that lead to sustained investment.

Porter enunciated his theory for nations. But with slight modifications it can be applied to subnational regions. Again, it may seem that the theory of competitive advantage is applicable only to developed economies or at best to the organized sectors of the advanced regions of the under-developed countries. But the fact is that even for the North-Eastern Region which is a relatively backward area of the less developed economy of India, the theory of competitive advantage has important policy implications. Because, the theory can dispel a number of wrong conceptions about the root cause of underdevelopment of this region and the ways to overcome it.

This will become obvious if we accept Porter's extremely reasonable stand that only meaningful concept of competitiveness is the productivity. Of course, in order to apply Porter's theory to the North-Eastern Region, one has to examine the question of competitiveness of this region *vis-a-vis* other regions and also *vis-a-vis* the rest of the world.

Porter's main conclusion that a society's prosperity is created and not inherited will provide an answer to those who wonder why the North-Eastern Region is backward in spite of its vast natural resources and to those who find the explanation wholly in the Centre's apathetic attitude to the region. According to this theory, even small scale of the region's productive organizations cannot explain its backwardness or comparative disadvantage as the important factor behind prosperity is not the economies of scale but capability to innovate and change on the part of the enterprises. The pioneering role of the NE Region in petroleum and tea lost much of its impact in the absence of this capability to innovate and change on the part of its enterprises. The question is one of sustainable advantage which means that one cannot rest on one's laurels but create new fields of advantages making the existing advantages obsolete.

Porter's concept of the diamond of competitive advantage can help to solve the so-called paradox of poverty in the midst of plenty in the North Eastern Region. Factor conditions—the first element of the diamond of competitive advantage in porter's theory does not consist of basic factors such as local raw materials in which the North-Eastern States are rich; it consists of highly specialized factors like scientific institutes and venture capital. Even the traditional craftman's specialized skill is of no avail if it cannot change along the changing demand and changing products of the rivals or if it is not supported by market research and market-promoting drives. This is why the rich village industries of the North-Eastern Region like silk, metal wares and woodcraft are on the wane.

Porter's assertion that static disadvantage may be a source of dynamic advantage through increase in efficiency and spurt of innovation has also important lessons for the gloomy prophets who see hardly any bright future of the North-Eastern Region as it is geographically isolated and inaccessible in many of its parts. Given the proper spirit of innovation, this difficulty may give birth to low-weight high-price products. Moreover, the relative geographical isolation also gives the North-Eastern Region some sort of protection against commodities that are produced outside or impetus for co-operation between the states of the region in respect of development schemes.

Unfortunately, owing to lack of dynamism, the productive enterprises in the North-Eastern Region are now unable to compete with goods imported even from other regions of India not to speak of the internationally imported goods. This is driven home by the flooding of the North-Eastern market by regionally imported products ranging from simple goods like rice and fish to sophisticated goods like electric equipments and electronic gadgets.

The second element in Porter's diamond of competitive advantage, *i.e.,* demand conditions are also of relevance in explaining low competitive advantage of the North-Eastern Region. Although it cannot be said that the North-Eastern consumers in urban areas are less demanding than their counterparts in the rest of India, it is true that isolationist environment, agricultural backwardness, rural and inward looking non-assertive culture of the region have all obstructed the growth of appropriate demand conditions for the enterprises which do not face any pressure from their buyers to improve and innovate. The region is virtually characterized by seller's market. Indeed, there is a pressing need for building up a strong consumer's movement in the region.

The North-Eastern buyers cannot shape the pattern of demand emanating for their product as the region suffers from not only geographical but also socio-cultural isolation.

Porter's stress on the related and supporting industries has much meaning for building up the development potential of the North-Eastern Region. The North-East has important industries like petroleum, gas, plantation, plywood, and jute. It has also traditional industries like handloom, silk and craft. But economic relation between them is extremely weak.

In this connection, Sharma and Sahoo[2] have observed, "The backward linkages of these industries are rather limited while their forward linkages are with the industries located in the big metropolises elsewhere. The result has been the emergence of an enclave-type economy, *i.e.,* few modern industries in the midst of traditional industries having very little or no interactions between the two." Had hydel power development and tourism been developed in greater intensity, these would have not only generated important backward and forward linkages but also utilized the critically scarce resources. This would create competitive advantage for the region without much difficulty. A similar stimulus for agro-industries would be created by a really meaningful green revolution in the zone.

Porter has also shown that firm strategy, structure and rivalry play a key role in creating competitive advantage. In the North-Eastern Region most of the productive enterprises are local and regional in character and even globally oriented industries like plantation lack dynamism. The public enterprises in the spheres of road transport, power generation, paper and pulp etc. are not prepared for competition but view themselves like monopolies. This is one of the important reasons for their inability to obtain competitive advantage. This means that one has also to take lessons from Porter's point about firm strategy, structure and rivalry.

Porter's theory also pinpoints that industrial development depends more on the endogenous factors than on the exogenous factors. In the North-East, scant attention has been paid to the endogenous factors like development of skill and enterprise, removal of social barriers like narrow localized outlook, research on production methods, product improvement etc. On the other hand, it has been assumed that the government can achieve wonders only if enough resources flow into the region. The myth has been exploded by the fact that in spite of high per capita plan expenditure, the region has not been able to achieve breakthrough in any area of productive activity in a manner that can provide it a sustainable base of development.

Needless to say, no one can deny the special role of the government in a backward region like the North-East. Porter's theory only implies that the governments in the North-East have unnecessarily extended their activities to the industrial arena when they have failed to ensure minimum environmental support to trade and industry by maintaining law and order and by developing appropriate type of human resource.

The power-and-transport scenario in the region has also not been conducive to competitive advantage of industries.

Although special tax incentives and subsidies have been declared for setting up industries in the North-East, they have failed to generate enthusiasm because the diamond of competitive advantage operates as a system. Unless other elements of the diamond like creation of specialized factors like skilled labour and enterprises, generation of a cultural movement in favour of competition rather than protection etc. are combined with the incentive and unless investors are sure of their fruits of investment in a secure atmosphere, regional competitive advantage cannot be generated.

The policy prescription that can be derived from the forgoing analysis is as follows :

1. Fight the problem of poverty mainly through the process of making the poor more productive. The conflict between equity and efficiency can be resolved to a great extent by concentrating efforts of innovation and change in the poverty-stricken segments of the economy.
2. Reject those values and attitudes which stand against innovation and change. This is a difficult task which can succeed only through sustained social movement. The concept of maintenance of tribal identity in the North-East must be given a new interpretation in terms of development needs of the poor and the disadvantaged in these societies.
3. Give a new direction to government activities concentrating on two fronts :

   (a) infrastructure creation and extension activities;

   (b) human resource development through a massive programme of training labour and enterprises along with re-orientation of institutional education and research towards practical needs of agriculture and industries in the region.
4. Find by techno-economic and market research, a set of mutually supporting industries which can attain competitive advantage, and exhort investment in them. Two separate phases of development may have to be crossed by the enterprises of the region to attain competitive advantage in national and global arenas.

5. Ensure security to enterprises and economic agents and provide fiscal and monetary incentives for innovation, change competition.

References

1. Porter, Michael E. (1990), "The Competitive Advantage of Nations", Harvard Business Review, March-April.

   The paper was later expanded into a full book of the same title published in May 1990 by Free Press.

2. Sharma, Atul and Sahoo, Amarendra (1992), "Zonal Planning in Industrialization" in Adiseshiah, Malcom S. (ed), *Planning Perspectives for the North-Eastern and Eastern Zone,* Lancher Publishers Pvt. Ltd., New Delhi, pp. 108-138.

Chapter 8

Liberalization and Internal Periphery : Understanding the Implications for India's North-East

Gurudas Das

To talk about the implications of liberalization for north-eastern region (NER), which has been aimed at here, is to asses the local impact of a global event. It is extremely difficult to asses the local impact without a stock taking of various dimensions of the global event and their consequent implications for the national situation.

As there is little scope to elaborate upon the factors responsible for launching the twin projects of 'globalization' and 'democracy promotion' by the world's core under U.S. leadership, how they are going to establish a new world order under the metropolitan hegemony, what impact they already have upon the world's peripheries and what may be likely consequences for India's attempt to go global, our analysis is based upon the following premises:

1. As the laws of capitalist development form the building blocks of the globalization project, the problem of uneven development between the core and peripheries will not only continue to persist—it may rather attain an altoge-

ther new heights—at both national as well as international levels.

2. Any successful transition from state capitalism to market capitalism following the neo-classical grammar of liberalization necessitates the existence of mature capitalism at home having acquired the strength of global competitiveness. At the local or regional level, the presence of a competitive entrepreneurial class is a prerequisite for any benefit to accrue to the region out of liberalization of the national economy.

3. Globalization project is certainly to reduce the direct role of the national government in productive activities. National governments particularly of the developing nations, instead of acting as entrepreneur, will assume the role of sales manager in the global capital market in their bid to attract the resources of Multinational Corporations and International Financial institutions. In post-liberalized India, as the central government does not influence the industrial location any more, the competition between the state governments in attracting private investment has intensified many fold. Hence, the local/regional benefits from liberalization largely depends on the relative strength of the states and efficiency of the state managers.

II

THE POLITICAL ECONOMY OF DEVELOPMENT OF NORTH-EASTERN REGION(NER) UNDER STATE CAPITALISM

As the effects of globalization project on a particular country largely depends on its historical contextuality, the impact of liberalization on a particular region of a country much the same way primarily depends on the state of historical development of the area and the people therein. As a result, it is important to analyze the basic nature of development of NER in pre-liberalized era before making any attempt to asses the implications.

The Indian State and NER : The Peripheral Syndrome

That the NER became a periphery of the Indian state following the partition of the country in 1947 and whatever state sponsored economic development carried out here exhibits certain peripheral syndrome have already been discussed elsewhere (Das : 1994). As the periphery being an area depended on the core/centre, the peripheral economic structure develops as a complimentary to the core, not competitive and hence remains exposed to exploitation (Das; 1996b). In the era of state capitalism, the region received very less investment in public sector and that too in extractive industries. Whatever private investments were made that too remained confined only in plantation and wood processing. The colonial structure of production was allowed to continue which has led some scholars to formulate a case for internal colonial syndrome particularly in Assam (Pardesi : 1980; Misra: 1980; Borgohain : 1995).

The working of the peripheral processes in the region is only evident from the pattern of resource exploitation and consequent production structure which has largely been evolved in response to the needs of the growing national economy. Although the exploitation of resources like oil, coal, limestone, timber, tea and hydro-power potential has increased many fold, since independence, under the active initiative of both the state and private capital, the surplus generated from these extractive activities has largely moved out of the region. This has resulted into a wide gap between resource exploitation in, and production structure of the region. Production structure remained, by and large, stagnant in spite of large scale exploitation of resources and thereby weakened the linkage between primary and secondary sectors in the local economy. The region, as a whole, is still a supplier of raw materials and importer of manufactured consumer goods.

The working of the peripheral processes becomes more evident from the different forms of extraction of surplus from the region to core areas. Some of the insights of the world-system analysis (Geschwender : 1982) may also be gainfully used in identifying the underlying mechanism of surplus extraction from NER to the core areas.

The surplus generated from extractive activities in the region is being extracted by core capital in a variety of forms. In some cases, *e.g.*, tea and plywood industries in Assam, core capital directly extracts the surplus from local labour. Whereas in case of trade in timbers (particularly in the hills where forests are owned privately) and agricultural products, local merchant class directly extracts the surplus from local producers through unequal exchange. These merchants then lose the major portion of the surplus so extracted to core capital through unequal exchange. Again, in the privately owned coal mines in the hills, local merchants extract the surplus from non-indigenous labour and then lose a substantial part of it to core capital through unequal exchange. Whatever may be the forms of surplus extraction, the net result is that it is no longer available to fuel the development of the region.

However, unlike core private capital, the extraction of surplus from the region by the state capital through central agencies like Oil India Corporation, Coal India Ltd. etc. has not been unilateral. Besides royalties on raw materials extracted by these agencies, transfer of resources from the center to the states through planning and other development agencies more than compensates the loss incurred by the region on this count. In fact, the states of NER, being the special category states, get much more from the federal exchequer in proportion to their contribution to it. This has made the internal-colonial thesis, advocated by some secessionist organizations and scholars in north-east, superfluous and illusory.

It may be noted, by way of digression, that the peripheries, in the context of world-system, have been colonized by the cores at different points in the history of world capitalist development. This, then, has made the peripheral process an integral part of colonial system. But after de-colonization, the peripheral process continues to operate in the newly independent countries. De-colonization by itself did not bring an end to the working of the peripheral process. Thus, the term periphery does not directly refer to any areas but to a particular process which structures the space (Taylor : 1985).

This process, as part of the world capitalist development, was in operation even before the advent of the colonial phase and continues to operate in the post-colonial era. In fact, both core and periphery processes exhibit two sides of a larger process of uneven capitalist development. The peripheral spatial structure may, at times, resemble to that of colonial structure particularly in relation to production, trade and distribution. Or the latter may, at times, continue to co-exist, at different degrees, even in the post-colonial era. This, then, often leads to misconstrue a peripheral syndrome as colonial one particularly in the context of a region internal to a sovereign multi-ethnic political unit.

Although much effort has not been made to apply the core-periphery model of the world-system variety to parts internal to a country, and much of the conceptual confusions involve in this area yet to be clarified, the broad features of internal periphery outlined here for our reference region, are, of course, subject to further modification and refinement.

However, the working of the peripheral process in NER is further evident from the degree of its dependence on the core areas for necessities. Whatever central fund is made available to the states of NER, the lion's share of it goes out to buy goods and services from the core areas adding little to the local productive capacity.

Be that as it may, the Indian state has failed to protect its North-Eastern peripheries from backwash effects. Resources, skill and capital from the region continued to move out all along the era of state capitalism. The incentives offered by the central government for the development of the industrial sector were too insignificant to overcome the market impediments. In spite of being rich in natural resources, the NER remained one of the most industrially backward region in the country perhaps owing to its locational disadvantage.

The Indian state, indeed, did very little to counteract this backwash effects that resulted from the operation of market forces through public investment in NER. All these have created a condition which resembles Hirschman's case for "economic arguments for separatism" (Hirschman : 1958).

Both the politics of regionalism as well as the politics of secessionism that have rooted deep into some of the societies of NER get their sustenance from this spatial inequality that grew under state capitalism.

How far the transition of the Indian economy from state capitalism to market capitalism will be able to address the problems of under development of the peripheral areas, like NER, will be taken up in the next section.

Emergence of Local/Regional Bourgeoisie

Besides this peripheral syndrome, the process of integration of the NER through state sponsored development programmes has created a space for rent seeking activities for the local political elites and bureaucrats. That the non agricultural sectors of the colonial Assam were in the hands of the non Assamese and hence capital accumulation could not take place in the hands of the local people which, in turn, stood on the way of growth of indigenous entrepreneurial class had been discussed elsewhere (Das : 1996a). A small band of Assamese entrepreneurs emerged particularly in plantation and timber trade in colonial Assam (Guha : 1977; Baruah : 1995) were no match to that of the comprador merchant capital in the hands of the Marwaris (Timberg : 1978; Robinson : 1975; Guha : 1969). With the departure of the British, this merchant capital transformed itself into industrial capital and thereby bridged the gap between these two forms of capital by consolidating both the functions largely in the hands of the Marwaris, the strongest partner of Indian bourgeoisie (Das : 1996a).

That on independence, the Assamese elites, occupied the political space and a section of a power elites made a good fortune out of their position in the power structure in amassing huge money capital by way of commissions on allotment of licenses, contracts, government orders and other public privileges has been discussed elsewhere (Das : *ibid.*). This rent seeking behaviour of the power elites has led to the emergence of a nouveau riche class. In fact, before the emergence of this nouveau riche class, the power elites had little control over the economy of Assam. And, on the contrary, the economic elites hardly had any control over the political power. The emergence of this class, to certain extent, helped to bridge the gap and thereby gave birth to Assamese bourgeoisie (Das : *ibid.*).

While locating bourgeois elements in Assamese society Pardesi observed : "there are about a dozen Assamese planters and a few medium scale industrialists; the rest of the Assamese bourgeoisie consists of contractors, transporters, professionals, bureaucrats and petty traders" (Pardesi : 1980). By way of digression, some corroborative information may be presented in this connection. As per Assam directory and Tea areas handbook 1990-1991, more than 150 tea estates are owned by the 130 Assamese companies only in the Assam valley (Baruah: 1995). Baruah and Associates, the largest Assamese tea company, has an annual turnover of about Rs. 50 crores (Baruah : *ibid.*). There are many non-registered small tea growers which are not counted while arriving at the directory figure. According to an unofficial estimate there were more than 500 small tea growers in Assam in 1994 and more than 80 percent of them are Assamese (Baruah : *ibid.*).

Besides the categories mentioned by Pardesi, Assamese entrepreneurs can commonly be found in thriving hotel industry, real estate business, LPG distribution as well as timber business in Assam. The overwhelming presence of the Assamese entrepreneurs in printing and publishing business in Assam only indicates their monopoly over the cultural resources of the state. Apart from these, a significant section of the *nouveau riche* class earn substantial amount of rent acting as sleeping partner in business run by the non Assamese in Assam. What all this indicate is that the size of the Assamese bourgeoisie is not as insignificant as it is often thought of.

That the process of integration through state sponsored development programmes in post-independent Assam not only intensified economic inequality within the Assamese community but also widened the social inequality between the communities, *i.e.*, between Assamese and tribal communities, leading to the reorganization of Assam has been elaborately dealt upon elsewhere (Das : 1997). What is important here is that the "contractocracy" played a more dominant role behind the emergence of the *nouveau riche* class in the newly formed hill states. The role of political power in enhancing economic position in these states, by and large, resembles the Arunachal Pradesh experience as has been cited elsewhere (Das : 1995a).

Besides public rent seeking activities, large scale exploitation of natural resources particularly of timber and coal in collaboration with the merchants from outside enabled another section of tribals to amass huge money with no time. The fact that the daily transaction of timber exports in Meghalaya is of the tune of Rs. 20 lakhs (The Shillong Times: 16-04-1997), the entire trade being in the hands of the local tribals, provides a clue as to how they have made a quick fortune.

How far this *nouveau riche* class is capable of utilizing the opportunities arising out of liberalization will be taken up in the next section.

State Strength and the North-Eastern States

That the role of the non-economic—particularly political—institutions are vital in the economic development of the society (Gerschenkron : 1965) as well as in the development of modern market economy (Polanyi : 1964) is well established in economic literature. Although the mainstream literature in this area refers to the role of the nation states, the same for the constituent states in a federal system in developing their respective territorial space cannot be ignored. Perhaps the neo-statist aphorism that "strong economies require strong states" (Weiss and Hobson : 1995) is also applicable, to a large extent, in case of constituent states in a federal system as for the union. As a result, it is important to analyze the relative strength of the states, of which, in turn, largely determines the implications of liberalization for, NER.

Out of the seven states in NER, while Assam, Manipur and Tripura emerged from historical continuity, the states of Nagaland, Mizoram, Meghalaya and Arunachal Pradesh were created much later to accommodate the aspirations of the tribal elites in the hills. On reorganization of NER in the early 70's, political expediency prevailed over the criterion of economic viability. In fact, none of the states in NER is economically viable.

The share of the central grant-in-aid to total revenue receipts in Meghalaya during 1990-1995 ranged between 55 to 61 percent (Report of CAG, Meghalaya : 1995). The same for Arunachal Pradesh during 1991-1996 ranged between 64 to 71 percent (Report of CAG, Arunachal Pradesh : 1996). For Mizoram grants constituted 58 to 72 percent of the total revenue receipts during 1991-1996 (Report of CAG, Mizoram: 1996). Needless to mention that similar is the experience for Tripura, Manipur and Nagaland. A seminar on the problems of development of Nagaland, organized by the Nagaland Thinker's Forum, Kohima, on May 26, 1982, observed that out of every rupee earned by a Naga, as much as 87 paise comes from the center in the form of cash, dole, subsidy and other form of grants (Goswami : 1985). However, Assam's dependence on the central grants is much lesser compared to the hill states. The share of central grants to total revenue receipts in Assam ranged between 33 to 40 percent during 1989-1991 (Report of CAG, Assam : 1991). As the relative strength of a state is usually measured in terms of its "extractive capacity" or the amount of revenue it can extract, the states of NER are, indeed, very weak. Perhaps this is why they utterly failed to generate any growth impulse even under state capitalism.

One of the reasons of their abysmal performance in mobilizing resources is, perhaps, their insignificant "penetrative power". 'Penetrative power entails the ability of a state to reach into and directly interact with the population' (Wiess and Hobson : 1995). As, unlike other states of Indian union, Assam, Meghalaya, Mizoram and Tripura come under the purview of the sixth schedule of the constitution, district councils having constitutional power operate as a parallel political institution occupying much of the space between the state and people.

A study on the political system of Meghalaya has shown that both the state and the district councils operate parallelly with overlapping legislative power in relation to land and people within a single, socio-political field. As the sixth schedule has empowered the district councils to regulate and supervise the traditional political institutions at the village level, the state exercises its authority without having much direct linkage with the grass root level (Das: 1995b).

Even in the states like Arunachal Pradesh, Manipur and Nagaland, where there is no district councils, the penetrative power is no better. In fact, there is no effective uniform legal code in relation to land and people on these states as the different tribes and sub tribes, occupying the territorial space, are in fact governed by their respective traditions and customs.

Thus, because of their pitifully weak penetrative power, the states of NER hardly have any significant command over the resources available within their respective territorial boundary. This effective 'isolation' of the states has made them incapable to convert their wishes into practice. What role they could play in post-liberalized era in promoting economic development will be taken up in the next section.

III

IMPLICATIONS OF LIBERALIZATION

Market Competition Vs Regional Imbalance

That the nature of competition between countries in the international system has undergone a sea change, *i.e.*, from 'control over territory' to 'control over market share in the world economy' and hence industrial and trade policies are now more important than defense (Strange : 1995)—these observations need no repetition. The severe competition between the developing countries in attracting foreign direct investment (FDI) has resulted into a war of incentives where every national government is offering lucrative incentive package in order to be competitive in the race as well as to encourage the home industries in mobilizing additional investment fund.

The declining corporate tax, tax on royalty payment, abolition of surcharge on corporate income as well as tax on company dividend in post-liberalized regime in India is surely to reduce the share of direct tax to the total national revenue.

In order to compensate this loss, central government , in view of the narrow tax base, has to increase the level of indirect taxes on goods and services, reduce or phase out the volume of subsidies, cut the expenditure on social sector leading to a general rise in the price level. Needless to say that both developed and under developed regions have to bear the burden arising out of inter-country competition for FDIs.

Similarly, the states in Indian union are also engaged in an intense competition in attracting private investment in their respective territories. With the withdrawal of industrial licensing, the central government could hardly play any role in regard to industrial location. As a result, the role of states in attracting private investment has become very crucial. In this race, the developed states having better infrastructural facilities and more lucrative incentive packages are already far ahead than their underdeveloped counterparts who hardly have any competitive terms to offer. This inter-state competition for private investment has further aggravated regional imbalances in post-liberalized regime (Bhambhri : 1996). As the programmes of liberalization are designed to achieve higher growth rather than to lower inequalities (Das and Barua : 1996)—both interpersonal as well as inter-regional—withdrawal of federal intervention in favour of market mechanism is likely to widen the inter-regional disparity manifold in future. Thus, while the India's north-east, being one of the under developed regions, has to bear the pains of liberalization, the gains are going elsewhere. The peripheral syndrome of NER will not only persist rather it seems to become more prominent in post-liberalized regime.

Private Initiative : Its Nature and Strength

The new economic policy, putting succinctly, viewed economic growth to be the responsibility of those who have the resources, the major task of state policy is to remove the state control that had been imposed under state capitalism (Kurien: 1994). Whether India could gain in terms of growth or experience further deceleration in post-liberalized regime largely depends on the comparative strength of the Indian bourgeoisie particularly of industrial bourgeoisie *vis-a-vis* foreign multinationals (Patnaik : 1985).

Likewise, in spite of market impediments, the strength of the regional/local bourgeoisie will largely determine as to whether the NER will be benefited or not. As it has already been pointed out in the previous section that the regional bourgeoisie, except a small group in Assam, have primarily emerged out of their rent seeking activities, neither they have any industrial background nor any business acumen. Another section of them emerged through large scale exploitation of natural resources, *e.g.*, forest, coal, limestone, etc., acting as agents of national bourgeoisie. They are, indeed, capitalist without factory. This lumpen bourgeoisie, hardly having any link to the process of socio-economic reconstruction of their respective societies, have little commitment to the development of the region.

A significant part of the money that they have amassed, besides their lavish expenditure, is going out of the region through banking institution. Perhaps, this is one of the major causes as to why NER is having low credit-deposit ratio (CDR) that has been a concern for both the development agencies and politicians alike. As capital can not remain idle, in absence of any taker, it is only natural that it will move to areas wherever it is profitable. Thus, the low CDR not only exhibits the under developed nature of the regional economy, it also simultaneously indicates the risk aversive nature of the regional bourgeoisie. Moreover, the steady decline in NER's CDR from 49.5% in 1990 to 45% in 1991, 41.98% in 1993 and then to 37.71% in 1994 (Basic Statistics : 1995) may be indicative of negative effects of liberalization. As the industrial entrepreneurial class could not mature under state capitalism, there is hardly any private initiative to utilize the opportunities arising out of liberalization.

Protective Rent Seeking and the States' Capability

The role of the state governments, in absence of any private initiative, in attracting outside investors has become very crucial. But how capable are they for this task? A few words are in order.

The industrial policies of some of the states of NER do not allow the outside investors to run their business without local participation. In some cases, like Arunachal Pradesh, certain areas of manufacturing activities, besides small scale sector, are exclusively reserved for the local people (Industrial Policy of Arunachal Pradesh : 1994). In Assam, for a new medium or large scale unit to run, 90 percent of the managerial and 100 percent of the non-managerial cadres need to be recruited from the local people (Industrial Policy of Assam : 1986). The land tenure system in the hill states hardly allow outside investors to procure land. While industrial licensing has been withdrawn at the national level, the same still continues to exist in some form or other particularly in the hill states—only to be used for public rent seeking activities.

Besides public rent seeking activities, what is shaking the confidence of the private investors is the "protective rent seeking activities" by the socio-political forces operating in one form or other, in all the states of NER.

By protective rent seeking activities we mean the rent that is collected by the various socio-political organizations in general and insurgent groups in particular from the traders, entrepreneurs, professionals and even from the white collar employees against so called protection of the interest of the later in the respective areas of influence of the former. In Nagaland and Manipur, this protective rent seeking activities are so well organized that even the cobblers and barbers have to pay 25 percent of their earnings (The Telegraph : 08-04-1997). Unlike Nagaland and Manipur, collection of protection money in other states has not yet been institutionalized. In the tea belt of Assam, this protection money runs into crores in case of big gardens managed by the big business houses.

This protective rent seeking activities have tremendous impact on the economy of NER. Firstly, the huge money collected in this way is going out of the country to buy arms and ammunitions from foreign markets which could have otherwise been used for productive purposes. Secondly, the traders and producers who are paying the protection money, in turn, charges a much higher price for the goods and services that they sell and produce. This, in turn, eats up further the competitiveness of local production where production cost is already much higher than the rest of the country. As a result, trading is more profitable than production, which only helps in the making of a dependent economy. Thirdly, many entrepreneurs, like the Kannadiga hotel owner of Thoubal district of Manipur (The Telegraph : 08-04-1997), who do not comply with the demands of the militant groups have to quit their business leading to a migration of entrepreneurs from the region. Fourthly, this rent seeking activities act as disincentive to additional investment, particularly in fixed assets, in existing business. The entrepreneurs keep their infrastructure as minimum as possible so that, if required, they can move out at short notice without incurring much loss. Fifthly, because of the socio-political uncertainties arising out of this protective rent seeking activities, many entrepreneurs are diverting their business to safer areas leading to a further flight of resources from the region. The general attitude of business is to invest as minimum as possible and earn as maximum as possible within short time. This attitude of business, instead of industrialization, only can lead to deindustrialization of the region as there will be hardly any long term investment in the productive sector.

The socio-political disincentives are far stronger than the economic incentives provided by the states of the region. Because of their weak "penetrative power" and relative "isolation" from the society, these states are handicapped in establishing rule of law without which the confidence lost cannot be regained. The business confidence in this region, as it is today, will make way for further flight of resources instead of bringing them in in post liberalized regime.

IV

CONCLUDING OBSERVATIONS

Besides this loss of confidence of the business, the problem of unemployment in NER will assume a new heights in post liberalized regime. As the absorption capacity of the state will reduce sharply, reservation of jobs for the scheduled tribes, the major population group in the hill states, will largely loose its relevance. Because there will hardly be any job in the public sector. Whatever job opportunities are being created in the private sector elsewhere, are, basically, skill based and highly competitive for which the unemployed youths of the region are not well equipped. As the states of NER, having much higher rate of growth of population than the national average, have little option to tackle this unemployment problem, the social tensions and conflicts are only to escalate in the days to come.

These circumstances are leading to a loss of authority of those who govern and have created a situation what Habermans, in the context of nation state, calls a double crisis of "rationality", where the state cannot protect its citizens in ways they have been used to expect, and a crisis of "legitimization" where the state cannot any longer rely on the loyalty of its citizens (Cable ; 1995).

Unless the penetrative power of the states of NER is strengthened, no amount of sweeteners, in the form of economic aid, from the center could make the region investment friendly. However, it does not mean that economic aid is not important, but without political and social aids it is unlikely to bring desired results. A shift from the policy of "social control from above" to "social control from below" may go a long way in extending the penetrative power of the states of NER.

References

Baruah, Anjan, 1995, Assamese Businessmen, Meenakshi Kashyap Baruah, Jorhat.

Bhambhri, C.P., 1996, *"New Economic Policy : Indian State and Bureaucracy"*, in Social Scientist, Vol. 24, No. 1-3, January-March, 1996.

Borgohain, Homen, 1995, *"Aupanibeshik Soshanar Biruddhe Asomar Sesh Sangram"*, (Assamese), (reprint), Asam Bani, Nov. 24, 1995.

Cable, Vincent, 1995, *"The Diminished Nation-State : A Study in the Loss of Economic Power"*, in Daedalus, Vol. 124, No. 2, Spring, 1995.

Das, Gurudas, 1994, *"Understanding the Underdevelopment of North-Eastern Region of India"*, in the Journal of Anthropological Society, Vol. 29, No. 1 and 2, March/July, 1994.

Das, Gurudas, 1995(a), Tribes of Arunachal Pradesh in Transition, Vikas, New Delhi.

Das, Gurudas, 1995(b), *"Social Change and Traditional Tribal Political Systems in Meghalaya"*, paper presented at the Sub-regional workshop on Panchyati Raj, October, 1995, ICSSR-NERC, Shillong.

Das, Gurudas, 1996(a), *"Migration, Ethnicity and Competition for State Resources : Causes of Social Tension in the North-East"*, in Mehtabuddin Ahmed and Prosenjit Chowdhury, (eds.), 1996, The Turbulent North East, Akshar Publications, New Delhi.

Das, Gurudas, 1996(b), *"Limits to Economic Development of North-Eastern Region : An Analysis of Contradictions Between Economic Goals and Social Choices"*, paper presented at the seminar on Sociological Constraints to Industrial Development in North-East India, 27-27 July, 1996, NEICSSR, Shillong.

Das, Gurudas, 1997, *"Understanding the Insurgency Phenomenon in India's North-East : An Analytical Framework"*, in B. Pakem, (ed), Insurgency in North-East India, Omsons Publications, New Delhi.

Das, Sandwip Kumar and Alokesh Barua, 1996, *"Regional Inequalities, Economic Growth and Liberalization : A Study of the Indian Economy"*, in the Journal of Development Studies, Vol. 32, No. 3, February 1996.

Gerschenkron, Alexander, 1965, Economic Backwardness in Historical Perspective, Frederick A. Praeger, New York.

Geschwender, James A., 1982, *"The Hawaiian Transformation : Class, Submerged Nation, and National Minorities"*, in Edward Friedman, (ed.), Ascent and Decline in the World-System, Sage Publications, Beverly Hills.

Goswami, Atul, 1985, *"Contents of Economic Development for North East India"*, in K.Alam, (ed.), Planning in North-East India, Omsons, Guwahati.

Guha, Amalendu, 1969, *"Socio-Economic Changes in Agrarian Assam"*, in M.K. Choudhury, (ed.), Trends of Socio-Economic Change in India, 1996, AIIAS, Shimla.

Guha, Amalendu, 1977, Planter-Raj to Swaraj, Indian Council of Historical Research, New Delhi.

Hirschman, Albert O., 1958, The Strategy of Economic Development, Yale University Press, New Haven.

Industrial Policy of Arunachal Pradesh, 1994, Dept. of Industries, Govt. of A.P.

Industrial Policy of Assam, 1986, Dept. of Industries, Govt. of Assam.

Kurein, C.T., 1994, Global Capitalism and the Indian Economy, Orient Longman, New Delhi.

Mishra, Tilottoma, 1980, *"Assam : A Colonial Hinterland"*, in EPW, Vol. XV, No. 32, August 9, 1980.

North Eastern Council, 1995, Basic Statistics.

Pardesi, Ghanshyam, 1980, *"Internal Colony in a National Exploitative System"*, EPW, Vol. XV, No. 23, June 7, 1980.

Patnaik, Prabhat, *"On the Political Economy of Economic Liberalization"*, in Social Scientist, July-August, 1985.

Polanyi, Karl, 1964, The Great Transformation, Beacon Press, Boston.

Report of the Comptroller and Auditor General of India (CAG), Arunachal Pradesh, 1996.

Report of the Comptroller and Auditor General of India (CAG), Assam, 1991.

Report of the Comptroller and Auditor General of India (CAG), Meghalaya, 1995.

Report of the Comptroller and Auditor General of India (CAG), Mizoram, 1996.

Robinson, William, 1975, A Descriptive Account of Assam, (reprint), Sanskaran Prakashak, Delhi.

Strange, Susan, 1995, *"The Defective State"* in Daedalus, Vol. 124, No. 2, Spring, 1995.

Taylor, Peter J., 1991, Political Geography, Orient Longman, England.

Timberg, Thomas A., 1978, The Marwaris, Vikas, New Delhi.

Wiess, Linda and John M. Hobson, 1995, States and Economic Development : A Comparative Historical Analysis, Polity Press, Great Britain.

Chapter 9

Liberalization and Development of India's North-East : Learning from Experience

—H. Srikanth

The Congress Party at one time convinced the Indian citizens that its avowed goal of socialistic pattern of society would ensure economic growth and at the same time eliminate poverty, unemployment, and inequalities in the society. After having experimented the so-called mixed economy model for more than three decades, of late, the Congress leaders seem to have realized that it is the command-style economy which has arrested the economic development all these years and hence, started prescribing liberalization as the panacea for all economic problems confronting the nation today. It is said that the withdrawal of state controls, free play of market forces, freedom for private capital, entry of foreign multinationals, privatization of public sector units and production for external markets would encourage competition, facilitate free flow of capital and bring about all round development of economy. Although it was again the Congress party, the most dependable ally of the Indian big bourgeoisie, which initiated the policy of liberalization, today all parliamentarian parties, starting from BJP to CPI(M), Janata Dal to Akali Dal, AGP to TDP, all of them are bowing their heads in respect of their new found religion and singing in praise of economic reforms aimed at liberalization and globalization.

What and Why of Liberalization ?

Before accepting or admonishing the process of liberalization, it is essential to keep in mind that in all class divided societies, the economic policies are pursued basically in the interest of the ruling classes. Just as there was nothing socialist in the socialistic pattern of society, there is hardly anything liberal in the liberalization pursued today. Apparently contradictory, yet both planned economy and liberalization are advocated and implemented only to pursue capitalist path of development. At one time planning, development of public sector, regulation of private sector and foreign capital were seen by the bourgeoisie themselves as means to consolidation and strengthening of the capitalist base in India. So long as the national bourgeoisie were weak, they accepted the leading role of the state. After having developed to its full strength under the umbrella of the state capitalism, masquerading itself as socialism, the monopoly faction of the Indian bourgeoisie has started looking for new avenues of growth within and outside the country. It is basically for the unrestricted development of this section of the Indian bourgeoisie, which is becoming more and more cosmopolitan in character, that the Indian state has initiated structural reforms in Indian economy. The globalization process aiming at integrating the national economy with the world capitalist economy, is a logical culmination of the liberalization process. Although the Indian state has been citing the problems of foreign exchange crisis, fiscal deficits, balance of payments problem, non-performance of the public sector, increasing foreign debts etc., as the causes compelling it to liberalize the economy, it should be clear to all that these problems are basically the problems of crisis-ridden capitalist path and they have nothing to do with socialism. By projecting the option open to the Indian monopolies in the given national and international context, as the only option available to the whole nation, the Indian state is successfully selling the policy of liberalization with the help of mass-media and political parties, even to those who gain little or no benefit out of this policy. Expectations that many scholars and people in Northeast India have of liberalization and globalization only show the marketing ability of the Indian monopolies to sell their products.

Impact of Structural Adjustment Programmes in Select Developing Countries

Liberalization, whether implemented at the behest of external compulsions or due to internal drives, would have similar effects on economy and society. In the name of Structural Adjustment Programmes, the IMF and the World Bank have been prescribing liberalization policies as anti-dote to underdevelopment. The experiences of some of the developing countries which pursued liberalization policies indicate that their problems got complicated after following the Structural Adjustment Programme. For example, Ethiopia, once a fertile land with rich forests and diligent people, have now become a symbol of world hunger. The process started with accepting the 'generous' World Bank assistance to build up huge dams aimed at generating power and providing irrigation facilities for the development of agriculture. For facilitating the construction of dams, the government destroyed the forests, cleared the pasture lands and drowned the cultivable lands, and made lakhs of people homeless. The use of fertilizers and insecticides supplied by the imperialist countries led to the decline of fertility of the soil. Production of cash crops like cotton and sugar canes for export deepened the food crisis and led to perpetual famines, forcing Ethiopia to beg for food. Similarly, Morocco which started producing citras and other cash crops for exports to the western countries, is compelled to import millions of tons of wheat from USA. To put in other words, Morocco does not produce that she eats and does not eat what she produces. Because of such wrong policies, foreign debts increased, forcing Morocco to accept the IMF prescribed structural adjustment policies, which subsequently led to retrenchment, migration of rural labourers to the cities, proliferation of slums and increase of riots and anti-social activities. Ghana another African country which implemented the structural adjustment programmes to overcome what the IMF and the World Bank had characterized as the fiscal mismanagement, also had to pay heavy social costs. Slashing of subsidies in education and medical care resulted in increase of school dropouts and rise in different kinds of diseases. The devaluation of currency affected the local fishing industry and the emphasis on cash crops like cocoa benefited only a section of the rich farmers. Likewise, the futility of expecting the MNCs and foreign capital to generate growth and all round development of the indigenous people, become evident from the experience of many developing countries, like Bolivia, Zambia, Cyprus etc.

Capitalist Development and Indigenous People : A Study of Jharkhand

Modernization, industrialization and technological advance–ment need not necessarily ensure improvement in the living standards of the indigenous people. A study of the experience of economic development of Jharkhand region, comprising the tribal areas of Orissa, West Bengal and Bihar states, clearly indicates what is there in store for the tribals and dalits elsewhere during the liberalization phase becomes clear. In Jharkhand region industrialisation began during the British period itself. After independence many Indian private monopolies and public sector industries, like Coal India Limited (CIL), TISCO, DVC, NMDC, Hindustan Copper Ltd. etc., started their business ventures in the region. Many industries sprang up in and around Jamshedpur, Rourkela, Ranchi, Bokaro, Dhanbad and Ramgarh. Different hydel projects and thermal power generating units came into being. Urbanization which was less than 2 per cent at the beginning of the century reached 21.25 per cent in 1991. The number of urban inhabitations increased. In Dhanbad district, for example, number of towns increased from 3 in 1951 to 40 in 1991. But all these developments, instead of improving the living standards of the indigenous people, *i.e.*, the tribals and the dalits, made their lives worse than before. The indigenous ethnic groups were systematically and methodically dispossessed of the ownership of the means of production and thereby their very means of human existence. They were alienated from their lands and forced to work as contract workers or bonded labourers. In many cases, compensation offered to them was unjust and inequitable and failed to give them alternative means of livelihood. Urbanization led to immigration of people from the plain areas, making the indigenous inhabitant minorities in their own land. Because of illiteracy and lack of skills, the tribals could not avail better opportunities thrown open to them by industries, and had to confine themselves to the position of wage labourers. Most of the employers coming from outside the region, transferred their profits elsewhere, instead of diversifying production within Jharkhand. As a result, although urban centres could develop as enclaves of prosperity, the peripheral villages continued to thrive in poverty without minimum basic facilities. Agricultural lands and rich forests belonging to the indigenous people have been laid waste. The destruction of flora and fauna, soil erosion, silting of water courses and subsidence of land have made land unsafe for habitation, agriculture and grazing. Acid-mine drainage, liquid effluents and radio active chemicals have polluted even the drinking water sources also. As such, the capitalist development initiated in the name of national interests, reduced majority of indigenous people to destitution, destroyed their sources of livelihood, perpetuated poverty for the benefit of a few and brought the whole region to the brink of ecological disaster. Jharkhand is not an isolated case in India. Whether it is the construction of Narmada dam, or commercialization of forest resources in Dandakaranya or transition to formal sector in Orissa, the first sacrificial lambs were the indigenous people, the tribals.

Specificity of Northeast India

These experiences of the underdeveloped countries and backward regions within India should not be overlooked in determining the path of development for the Northeast India. At the same time the ethnic groups in the Northeast India should not be mechanically equated with the tribals in the mainland India. Because of the innerline regulations and the autonomous district councils, the ethnic groups could escape colonial and capitalist plunder to a considerable extent. Their xenophobia and ethnic philistinism, no doubt, prevented them from taking advantage of the fruits of modernization, but they also helped in avoiding, to some extent the sense of alienation, deprivation and dehumanization to which indigenous people of other regions in India are subjected to. While condemning the tribal militancy, to the extent theil acts are self-destructive or directed against innocent human beings—whether tribals or non-tribals, it should be recognized that their militancy helped them gain better bargaining position *vis-a-vis* the government of India. Despite poverty and economic backwardness, status of the tribals in the Northeast are better off than their counterparts in other regions in terms of human indicators like literacy rate, health standards, economic status and organizational strength.

Strategy for Economic Development of the Northeast

While taking note of these specificities, we should, however, avoid romanticizing economic backwardness and narrow ethnic identities. The Northeast lags behind the rest of the country in terms of economic indicators, like industrial growth, urbanization, power supply, fertilizer consumption, credit flow, communication facilities, transport net-work etc. The people of this region, therefore, have every right to demand development of necessary infrastructural facilities, establishment of basic industries and modernization of agriculture. It is true that what the state governments and North-Eastern Council (NEC) could accomplish during the earlier plan periods falls short of the expectations of the people. The critics are right in pointing out that crores of rupees pumped into these states by the central government are being spent mostly on unproductive purposes, benefitting a handful of politicians and bureaucrats. But as has been pointed out earlier, mere development of infrastructure, industrial growth, modernisation of agriculture, exploitation of forest and mineral resources need not necessarily ensure improvement of the living standards of the indigenous people. If economic development has to be meaningful, it has to meet the specific needs of the region. In case of the Northeast, priority should be given to increase agricultural production and achieve self sufficiency in the production of food grains and other agrarian products. There is a need for developing an indigenous entrepreneurial class capable of utilizing the local resources and managing the firms profitably. Basic industries like iron and steel, cement, chemicals etc. should be established in different regions in the Northeast. Import of goods from outside should be discouraged in areas where the local industries are competent, by giving preferential treatment to the local entrepreneurs in terms of duties, bank credits and market incentives. Flight of capital needs to be checked and central government funds should be utilized for productive purposes. Efforts should be made to generate internal resources, without depending parasitically on the grants and special assistance from the Government of India.

Likely Impact of Liberalization in the Northeast

Had the central and state governments taken appropriate measures in the directions mentioned above, the Northeast could have achieved better results. The desire to catch up with the rest of India would, however, remain a distant dream. As long as India follows the capitalist path of development, it is not possible to overcome uneven and sporadic development. Certain regions are bound to develop at the cost of others. Although it is not possible to bridge the gap within the given structure of economy, centralized planning, to some extent promotes the development of the backward regions. But liberalization is a negation of planned and state controlled development. In essence, liberalization is an unrestrained capitalist growth. It calls for unrestricted play of market forces and free flow of capital. The policy expects the state to relieve itself of all its commitments to balanced regional development and delegate the responsibility of economic development to the omnipotent and omnipresent monopoly capital. What would happen, if such liberalization becomes the guiding force of future development in the Northeast? At the first instance, the government will have to invest crores of rupees for creating those infrastructural facilities necessary for attracting capital. The government has to take tough measures to ensure law and order in the region. As no Indian monopolies or foreign monopolies would enter the region unless they are assured of maximum profits, the Northeast should have to change its priorities to suit their interests. Agricultural growth should be tuned to the needs of external markets, which means giving priority to cash crops instead of food grain production. Forest and mineral wealth should be allowed to be exploited for the benefits of the greedy investors. Once the capital intensive industries which have very little ability to absorb the jobless, are permitted, they will destroy even the existing small-scale and medium industries.

All these developments will have serious repercussions on the already volatile social and political situation in the Northeast. A section of the elites closely associated with the liberalization process no doubt gets some benefits. But majority of the indigenous people will be exposed to the problems of land alienation, displacement, proletarianisation and unemployment. Due to lack of social commitment, the private capital mercilessly plunders the natural wealth and creates serious ecological problems in the region. Further, liberalization will widen the regional imbalances even within the Northeast, benefitting certain regions and groups at the cost of others. Industrialisation and modernisation will accentuate class differentiation within the society. Sooner or later class formation in the tribal societies is unavoidable. But in the absence of class based all India parties capable of uniting the oppressed and exploited masses of all nationalities and ethnic groups in the region, the people's anger and frustration with the process of change are likely to ventilate in the intensification of self-destructive ethnic movements demanding secession from the Indian Union.

References

Anand Kumar Yogi, *Development of Northeast Region : Problems and Prospects*, Spectrum, Guwahati, 1991.

Ashish Kothari, *"Environment and New Economic Policies, Economic and Political Weekly"*, April 29, 1995.

Bikram Narayan Nanda, *Contours of Continuity and Change : The Story of Banda Highlanders*, Sage, New Delhi, 1994.

B.L. Abbi (ed.), *Northeast Region Problems and Prospects of Development*, CRRID, Chandigarh, 1984.

B.K. Ahluwalia and Shashi Ahluwalia, *Socio-economic Development*, Indian Social Institute, New Delhi, 1986.

Mathew Aneeparampil, *Tribals of Jharkhand : Victims of Development*, Indian Social Institute, New Delhi, 1995.

Walter Fernandes, *National Development and Tribal Deprivation*, Indian Social Institute, New Delhi, 1992.

________, *Structural Adjustments : Who Really Pays*, Public Interest Research Group, New Delhi, 1994.

________, *Imperialism : The Deadly Octopus*, Annyachoke Parishad, Calcutta, 1995.

Chapter 10

North-East India in the Wake of Economic Reforms and Liberalization

—R.K. Choudhury

The new economic reforms policy with a globalized and market-friendly economic structure which India has been experiencing for the last six years is yet to make a noticeable score in the country, while it has even failed to make the North-Eastern region properly feel its existence and operational network. What is important here to note is that since the economic base of North-Eastern region is known to be one of the poorest in the country, the impact of economic reforms to establish a strong developmental base should have, in fact, been vigorously felt here in the last six years, and, if the economic reforms were meant for economic development, the top most priority should, in fact, have been accorded to the backward regions like North-East India.

Basic Economic Structure of North-East

The region with a population of around 31.4 million has a geographical area of over 25.5 million hectares and 90 percent of people living in rural areas. Agriculture is the primary occupation giving livelihood to 78 percent of population of which 60 percent are cultivators, 10 percent agricultural labourers and 8 percent remain engaged in allied farm sector.

Shifting cultivation is the traditional way of life of hill states with 2.7 million hectares under it. Needless to mention, the fate of the region's economy is inseparably linked with that of the agricultural sector. The irrigated area as proportion of cropped area except in Manipur (39.1 percent) ranges between 11 percent and 28 percent as against 35 percent in the country as a whole and 95 percent in Punjab. Mechanization of agriculture is yet to take root in the region. Fertilizer consumption per hectare as in 1994-95 in the North-Eastern states ranges between 1.2 kg in Arunachal Pradesh and 19.5 kg in Tripura as against 175 kg in Punjab and 75.7 Kg in the country as a whole. The number of irrigation pump sets in the region comprises less than even half of a percent of the country and the tractorised tilling ranges between 0.01 percent and 0.80 percent of all India total. With high growth of population, the north-eastern states have for long been a heavily food deficit region where the production of food grains as in 1990-91 is only 49 lakh tonnes as against 31.4 million people. The per capita per day net production of food grains in the region comes to only 365 grams as against the requirement of around 470 grams as against 510 grams in the country. Hence, food grains to the extent of 25 percent of production has to be imported from outside the region. Per capita income in the region is much lower than the all India average and such difference at current prices has registered a rise from Rs. 269 in 1980-81 to Rs. 2147 in 1994-95 in Meghalaya and from Rs. 346 to Rs. 2284 in Assam during the same period.

Agro Sectoral Reform

It is uncomfortable to note that agriculture has received the least attention of liberalization and since the backbone of North-Eastern region's economy is the farm sector, the impact of total liberalization process is almost absent in the region's economy. It may be noted here that the market-friendly new economic policy envisaged gradual privatization in mechanization of agriculture, but in fact, government subsidy in the farm sector particularly with respect to food, fertilizer and other inputs has been on the rise. The Union budget for 1997-98, for example, has provided for an increase in food and sugar subsidy to Rs. 7,500 crores from Rs. 6,066 crores in

1996-97 and fertilizer subsidy to Rs. 9,910 crores from Rs. 7,767 crores in 1996-97.

While it is a fact that privatization of farm inputs in totality should not be forced at the moment, but there are segments of agriculture which have now become highly rich and deserve to be completely privatized. Hence, such subsidy should be area-specific and farmer-specific. The practice of spending hard-earned money of tax-payers in the form of fertilizers and other input subsidy has widened the gap between poverty and prosperity in the farm sector. It may be noted that 75 percent of the subsidy on agriculture is utilized by the richest state of India—*i.e.,* Punjab alone. Again, the supply of free electricity to farmers in Punjab has been vehemently criticized by the World Bank.

In so far as North-Eastern States are concerned, agro-sectoral reform needs the largest attention of government. Here the strategy should be improvement of production technology farm management and marketing structure under the direction, guidance and budgetary help of public authorities. The time for market friendly liberalization is, perhaps, long yet to be ripe in the region. Agro-Sectoral reform structure needs to give a high priority to allied activities like diary farming, poultry, fishery, horticulture, etc. which have a tremendous prospect of development in the region. The flow of credit to farm sector should be enhanced at any cost and proper utilization of the same ensured. The Union Finance Minister's call for doubling the flow of credit to agriculture and agro-industries within five years and the necessary provision made should be utilized. The union budget for 1997-98 has raised the quantum of facility by 30 percent from Rs. 22,000 crore in 1996-97 to Rs. 28,600 crore. The benefit of Rural Infrastructure Development Fund which was created in 1996-97 with a capital base of Rs. 5000 crore should flow adequately to the North-Eastern region.

Development of Infrastructure

One of the main reasons for economic backwardness is the poor level of infrastructure in the region. Transport sector is very weak. The region is still to go a long way in building up of proper road transport system in the rural areas. The railway network is yet to make an inroad into most of the states of the region. The railway transport which mainly operates in Assam and partly in Tripura is also at a very low level of efficiency, regularity and adequacy. Power generation and energy consumption in the region is the lowest in the country though there is a vast hydro-electric potentiality in the region. Even though the new economy policy has opened up infrastructural sector to private investment participation, the impact in the North-Eastern region is minimal—almost absent. Fiscal incentives like period tax holiday has failed to attract private investment in the region. The power sector investment is yet to take a root in the private sector though the potential is vast.

It is only in the communication sector that some benefits may be received from economic reforms in the region. While some improvement in the telecommunication sector has visibly flown to the region in the form of improved telephone facilities, it is heartening to note that the region will now have an access to global information network. Guwahati, the gateway to North-East, is the 13th city in India to have access to information super highway with effect from April 21, 1997.

Liberalization in Oil and Service Sectors

The Union budget for 1997-98 which makes a supplementary effort to speed up liberalized economic reforms has given a special thrust to the aspect of oil exploration, health insurance and pension services. Thus, in addition to announcement of a new oil exploration licensing policy to boost up foreign as well as domestic investment in exploration task, the budget has extended a five-year tax holiday to oil exploration as well as industrial parks along with the benefit of other infrastructure projects. The budget has also provided for deemed export benefit for supply of goods to oil, gas and power projects. This is a great incentive to development of export—substituting industries in north-eastern region since many projects in gas, oil and power sectors are either in operation or are going to be taken up in the days to come.

From the opening up of health insurance sector to Indian private companies and re-casting of Employees Provident Fund and Gratuity scheme and setting up of a full-fledged pension fund by the Unit Trust of India, the North-Eastern region along with other states is supposed to be benefitted if the schemes get through successful implementation. It is again important to note here that the union budget for 1997-98 has identified nine public sector enterprises to become global giants and the Indian Oil Corporation, Oil India Limited and Oil and Natural Gas Corporation—which are the main operators in the oil sector of North-Eastern region are among them. As such, North-East India on this account might expect additional flow of investment in these sectors.

Foreign Direct Investment in North-East

The experience of post-liberalization period in regard to foreign direct investment (FDI) in the north-eastern region is unhappy indeed. This is in spite of vast potentiality in power generation, oil sector, food processing, tourism etc. After introduction of liberalization policy in 1991, it is important to note, only seven states, *viz.*, Maharashtra, Karnataka, Gujarat, Tamil Nadu, Andhra Pradesh, West Bengal and Orissa alone have accounted for 80 percent of the total FDI flow of Rs. 25,490 crore between 1991 and 1996. Investment in the region being too low, the Assam state committee of All India Bank Officers Confederation has appealed to the government of Assam and other states of North-East to take all possible steps to lure direct foreign investment to enhance development through economic growth, employment and income generation and promotion of exports and tourism. To establish intensive trade relation with neighbouring countries, the centre should set up an EXIM Bank in the region.

Apart from foreign direct investment, private investment from other states of India is also shy in the region. It is important to note that socio-political unrest on the one hand and insurgency operation of militant outfits on the other have been an obstacle to the flow of private investment in the region. Needless to mention, the other important unfriendly situation is created by the poor level of infrastructure facilities.

Industrial Sector Reform and North-East

The main thrust of the liberalization policy is to boost up industrial development of the country through large scale abolition of licensing restrictions, creation of market-friendly structure under a globalized set up, invitation of foreign capital and foreign industries, encouragement of free competition and measures to liberalize trade and foreign exchange market. The North-Eastern region having a very poor industrial base is not expected to benefit much from the industrial sector reform. The main industries in the region, particularly of Assam, are the tea, oil and paper industries. In the tea sector, there is no visible impact of liberalization and the benefits in the form of larger investment, larger productivity or larger employment are not noticeable. Had there been new plantation factories and import of equipments from foreign market, there could have been benefit through import liberalization measures of the new economic policy. On the other hand, however, devaluation of rupee as a consequence of the liberalization policy could boost up exports of tea from Assam and, hence, foreign exchange earnings. But it is not only that production is more or less stagnant and the domestic demand has been rising enormously but also that Indian tea is facing heavy competition in the foreign market. As a result of this coupled with lower value of rupee, the foreign exchange earnings from the tea industry of Assam in the post-liberalization period is not at all encouraging. The oil sector has been discussed separately. In so far as paper industry is concerned, the liberalization policy could help the least. Almost all the paper units of the region—two units in Assam and one in Nagaland—have gone sick and no determined attempt at their revitalization is in sight. If the scope of expansion in the large industries sector is the least in the north-east, the scope for expansion of the small scale sector is tremendous. This is the only sector which, when developed optimally, could transfer the economy into a high income region with full employment of excess labour of primary sector.

It is well known that the policy of liberalization does not contain enough elements to boost up the small scale sector.

Moreover, about 40 percent of the small industrial units in the region is utterly sick and no sustainable attempt is in the government agenda for their revival. However, the new industrial policy, 1997 of Assam has made an attempt to develop the sector in the state and has identified 19 priority areas for the purpose. The policy seeks to create conditions favourable to the use of maximum local materials and man power together with competitive advantage under a market friendly set up under which food processing industry, rural non-farm sector, export-oriented units and balanced regional development would be promoted. For the purpose, the government will be arranging industrial land allotment, setting up of three growth centres, completion of power generation projects, removal of transport bottleneck of the industrial areas, strengthening of district industries centres, extension of power subsidy and tax holiday on sales of finished product and purchase of raw materials. The other states of the region should make such an attempt and sincerely implement the strategy.

Reform of Public Enterprises

It is important to note that the World Bank is unhappy over the pace of progress in reform of Public Enterprises in the country in general. The position of state level public enterprises in the North-East is still worse due to a number of reasons like poor management, excessive fixed cost of running business, absence of monitoring activity, total indifference to accountability etc.

The original idea was to make the management professionally competent and free from political and bureaucratic control. However, in most of the state level public enterprises of north-eastern region, the top management positions are occupied by either politicians or bureaucrats. Instead of enjoying independence, these enterprises suffer from political decisions and bureaucratic influence forced on them. Excessive man power recruited indiscriminately under these influences, irregularity in the supply of finance and consequent time over-run and loss over-run, excessive administrative expenses, total lack of accountability and monitoring and, above all, inefficient management—all these have made most of the state level public enterprises chronically sick units. On the other hand there is no sincere attempt on the part of government for their revival.

The exit policy of economic reform has already proved to be a failure. Any attempt to wind up even the economically most unviable enterprise will be vehemently obstructed unless alternative employment avenues are created for the oversized labour structure. Hence, the impact of liberalization on these enterprises in the North-East is the least. In order to revive them there is the urgent necessity of strengthening management of these enterprises through dynamic leadership and excess labour must be redeployed to associated areas of gainful productivity. Again, since, the memoranda of understanding are silent about responsibility of government but are only vocal about the obligations of enterprises, they should be amended to give real autonomy on the one hand and clearly state the obligations of government in the task of proper running of the enterprises.

What is clear from the above is that the impact of liberalization is almost non-existent on the economy of the north-east till date. It is perhaps neither desirable at the moment since the circumstances are yet to be ripe to absorb profitably the inputs of liberalization strategy. The reform measures at the moment should be initiated by the government and implemented properly by removing the defects that have so long kept the region in a backward state. Liberalization policy could better benefit the region only when it attains a favourable grounding frame.

References

Annual Report of the Asian Development Bank, 1994.

Assam Industrial Policy, 1997, Government of Assam, Dispur, March, 1997.

Chief Minister's Budget Speech, 1997-98 budget, Government of Assam, Dispur, March 1997.

Economic Survey, Government of India, New Delhi, 1993-94 and 1996-97.

IBRD country Report on Indian Economic Reforms, 1994.

R.K. Choudhury, "Market-Friendly Liberalization of Indian Economy: Some Structural Problems", Guwahati University, Journal of Arts, Guwahati University, 1996.

The New Industrial Policy, 1991, Government of India, New Delhi, July 1991.

World Bank Development Report on "Recent Economic Development and Prospects", June, 1994.

Chapter 11

Resource Mobilization, Distribution Effect and Economic Development of the North-Eastern Region

—Sujit Sikidar & Devadas Bhorali

Resource mobilization has assumed a key word in financial management of the government. The Central Government is under constant pressure : to raise additional financial resources needed for financing the plan development efforts and budgeted projects, to ensure attainment of 7 pc growth rate, to bring down the fiscal deficit to 5 pc of GDP; to reduce revenue gap; to reduce the income tax rate, to widen the tax base by bringing more people within the tax bracket and to ensure strict enforcement of tax administration and better compliance with the tax law by the assessee and to reduce unproductive expense beyond the financial means of the public revenue. The same tenets are equally applicable in respect of states also.

Objective

Considering the above broad national parameters it has been decided by the present researches to make an analysis of the resource mobilization efforts and avenues of the states in the north-eastern region and then to highlight the norms stipulated by various Finance Commissions (FCs) while giving their award for resource sharing by the states.

Methodology

For the purpose of meeting these objectives some selective variables affecting the state finance of the N.E. region have been collected. Some analytical light has been thrown on those variables and finally several concrete suggestions have been offered.

In this context let us now look into the constitutional provision as regards mobilization of resources by the states under the federal structure, as discussed hereunder.

Tenth Finance Commission (TFC) and its impact on N.E. Region

(a) Opening of border trade with Myanmar and Bangladesh would open large markets having potential for extension upto the entire South East Asia. Despite tax holiday scheme, and a strong 32 million market, the region could not earn the confidence of industry. The region enjoys a basic advantage on account of easy accessibility with South East Asia. The FC should provide special grants-in-aid for flood protection, gauge conversion of railway, electricity generation, wherever possible through private participation. Special assistance should have been included by the TFC for rubber cultivation in Meghalaya. Under backward area improvement programme the TFC could not make any worthwhile recommendation. Out of total government investment in public sector, only eight percent has gone to ten special category states, which includes the seven sister states. As a result these states are deprived of investment, both from public and private sector.

(b) The overall allocation of resources to the states of Assam has been fixed by the TFC as per the conventional norms of devolution. But the TFC could not give due weightage to the fact that devolution under intra-state administrative agencies has increased many fold particularly in Assam and Tripura, as the governments of these states have to make allocation from its own common pool to the District Councils under Sixth Schedule of the constitution, and above all, to the various tribal autono–

mous councils set up by virtue of an agreement between tribal leaders and the state government; to enhance the prospect of self government in the tribal areas. So the FC and the planning commission ought to have recognized the inter state and intra-state financial requirement for public administration.

(c) Following the imperative need of improving law and order situation, smuggling of drugs form across the international border and to fight AIDS and drug trafficking in the states of Assam, Manipur, Tripura and Meghalaya, substantial portion of resources of these states is spent in paying the hire charges of security forces and police commandos borrowed from the centre. This expenditure enhances the quantum of non-plan unproductive expenses of the state and causes severe erosion in their resources. The TFC, however, could not spell out anything in this regard; on the plea of maintenance of law and order is a state subject. The present authors contest that when law and order situation has been worsened from across the international border, it assumes a national problem, on the other hand, the centre also cannot be expected to assume additional non-plan expense burden over and above its own fiscal deficit. This is a vicious circle engulfing the inter-state resource harmonization.

Even the central government cannot contain its increasing expenditure against limited receipts. The available data reflect that central government's interest payment as a proportion of tax revenue has gone up from 53% in 1991-92 to 69% (budget estimate) in 1995-96 and as a proportion of total revenue from 40% to 51.5% for the said two years. The states' plan outlay, including Area Programmes for 1995-96, comprising the approved outlay in respect of all the 25 states, accounts for 18.5 % shortfall of the approved Eighth plan outlay, which is less than the pro rata level of 20%. The shortfall *vis-a-vis* approved outlay, in the case of states, is due to their inability to raise resources on the scale necessary to overcome the erosion in resource base caused by the negative balance from current revenues (BCR). Hence the state of Assam should endeavour to overcome shortfall in plan expenditure by minimizing non-plan, unproductive expenditure.

The state of Assam has been demanding two-year moratorium on repayment of central loan assistance for flood. The total accumulated debt under the central loan assistance (CLA) of Assam was of the order of Rs. 179.21 crore. The state also appealed to the central Finance Ministry for higher allocation and conversion of central loan assistance into grants to deal with the colossal damage caused by recurring floods in the state.

Schemes to control floods in Assam are now financed through the state's plan fund and from CLA, which was cent percent loan and was repayable at the annual interest of 12% plus 2.75 % for default. During the last three years of the Eighth plan (1992-93, 1993-94, 1994-95), Rs. 5.91 crore had been obtained by the state under CLA after deduction of principal and interest, although the total sanction was Rs. 75 crore. The net effect of two-year moratorium on loan repayment for 1995-96 and 1996-97 would be that the entire amount of Rs. 25 crore each would be available to the state during 1995-96 and 1996-97. Most of the state Finance Commissions (SFCs) set up under the 74th Amendment have also confined themselves only to the non-plan aspects.

Tax Structure and Assam

Unequal tax structure costs the state of Assam heavily. For instance, the rate of taxes in the neighbouring states is very low as compared to Assam. Thus taxes on expensive items like vehicles and other motor parts are almost nil in bordering areas.

Although Assam produces commodities like tea, plywood, crude oil and jute, it hardly earns any revenue from these. It may be suggested that if a turnover tax is introduced then the state could collect about Rs. 200 crores annually.

Assam produces plywood worth Rs. 700 crore of which only about 5% is sold in the state; *i.e.*, 95% goes out of the state. Assam gets only 2% of the tea sold through the Guwahati Tea Auction centre while most of the tea produced in the state is sold outside the state leaving very little for levying state tax.

The state of Assam has, as in September 1995, about Rs. 1,809 crore as outstanding dues towards the centre which was deducted at the rate of about Rs. 60 crore every month. The national committee on uniform tax structure has recommended in August 1995 that the tax structure in the country has to be changed so that the maximum rate of tax will come down to 20% for items like liquor, narcotics, molasses, rectified spirit and petroleum products other than diesel. Thus the highest rate of tax will be only 20% applicable to five items. As per the committee recommendations maximum number of items will come under 8% tax numbering 72 and 64 items under 12% tax. 25 items are fully exempted from tax like rice, flour, artificial limbs, cereals, pulses, eggs etc., and 55 items fall under 4% tax rate. Those states where the rate of tax is low at present will be compensated by the Union government by equal amount which can be used for developmental activities within the state for the welfare of the people. With the introduction of uniform tax structure and value added tax in the country, it is hoped, all the states are going to get equal benefit and this will also stop cut-throat competition which is prevailing in all the states as in September, 1995.

Finance Commission and Finance for Flood Control in Assam

The resources of the state flood control department was not adequate in 1995-96 because of drastic cut in central assistance on account of flood control. Being unable to meet the demand for state flood control, the centre had given instructions that the DRDA projects could be used for earth work such as repair of embankments and other related works. The severe shortage of flood control resources to meet expense on this count may be understood from the following fact. Assam was entitled to a loan of Rs. 25 crore a year for flood control, but in 1994-95 the amount received after various deductions was only Rs. 1.04 crore; consequently embankments damaged by floods were repaired using DRDA funds, as the flood control department did not have funds of its own.

The state of Assam was also entitled to Rs. 47 crore per year to combat natural calamities as per the recommendations of the finance commission. Out of the amount, the total drawal in the current year (1995-96) up to July 1995 had been Rs. 23 crore, of which Rs. 17 crore had come from the centre and Rs. 6 crore had been contributed by the state government.

Borrowing Power of the States

All the states are allowed to resort to market borrowing under Article 293 of the constitution. But when a state is indebted to the centre, as is the common case with all the states, it shall seek prior approval from the centre. The states have virtually no choice in determining their market borrowing. Second, the Planning Commission in consultation with the Finance Ministry and RBI determines the total quantum of borrowing and allocates each state's share. Thus the poorer states like Assam, Tripura, Nagaland enjoy negligible support from the market as regards subscription of their bonds even 1% of the value price of the bond issued. Thirdly, the RBI being the manager of the states' public debt determines the timing and the rate of interest on the loan raised by state government. They enjoy little respite from precarious financial condition. It is only through RBI's insistence that the commercial banks subscribe to states' bond issue.

Unnecessary government spending has to be controlled to avoid slippage of the benefits of economic reforms and to take advantage of private investment in development projects, specially in Assam and Meghalaya. This is needed in connection with developing power generating projects in collaboration with private parties. The state of Assam may try to reduce her dependence on centre by expanding her export specially in South-East Asian nations, dispatched from Guwahati air port. There prevails some export potential as the country's export growth in first three months (April-June 1995) of the fiscal year 1995-96 marked a healthy 27.2% growth. We have to enhance our export because we are not a prosperous country as our per capita income is only $300, as against $550 in Sri Lanka, $3,000 in Mauritius, $13,000 in Singapore, $28,000 in Japan and $38,000 in Switzerland.

Financial Discipline and Assam

While VP Singh Government during the AGP rule in the state adopted 90% grant and 10% loan formula, the state of Assam, however, could not derived much benefit from this formula. Because the state had to redeem huge loan liability incurred by successive congress governments, despite Assam was accorded a special category state. The state's indebtedness to the central government as in August 1995 was around Rs. 4,000 crore besides financial obligation to clear contractors and suppliers bill aggregating about Rs. 1,500 crores.

The amount of unproductive expenditure has been increasing by leaps and bounds, contrary to the government's claim over improvement of law and order situation, the state had to spend around Rs. 892 crore on this head alone during 1991 to March 1995.

DA package to state government employees including public sector enterprises amounted to about Rs. 2,400 crores a year according to an estimate submitted to TFC. This sum is also not supported by corresponding hike in productivity and work efficiency. Stoppage of overdraft facilities with the RBI exhibits the day to day mis-match between government receipts and payments and further reflects the unsound financial management implying living beyond means.

The problem has been accentuated by the huge arrear loan obligation for which a large portion of central plan assistance has been reduced and adjusted against the debt servicing obligation of the state government. For instance, during the period 1992-93 to 1994-95 the total plan allocation was Rs. 3,040.72 crores out of which an amount Rs. 2,199.64 crores was deducted at source by the centre, leaving a meagre sum of Rs. 841.08 crores available for development works of the state. Persistent reliance on borrowed funds to finance ever growing expenditure, keeping the revenue flow constant, has ultimately landed the state of Assam in a veritable debt trap where it has to borrow every time to finance her non-development expenditure.

Assam and northeastern region could not reap the benefit of liberalization. Out of the 1,650 proposals cleared by the

Union Government between January 1993 and October 1994, Assam's share is only 2 while Maharashtra heads the list with 283 proposals. Out of Rs. 3.5 lakh crore foreign investment in the country, only five percent has filtered down to the eastern region, though this area represents 26% of the country's population. Out of this, the north-eastern region's share is almost nil. Foreign investment has gone into those areas which have three factors namely, infrastructure, a proper work culture and peace. Meghalaya State Electricity Board is the first such concern to be privatized with partial foreign assistance as in September 1995.

Performance-linked Grants to States

Following the deterioration of tax efforts of the states, RBI study suggested a system of performance-linked grants to states. Study entitled 'Fiscal Efficiency—in the Indian Federation', in September 1995 points out that fiscal responsibility requires decentralization of tax and expenditure responsibilities. A balance should be maintained between decentralization, efficiency and equity in tax collection. There is a rationale for resource transfers from higher to lower levels of government. During 1982-92 period, the tax productivity index (TPI) has been positive only during 1985-90 period—that is the seventh plan period. TPI measures the aggregative implications of variations in fiscal efficiency of different states.

There was a decline in TPI in the late eighties. The negative drift of the TPI for states in recent years occurred around the time when stress on tax efforts and fiscal management for distribution of central assistance was brought down. Fiscal transfers should be used to encourage states to improve their tax efforts. Improvement in tax collections will improve welfare if such an effort is accompanied with lower distortionary costs of taxation to the economy. Achieving such efficiency will require at least two steps : *(a)* States should be induced to improve tax efforts by placing a larger weight on tax effort in the devolution formula, and *(b)* there should be a movement towards more efficient taxes and central value added tax (VAT).

The present high level of fiscal stress in states is partly explained by the decline in tax productivity in recent years.

Given the upward trend in state expenditure, improvement in tax efforts assumes crucial importance for future reforms in state finances (The Economic Times, dated 17 September 1995.)

The Annual Plan Outlay for the year 1997-98 for Assam has been fixed at Rs. 1,500 crore although it is marginally higher by 4.6% over the current (1996-97) year's outlay of Rs. 1,434 crore. The central support also includes Rs. 80 crores for financing the externally aided projects. An amount of Rs. 217 crore will be met out of state contribution. State's contribution has been proposed to be met from small savings, loans, market-borrowings, net accretion to State's provident fund and other institutional borrowings. The plan outlay for Assam also includes Rs. 88.61 crore under award of the 10th Finance Commission for implementation of various upgradation schemes.

It may be suggested that development needs and priorities of special category state like Assam should be on the basis of plan funding delinking it from the resource raising ability of the state. Due consideration ought to be given to the state's constraints in resource mobilization for financing the plan. Assam has very limited tax potential owing to poor industrialization of the state. It has been further suggested that crude oil royalty be fixed at minimum 10% of the intrinsic value of the crude based on international price and not on the administered price, as is currently done. The period of revision may be reduced from three years to two years. The Union government has in 1996 fixed the royalty at Rs. 570 per MT, as against the demand of Rs. 1,204 per MT. Following the special category status accorded to Assam during the Ninth Plan need be continued. Considering the heavy debt burden of the state, the existing central assistance pattern of 90% grant and 10% loan may be converted to 100% grant during the Ninth plan period. But a cabinet decision of the central government in February 1997 to slash aid to NE states may half the tempo of growth when the central plan outlay would be deducted at the rate of 15% annually towards the NE states' arrear dues to the centre. The state governments of Assam owe Rs. 222.45 crore; Arunachal Pradesh Rs. 3.50 crore;

Meghalaya Rs. 10.77 crore, Manipur Rs. 65.04 crore; Mizoram Rs. 29.88 crore and Nagaland Rs. 25.10 crore. The cut would be effective from Ninth Plan and amounts were due to various central undertakings for supply of power, coal, atomic energy and railways. Different states owe the central undertakings over Rs. 15,000 crore of which dues to power sector alone was about Rs. 9,000 crore. The aim of the central scheme was to enable the government to introduce cash and carry scheme for the states. The Assam government's demand for sanction of Rs. 20,000 crore as Annual Plan Outlay for 1997-98 has already been slashed down by the planning commission to Rs. 15,000 crore.

For Meghalaya the state government has demanded to the Planning Commission that a special central assistance of Rs. 132 crore would be required during 1996-97 for the implementation of infrastructural development projects. The High Level Commission has been reviewing the formula for allocation of central assistance for the Basic Minimum Services. Meghalaya Government has laid emphasis on the implementation of Basic Minimum Services.

Diversion of Funds

About 20% of the allocation to the states in NE region under the centrally sponsored schemes go unutilized. This is, however, common in other states as well. Several state governments deliberately delayed the tabling of CAG reports on the floor of the Assembly. The CAG has proposed to the central government that reports of the CAG should be 'deemed to have been laid on the table of house' to avoid the delaying tactics of the state governments. Once the proposal is accepted, it would enable the Public Accounts Committee of the state assemblies to immediately go into the reports.

Perturbed by increasing incidence of states diverting funds towards non-plan expenditure, the Ninth Plan draft approach paper has sought greater expenditure discipline and fiscal prudence to realize the fruits of planned development. The NE states are even diverting planned funds for disbursal of salaries and other administrative expenses. As a result of an expenditure shortfall and diversion of planned funds, the states have not been able to complete the projects and the resulting delays have cost the exchequer heavily, besides stalling the development process. The Meghalaya government failed to utilize even 20% of the total allocation of centrally sponsored schemes. The CAG Report 1997 has proposed for enhancing CAG's power to bring autonomous bodies under its audit.

The management of oil sector signifies disparities in union-state relations. Although the article 294 of the constitution recognizes the proprietary rights of states in respect of all mineral resources including crude oil and natural gas, in actual practice the central government does not adhere to. For instance, the Oil Field (Regulation and Development) Act 1983, provides that the rate of royalty on mineral oil shall not be enhanced more than once during any period of three years. But there is no such stipulation fixing time limit for the revision of the oil development cess or price of petroleum and petroleum products. Thus the state has hardly any freedom in earning revenue from crude oil. The Assam government has been demanding for 'automatic annual revision of royalty', which is to be paid on the value of crude oil for the previous year, with provisions for final settlement based on the average prevailing international market price of the current year. Timely revision of oil royalty after every three years is a basic obligation. It has been estimated that owing to inordinate delay in revising the oil royalty the state of Assam Exchequer has lost about Rs. 64 crores at a nominal annual interest rate of 10% between 1984 and 1991. Out of the total cess of Rs. 30,000 crores collected from the oil sector, over Rs. 26,000 crores of cess collection has been deposited into the consolidated Fund of India. The state may legitimately demand a share of it.

References

The Assam Tribune, Dated January 19,20, 1997.

The Report of the CAG, January 1997.

Personal interview with Finance officials of the respective state governments.

Chapter 12

LIBERALIZATION AND THE NORTH-EAST INDIA

—Rakhee Bhattacharya

Liberalization as commonly understood relates to relaxation of Government controls and regulations upon economic activities, in order that the growth, efficiency and resource allocation within the economy may improve in response to market forces of demand and supply. As Shri R.N. Malhotra, the Ex RBI Governor has rightly visualized, the present phase of liberalization in India not mark an ideological divide and can more appropriately be looked upon as an evolutionary movement which has been underway for some time and has now gathered some momentum and become more comprehensive.

The policy of liberalization in India can be traced to the mid sixties with the introduction of export incentives but it seemed to have ended soon with devaluation and limited decontrol of imports. The reforms in the mid seventies were undertaken in a more favourable economic scenario, with good foreign exchange reserves, a steady growth of GDP by more than 5% (1975-76 to 1978-79), a stable political system, and high credit rating in the international financial market. The policy of liberalization during that phase had been introduced in some isolated areas with varying degrees of relaxation, at a very slow pace. The Alexander Committee Report on Import and Export Policies and Procedures (1978) had made several recommendations to improve the access of manufactures to imported inputs and to simplify procedures. The goods covered by Open General Licenses (OGL) were expanded. In May 1979 the Dalgi Committee Report on government controls and subsidies came up with a somewhat broader and more inclusive mandate than the Alexander Committee. The report tried to link up the demands for trade liberalization. In the early 1980s, the economic policy focused more on stabilization measures in the wake of the second oil shock and severe worldwide recession. India suffered a sharp setback in 1979-80 due to steep fall in agriculture production and rising oil prices. A severe BOP problem had developed, but the country continued to have the same import liberalization policy without reimposing a highly restrictive regime.

While Indian economy entered the decade of the 1990s, with large imbalances both on the internal as well as the external front, which were actually exacerbated by the gulf crisis and disturbed situation in the domestic policy during 1990-91. The erosion of international confidence in India's credit worthiness led to massive outflow of deposits from non-resident's accounts. Growth in industrial production had turned negative due to severe imports squeeze, inflation rate had touched double digits severely affecting the domestic prices and savings of the country.Realizing the gravity of the situation, the Narasimha Rao Government which came to power in 1991, had immediately adopted a number of stabilization measures designed to restore internal and external confidence. It also announced a number of structural reforms in the spheres of trade, industry, public and financial sectors aimed at strengthening the growth of the economy in the medium term.

The macro stabilization policies basically aimed at reducing economic imbalances by attacking demand, while structural adjustment policies aimed at increasing growth and supply by imparting competitiveness, efficiency and dynamism to the system. The process is time consuming and complex, but will have to be completed in full to get the benefit of the structural reforms. In the transitional period and in the short term, the fiscal correction measures and tight monetary policies might slow down economic activities, but in the medium term and long term, the structural reforms are expected to eliminate economic inefficiencies, increase overall growth employment, achieve desirable price stability, ease the BOP pressure and consolidate the productivity gains achieved in the past. These, in brief, essentially constituted the liberalization package of 1990s.

The thrust of the present paper is on the condition of the economy of North East India and how far the above mentioned liberalization policy of 1990s is applicable to this far flung region of the country. Let us first try to understand the economic realities of this region through an analysis of the available secondary information so that the feasibility of liberalization policies can be clearly understood for this part of the country. This has been attempted in Table I where some of the major economic indicators of north-east India have been considered.

Table 1

ECONOMIC INDICATORS OF NORTH-EAST INDIA (1991-92)

States	*Net State Domestic Product*	*Share of real Output in NSDP from*		*% Share in All India NDP*	*CD Ratio*	*Large & Medium Scale Industry*	
	at Current Prices (Rs.Cr)	*Agri-culture*	*Manufac-turing*	*at Cons-tant Prices*	*of Comm. Banks*	*No*	*%**
Assam	8905	34.1	13.2	2.3	49.0	118	74.8
Meghalaya	795	31.0	4.1	0.2	20.0	7	4.5
Manipur	694	32.7	5.9	0.2	71.0	6	3.9
Mizoram	281	NA	NA	NA	26.0	1	0.0
Nagaland	561	21.5	1.8	0.1	40.0	16	10.4
Arunachal Pradesh	426	37.1	6.3	0.1	17.0	17	5.8
Tripura	933	NA	NA	NA	61.0	1	0.6

Source : Basic Statistics of North-Eastern Region 1995.

* Figures in this column indicate percentages of total number of large and medium scae industries in the north-east.

The figures in Table 1 depict a very gloomy economic scenario of the entire north-eastern region. The Net Domestic Products of all the states except Assam remain extremely low compared to states like Maharashtra (57,178), Gujarat (23,316), West Bengal (32,062). Even the hill states like Himachal Pradesh has higher NDP (2,429) than any of the hill states of north-eastern region. Shares of real output from manufacturing sector are also extremely low in all the seven states of this region compared to the states like Maharashtra (29.8%), Gujarat (27.7%) and Tamil Nadu (21.7%). Declining share of agriculture and increasing share of manufacturing and service sectors to the net income are accepted indicators of industrialization. We find that in these developed states, the shares of agricultural sector is much lower compared to the manufacturing sector. Thus the shares of agriculture in NSDP for Maharashtra, Gujarat and Tamil Nadu were respectively 16.0%, 19.0% and 21.6% in 1991-92 compared to the corresponding figures for north eastern states as depicted above. The percentage share in all India NDP similarly shows a very depressing picture. Coming to the credit-deposit ratio of all scheduled commercial banks, surprisingly we find that some of these border states have very high CD ratio, even higher than the national figure (60%) and of some of the states like Punjab (40.8%) or Maharashtra (72.2%). But since the credit absorption capacity in the economy is very low, given the low level of NSDP and poor infrastructure, the north-eastern states do not show any appreciable development despite the high CD ratio. The obvious conclusion is that the credit disbursed is not properly and fairly utilised for economic and productive purposes. Regarding industrialization, the entire region is awfully backward compared to the rest of India. Table 2 shows the level of industrialization in the different states in this region.

The figures of Table 2 shows an extremely low performance of industries in north-eastern states. The situation in Assam is comparatively better but can in no way be compared with that of any other states in the country. It has been argued that this entire region of north-east India except for some plain areas of Assam, is not viable for large scale industrialization. This is due to some basic problems like inhospitable terrains and very low and unsatisfactory performance of physical infrastructure. Along with these, lack of enough initiative towards industrialization amongst the people of this region can also be cited prominently and thus very low level of investment in this front has taken place so far.

Table 2

INDUSTRIES IN NORTH-EAST INDIA

(Value in Rs. Crores, 1989-90)

States	*No of factories*	*No of employees*	*Fixed capital*	*Value of output*	*Net value added*
Assam	1,585	1,22,063	974	2,981	749
Meghalaya	31	5,508	200	29	10
Manipur	40	356	1	1	1
Mizoram	NA	NA	NA	NA	NA
Nagaland	55	1,900	9	28	5
Arunachal Pradesh	NA	NA	NA	NA	NA
Tripura	322	15,534	71	48	8

Source : Basic Statistics of North-Eastern Region, 1995.

The following Table 3 gives the level of infrastructure of the states of north-east.

Table 3

CMIE'S INDEX OF RELATIVE DEVELOPMENT OF INFRASTRUCTURE

States	*Year (1992-93)*
Assam	93
Meghalaya	65
Manipur	81
Mizoram	63
Nagaland	71
Arunachal Pradesh	44
Tripura	63
All India	100

Source : CMIE, Basic Statistics relating to States, Sept. 1994.

The states like Punjab, Maharashtra, West Bengal, Tamil Nadu are in a much better position with regards to infra–

structure compared to these north-eastern states, whose relative indices are 214, 112, 116, 139 respectively.

In this dissatisfying economic, more specifically industrial scenario, if one at all desires to implement the policies of liberalization for the region's economic upliftment, it will not immediately make much sense. But truly speaking, it should now be urgently felt that the time has come to initiate some radical structural reforms in this region, so that it can achieve a certain minimum level of economic self sufficiency and can at least be compared with the rest of the country. Since the entire region lacks heavy industries, therefore none of the objectives of the New Industrial Policy will be practicable and achievable here immediately. The atmosphere and infrastructure for large scale industries and manufacturing units should therefore be created first. But there is one area where significant progress can be achieved even with the existing infrastructure. The new economic policy also speaks about the promotion of small scale sectors and this has an important role to play in the overall industrial development of the region on account of its inherent advantages like lower capital intensity and high capacity for employment generation. The entire north-eastern region has large potential in this front, since small scale and cottage industries are already well established in the region. Table 4 will highlight the position of SSI units in this region.

Table 4

PRINCIPAL CHARACTERISTICS OF SSI UNITS IN NER 1988

(Rs. Lakhs)

States	*No of Units*	*No of people Employed*	*Fixed Investment*	*Working Capital*	*Production*
Assam	4430	34475	9369	7746	30235
Meghalaya	587	3780	888	765	2700
Manipur	2078	10216	2078	723	2988
Mizoram	917	4223	1388	457	1470
Nagaland	183	3059	729	649	11247
Arunachal Pradesh	326	2771	703	631	2624
Tripura	809	10069	1479	972	2957

Source : Basic Statistics of North-Eastern Region 1995.

The trend of growth of small scale industries in the north eastern region is also appreciably high, which can be seen from Table 5 below.

Table 5

TREND OF DEVELOPMENT OF SSI IN NER

Year	*No. of Units*
1971	991
1981	9823
1985	13816
1986	16452
1987	19770
1988	20377

Source : Basic Statistics of North-Eastern Region 1995,

The tribes of north-eastern states are highly skilled in making a variety of indigenous products, which can be easily marketed and commercialized at a very high rate, both in the national and international markets. The major policy changes in this field under liberalization scheme of the country include a rise in investment ceiling on plant and machineries from Rs. 35 lakhs to 60 lakhs (with effect from April 2, 1991) and now to Rs. 3 crores w.e.f. February, 1997. The investment limits for ancillary and export oriented units were fixed at Rs. 75 lakhs, and also for the tiny enterprises the limit has been raised from Rs. 2 lakhs to Rs. 6 lakhs. To provide further access to the capital market and to encourage modernization and technological upgradation, it has been decided to allow equity participation by other industrial undertakings in SSI not exceeding 24% of the total share holding. Another policy under liberalization package for financing SSI is introducing an apex bank known as Small Industries Development Bank (SIDBI), which has become operative from April 2, 1990. In order to facilitate access to finance to a large number of entrepreneurs in the tiny sector, it has been decided to widen the scope of the National Equity Fund Scheme, and enlarge the Single Window Loan Scheme. It is proposed to set up factoring services and a Technology Development Cell within SIDBI. These and other benefits extended to the small scale industrial sectors under liberalization policy can easily be made operational in the north-east India by encouraging people to avail of these benefits. These investment opportunities should be properly utilized here to upgrade and standardize the small scale sectors, so that a competitive attitude can be developed amongst the people of this region. This not only will improve the economy of this region, but also will simultaneously increase the level of employment opportunities amongst the people. But this demands a positive response from the state Governments and financial institutions in the region.

References

Basic Statistics of North-Eastern Region 1995, North-Eastern Council, Shillong.

Gandhi P.J., *Economic Reforms in India : Mid-Way Reflections*, Interest Publications, New Delhi, 1994.

Gupta S.P., *Liberalization : Its impact on Indian Economy*, MacMillan India Limited, New Delhi, 1993.

Mahajan V.S., *Manmohan's India : And Other Current Writings*, Deep and Deep Publications, New Delhi, 1994.

Chapter 13

Implications of Economic Liberalization for North-Eastern Region

—*P.M. Passah*

Introduction

The economic reforms on globalization, liberalization and privatization have no impact on the north-eastern region of India. It needs to be recognized that the great constraints coming in the way of industrial development in the region are : (1) its geographical isolation, (2) lack of infrastructure, (3) shortage of power, (4) lack of proper transport and communication facilities. Both the Central and the seven State Governments in the region have been offering various incentives to encourage private participation. These include (1) introduction of state capital investment subsidy, (2) power subsidy, (3) interest subsidy, and (4) tax exemption. The Central Government has provided a 5-year tax holiday to industries in the 1993-94 budget proposals. It has extended transport subsidy for another five years upto 2000 AD to encourage industry in the region. Now the North-Eastern Financial Development Corporation has been set up exclusively to attract private investment in the region. Assam, the gateway to all other states in the region, has further been offering exemption to the tea companies in the state from agricultural income tax to the extent of their investment in the state's power and industry sectors. But in spite of all these incentives, the economic reforms have no impact and will not have any until the aforesaid constraints are overcome.

Capability Building

Almost half a century after Independence, the region continues to this day in a sort of isolation from the rest of the country. The 1962—Chinese aggression should have prompted the then Central Government to acquisition the entire chicken neck of 50x12 square kms in North Bengal connecting the Region with the main-land and to convert the same into a Union Territory while assigning a 10-km wide area each on the north and on the south for a Mountain Division of the Indian Army and a Station for the Indian Air Force respectively. The remaining portion of 30-km wide could then have been utilized for laying a multitract broadguage railway system and a multi-lane National Highway both opening up and directing towards the region. Provision for a canal could have also been made in this portion for the future diversion of river water from the Brahmaputra to the Ganges, thence towards southern India for the purpose of inland water transport. That could have removed long ago both the geographical and the emotional isolation of the Region and insurgency problem would not have raised its ugly heads as it has done today in the region. It is an irony of fate that the region having the potential of 30,000 MW of hydro-electric power, has been reeling under power crisis and even as it is the least industrialized area in the country. So far only 2.2 percent of the potential has been developed.

Capability Components

The States in the region are increasingly left behind in the field of capabilities, both at the individual and societal level. The nutritional inputs produced, even in the Assam Valley, are far below the all-India level. The yield of rice in the valley stands at 1330 kgs per hectare as against the all-India average of 1880 kgs in 1993-94. The Assam Valley could produce only 259.7 eggs per capita as against the National average of 289.6 eggs in 1993-94. The production of milk in the valley was only 36.78 kgs per capita as against all India average of 75.28 kgs. The per capita production of vegetables stands at 78.69 kgs as against all India figure of 84.2 kgs for 1992-93. The position of other hill states of the region is lower than that of Assam.

Other components determining the capability of individuals are education and health. To take again the case of Assam, being the gateway to all other hill states in the region, it may be mentioned that the educational expenditure of the state during 1974-75 to 1991-92 declined from 6.3 percent to only 2.79 per cent and the expenditure on health from 7.62 percent to 1.45 per cent. The real per capita social expenditure of Assam grew at the rate of 8.14 per cent during 1974-75 to 1984-85 but declined to a negligible rate of 1.0 percent during 1985-86—1991-92. All these might have further declined. Hence it may be inferred that in totality, the capability building of the region is far below the national average.

Implications of Liberalization

There has been a widespread yearning for development among the people of all states in the region. For instance, the chief Minister of Arunachal Pradesh and the ministerial team together with opposition leaders of Meghalaya had visited the countries of Europe to invite foreign investment in their respective states. Other states too had made contacts with foreign countries for the same purpose. Representatives of western countries, Australia and Japan also visited the States in the Region. The World Bank team had also visited the region in recent weeks.

The policy measures adopted under the new economic liberalization do consist of measures to take care of the needs of the socio-economically weaker sections of the population during the short-run stabilization and adjustment period. This would take care of the human capability building. But the measures did not envisage taking care of the interests and protecting the development prospects of less developed regions of the country like the states in the North-East. This should have been envisaged in the liberalization scheme considering in particular the insurgency problem of the region.

The implications of the liberalization policy in the context of insurgency have not been studied. Thus the ability of the economic reform measures to create the needed peace is not known. In this context, it is doubtful whether the leadership in the region itself has been capable of appreciating the implications of the liberalization policy.

To some experts, the strategy of human capability building should be distinguished from building up the economic infrastructure of the region. The development strategy to be followed in the region is to intensify the building up of economic infrastructure so that interactions within the region should first take place. This would enable the socio-economic changes to emerge from within the region.The endogenous changes alone are sustainable. On the other hand, other experts would wish that capability building should get the priority where education, health and nutrition are focussed so that the people would have the ability to participate in the development process. But in the ultimate analysis both the strategies are simultaneously required. The development of the region might have a bigger bottleneck than social capacity building but both contribute equally to the building up of the much needed infrastructure for the industrial development of the region.

Development Priorities

While expenditure on health and education should not decline, the region should thoroughly be opened up to the main-land with proper transport and communication network. The extension of the broadguage railway line up to Tinsukia in Assam is a must. The broadguage system should be branched out to the Barak Valley and to Kohima and Imphal the state capitals of Nagaland and Manipur within the shortest possible time. Except Assam, all other states are mountainous with hilly terrains. Since the region experiences heavy rainfalls during the long monsoon period from May to September every year, stable and all-weather roads have to be built. Each hill state should have an interstate road running along its central zone and linking with one or more states to serve as a lifeline both for its internal and external transportation and trade.

Lateral roads on both sides of the lifeline could then be constructed and made to converge on the lifeline. For instance, in Meghalaya such an inter-state road can be identified with no other than the Tura-Shillong-Jowai-Haflong Road passing through Williamnagar and Nongstoin—all these six centres being district headquarters in Meghalaya and Assam. This all-important inter-state road happens to pass west to east along the ridge of the Meghalaya Plateau which is part of what usually termed the Central Assam range. The major part of the road, *i.e.,* Tura-Shillong Road via Williamnagar and Nongstoin, is being maintained as a State Trunk Road. It should be widened to the NH standard and the distance could be reduced through further realignment. The Shillong-Jowai road is part of the National Highway—44 while the Jowai-Haflong road falling under two states has not been properly maintained by these states in spite of its economic importance. This road too needs widening to the National Highway standards and its distance shortened by further realignment. Meghalaya had long ago moved the Central Government to take over this particular road and to declare it as a National Highway as done to its middle portion *i.e.,* the Shillong-Jowai Road (NH-44). But the proposal had found no favour with the Central authorities. If the road had been taken over as a National Highway, the Central Plateau of the region falling within Meghalaya and Assam would have been immensely and economically benefitted.

The proposal for the expansion of the Guwahati airport could be beneficial to the region only if other state capitals are linked to it. Of course its conversion into an international airport would open up the region to the South Asian countries. Inland waterways along the Brahmaputra and the Barak rivers have not yet been developed to the desired level. The development of proper transport and communication system would intensify the interactions within the region thereby release the forces for development. The strategy should be to connect one state capital with another in such a way that one can commute between two capitals within ten hours either by air or surface communication.

The rich power potential of the region has to be developed before the industrialization process can start and be sustained. Although the North-Eastern Development and Financial Corporation has been set up with Rs. 5000 crores as capital for funding industrial and development projects within the region, yet skepticism is already being aired. Different voluntary organizations involved in industrial development in the region are of the opinion that the low credit-deposit ratio would change only marginally unless the terms and conditions of banks and financial institutions in the region are made flexible to the advantage of the young entrepreneurs of the region. Their experience is that most of the banks are not even prepared to provide information on the different schemes offered by the Government.

Conclusion

The foregoing discussion has clearly indicated that the region is still in the midst of the initial structural shocks while states in the rest of the country have taken full advantage of the reform measures. The states in the region are equally enthusiastic about the liberalization policy of our country. We have seen how they have been keen enough to encourage foreign direct investment. But when it comes to signing a memorandum of understanding (MoU), their efforts become fruitless. For instance, the state of Meghalaya had come into an agreement with the National Grid of the United Kingdom for the development of the power sector in the state. But the draft MoU to be signed between the State Government and the National Grid which was sent to the Power Ministry some time in the month of March 1995 did not get so far the clearance of the Ministry. This happens even as the Central Government had already cleared such MoU that was signed between the Arunachal Pradesh Government and the Snowy Mountain Engineering Corporation of Australia in New Delhi on 6 March 1993. According to the Central Government Liberalization policy, foreign investment in the core infrastructure sectors is welcome. The Government of India had accordingly notified as far back as October 1991 that foreign investment to the extent of 100 per cent will be permitted in the power sector by privately owned enterprises. But despite such radical policy initiatives of the Central Government, its Power Ministry has failed to clear the

Meghalaya's draft MoU with the National Grid of the United Kingdom which had already backed out due to immense delay. The Ministry obviously appears not inclined to agree to amendment of the Electricity laws in the case of Meghalaya.

It is hoped that the leadership in the North-East would arise to the implications of the liberalization policy measures and the fundamental weaknesses in the crucial sectors of the economy. The leadership should see that not only the investment in the core sectors should be augmented but the capability building of the people of the region is also taken care of by the central government. The Central Government will have to think beyond liberalization and strengthen the social sectors of the North-Eastern states of the country.

PART THREE

LIBERALIZATION : IMPLICATIONS FOR IDENTITY AND ETHNIC SITUATIONS IN INDIA'S NORTH-EAST

Chapter 14

ON THE POLITICS OF GLOBALIZATION : MANAGING ETHNICITY IN NORTH-EASTERN INDIA

—Samir Kumar Das

This paper proposes to review some of the major advocacies or pleas for opening up the north-east to global economic influences—a phenomenon popularly known as, globalization and tries to argue that most of them tend to offer a highly simplistic and albeit, static view of politics in India in general and the north-east in particular. In order to illustrate this point, it concentrates on the problem of ethnicity and shows how it affects or more accurately, is likely to affect the programmes of globalization in the region under review. While it would be definitely an exaggeration to say that globalization is incompatible with the present-day ethnic assertion in the north-east, a more nuanced view of their relationship is bound to draw our attention to some of the factors that unless taken care of and appropriately managed, might in their combination, prove to be a stumbling block to current economic reforms and structural adjustments. It is true that the economic rationale of globalization in the region has been subject to scathing criticism especially from such scholars as Archana Sarma of Gauhati University. Correspon–dingly, there has not been any political critique of the programme. This paper is a very modest attempt at preparing some of the major elements of such a critique.

The Politics of Opening Up

A vociferous plea is made in recent years for breaking up the relative isolation of the regional economy of the north-east—if there is any (for it seems there are many isolated economies without being integrated into a common regional economic framework) and also for integrating it into the South Asian economy and thereby into the global economic framework both by such organizations as Industrial Development Bank of India and Tata Consultancy Services as well as such eminent economists as Nitish Sengupta and Arindam Banik of International Management Institute, New Delhi and Arunoday Saha of Tripura University. As Saha writes : ".....(The) complete isolation appears to be standing on the way of industrialization of the region. If industrialization is to take place in this part of India than the North-East Region must be integrated with the neighbouring countries breaking the isolation of economic barriers".[1] One of the essential features of these pleas is its underlying economics whereby political factors—may we say, politics in general, are viewed as avoidable aberrations in the path of economic development that nowadays demands globalization. While it is said that the north-east has remained open to the East as well as the West since the year of 1793 when a commercial treaty was executed between Raja Gaurinath (1780-94) of Assam and Captain Welse, partition of India in 1947 and consequently the emergence of clearly demarcated boundaries making their violations illegal and a punishable offense have made it a bounded and what Saha calls, an `isolated region' and denied it of all the comparative advantages and returns that are seen to be associated with globalization : "One of the plausible reasons for the region for not being able to register itself as the industrially developed economy is that the partition of India in 1947 virtually cut off the whole North-East India from the rest of the country. The partition made the region completely isolated form the mainstream economy of India".[2] While Saha makes a strong case for opening up the north-east, both Sengupta and Banik have shown by way of citing what they think to be `a telling example' how both India and Bangladesh might benefit by working out `a proper transit route for the movement of bulk goods from India through Bangladesh to India's north-eastern provinces' instead of transporting goods through the Siliguri corridor.[3]

The problems with these pleas is not simply that they are insensitive to politics or for that matter, political factors but that they relegate politics to secondary importance. The economic gains according to its advocates, will go a long way in offsetting political differences. In the words of Sengupta and Banik: "Once the two countries (*i.e.* India and Bangladesh) decide on transit trade, and mutual cooperation in trade and investment, they will realize that political differences are of secondary importance".[4] In other words, economic rationality will have its own way of doing away with the political factors that separate one country from another and impede economic development for both of them. Here, political factors are expected to give way to the imperative of economic development. We all know that in real-life situations, `political differences' have proved to be far more resilient than what Sengupta and Banik would have us believe. Besides, the government of respective countries are supposedly embedded in what may be termed, certain old habits of mind. In an era of globalization, governments just cannot afford to be obsessed with their territorial boundaries, national sovereignty and forces that have a vested interest in protecting the country from foreign economic influences. Our attempts at discarding them as old—albeit persisting habits of mind only feed fat the expectation that the governments are bound to get rid of them—sooner rather than later. Indeed, very recent studies tend to show that such obsessions have not yet outlived their utility and the imperatives of globalization may not be strong enough to compel the governments to get rid of them. Hence, it is equally naive that old habits of mind will instantly give way to new ones believed to be conducive to the imperatives of globalization and economic development.

Moreover, all these pleas take an extra-ordinarily simple and limited view of politics for according to their advocates, politics is necessarily confined to the activities of respective governments. They also seem to create the impression that the governments can do whatever they want (as if they are both free and rational actors). In the words of Sengupta and

Banik : "What is lacking is the political will to give a trial to this concept (of globalization)". In a country like India (or for that matter any country of South Asia), so-called freedom and rationality of actors are limited and conditioned by a plethora of factors—of course political but situated beyond the organized domain of the modern government. In order to appreciate this point, Partha Chatterjee's distinction between the organized and unorganized domains may be instructive:

> *On the one hand there (is) the domain of formally organized political parties and associations, moving within the institutional processes of the bourgeois State forms introduced by colonial rule and seeking to use their representative power over the mass of people to replace the colonial rule by a bourgeois nation-state. On the other side was the domain of .... politics where beliefs and actions did not fit into the grid of 'interests' and 'aggregation of interests' which constituted the world of bourgeois representative politics. Seen from the former domain the latter could only appear as the realm of spontaneity, which was of course nothing more than to acknowledge that the specific determinants of the domain of .... political activity remained incomprehensible from the standpoint of bourgeois politics.*[5]

The main problem with the recently made plea for globalization is that it remains insensitive to the dynamics of inter-relations between the two domains and how they affect or are likely to affect the economy of the region. This paper proposes to take a more dynamic and complex view of politics of the region.

Ethnicity and the Unorganized Domain

The efficacy of what the government as the pivot of the organized domain seeks to do—in our case, integrating the region into the global economic framework, hence, will depend on the terms of relationship with the unorganized domain. The unorganized domain in a country like India and that too in a region like the north-east is constituted on the basis of ethnicity. Such a constitution implies two closely inter-related things : First, the identity of an individual is determined not so much by the community he belongs to : 'the individual is what he is by virtue of his community that makes him what he is'. His identification with his community is so intimate that he continues to identify him with it even when that is detrimental to his selfish interests including that of physical survival.[6] Should such a conflict arise between his identity and interest the latter gives in to the former. Secondly, and as a corollary to it, the individual's modes of thinking, actions and more importantly, evaluations are a priori in the sense that he has no freedom of shaping and influencing them. They are given to him as a result of his entitlement to community's common patrimony. In a region where community enjoys such a pre-eminent role, individual responses to the programmes of globalization have to do a lot with it. It is quite odd that no serious study is yet made to determine their relationship.

In a paper written not quite long ago, I have suggested that the world-wide phenomenon of ethnic assertion including that in the north-east is incompatible with the present accent on globalization.[7] I now realize that it is hazardous to absolutize the statement.[8] For even in the north-east, there are communities that are unlikely to be completely averse to these programmes. There are at least three reasons why ethnic communities in the north-east may not be obstinately opposed to the trinity of liberalization, privatization and globalization: First, these programmes as we all know, thrive on creating markets in far-off areas that have hitherto remained untapped by global capital. One of the tasks that is necessarily associated with the creation of markets is enhancement of people's purchasing power for unless this is enhanced in proportion to the expansion of markets and marketable products, globalization is bound to suffer a setback. It is however observed that since people's purchasing power does not expand as much as expected, it finds it difficult to keep pace with the products available in the market. Hence, the emphasis is : If it sounds difficult to enhance people's purchasing power without affecting the savings, then it may be easier to divert savings or at least a good part of it for consumption so that the volume of purchase goes up. The programme of globalization has therefore created a new social ethos of 'living out one's life'—of spending at present without saving for the future. This concern with the present has given birth to what in Social Anthropology is called, presentism. Many of the tribal communities of the north-east that by their own admission are situated beyond the so-called, Indian Varna-Hindu mainstream seem to be already imbued with the same ethos. This is evident from the extremely low and in some cases, declining savings rate among such communities as the Nagas and the Khasis.

Secondly, presentism defined as diversion of savings for consumptive purposes of the present crucially depends on the attractiveness that the goods and services made available by globalization holds out to the consumers. In other words, these goods and services have to be sufficiently attractive to them so much so that they feel it worthwhile to sacrifice their concern for the future in order to intensely live in the present by consuming them. The goods and services that are or are likely to be made available to them by the forces of globalization in many cases, are not at all unfamiliar to them. In other words, many of the tribal communities having the advantage of living at the borders and borders which by their very nature have been highly porous and permeable and are already exposed to the information about them—if not the actual goods and services—thanks to illegal transborder trades reportedly rampant in the region. In fact, we may argue that globalization helps in legalization of what hitherto has been rendered illegal in a very strange and surprising way. Because of their early familiarity with these goods and services, the responses of the communities are likely to be positive and favourable.

Thirdly and this is very important, globalization involves what is called, minimalization of the state for it is centred on the assumption that productivity and even distribution can be better managed if the government withdraws from it. The minimalization is accomplished at two levels : on the one hand, the government as the pivotal agency of economic development takes a backseat and the argument goes that it does well to withdraw from the economic sphere. The anti-government bias of contemporary economic reforms seems to go hand in hand with the gross depreciation of the government that characterizes present-day ethnic assertions.[9] On the other, globalization involves a fatal obliteration of territorial boundaries where the country's national sovereignty is seen to circulate. In the same vein, territorial boundaries have been subject to criticism from ethnic communities on two counts : One, their reorganization in the wake of partition has severely fractured what these communities consider to be their 'homeland' with the effect that they are now separated from their ethnic cousins across the borders. Two, the circulation of national sovereignty within the territorial boundaries has made them directly subservient to that of India. Before partition, a Naga did not have to be as much—if at all, an 'Indian' as he is required to be now. The obliteration of national boundaries and transit facilities thus will not only enable many ethnic communities to socialize with their across-the-border ethnic cousins but also go a long way in softening and mellowing the impact of India's national sovereignty and it will not hang too heavy on their shoulders.

Managing the Ethnic Factors[10]

By saying that I was wrong in assuming that ethnicity is incompatible with the phenomenon of globalization, I am not trying to prove that the opposite is the case. In fact, there is no one answer to this tricky question. While there are many ethnic factors that are at odds with the imperatives of globalization, ethnic communities are seen to contain other factors that do not have at least a strongly negative correlation with them. Hence, ethnicity is neither compatible nor incompatible with the imperatives of globalization. If globalization is to succeed, the ethnic factors of the region are to be managed in such a manner that they do not have any adverse impact on it and *vice versa*. That is to say, it has also to be ensured that globalization does not have any adverse impact on ethnic communities of the region. All this requires a very tender and careful handling of ethnic factors by the agencies of globalization. Any mindless programme of globalization that is insensitive to the ethnic factors and dismisses polities of the unorganized domain as an avoidable aberration may ultimately turn out to be counter-productive. The problem with our over-zealous advocates of globalization is that they in their hurry seem to be oblivious to these factors. They do not show any sign of having made serious attempts at coming to terms with them and such an insensitive and unhelpful attitude might in the long run force them to abandon their programmes at the midpassage.

In order to appreciate this point, it may be instructive to refer to a distinction between ethnic communities which show a 'correspondence of values' and those which do not—made by such scholars as Donald Horowitz and Leo Despres.[11] Translated into our context, the former type may be taken to mean communities which are favourably oriented to globalization for according to them, its gains outweigh the losses while the latter type is illustrated by communities which think that there actually cannot be any trade-off between gains and losses when their survival is at stake. There is no question of reaping the gains if it ceases to exist. In the second type the more these communities think in these terms, the greater will be the likelihood of their refusal. It is only obvious that the advocates of globalization will not under all normal circumstances, do anything that jeopardizes the very survival of these communities. In simple terms, that the programmes of globalization have been undertaken should not lead us to believe that they are necessarily corrosive of the foundations of these communities. The protests against proposed railway connection in Meghalaya serves as a case in point. While railway connection is expected to play a crucial role in breaking down the isolated nature of the concerned economy, it was also feared that this would open the flood-gates of immigration and the natives gradually would lose out their language and culture to those of the immigrants. In fact, there might be a time in the near future when they would be outnumbered by the immigrants in what they consider to be their homeland. The fear of losing out the identity determines many a community's response to the phenomenon of globalization.

How do the programmes of globalization become corrosive of the foundations of ethnic communities? There is a tendency on the part of many commentators to think that ethnic communities as they are known to us, pre-exist these programmes so much so that they are vulnerable to the onslaughts of globalization. But that ethnic communities also construct or are likely to construct their identities in keeping with the changing requirements of the situation is seldom taken into account. Despres has designated it as 'ethnogenesis' and defines it in these terms : "... ethnogenesis involves processes by which populations become more or less culturally differentiated as a consequence of their economic and social adaptation to different techno-environments.[12]" Viewed in this light, corrosion may be defined as a process whereby an ethnic community is dispossessed of its right to construct and reconstruct itself in keeping with the changing requirements of the situation. Hence, ethnic communities might not object to corrosion *per se* (of the prevailing form of the community) in the wake of globalization provided they are granted the right to construct and reconstruct themselves. While there have been occasions when Assamese identity has been defined in narrow and chauvinistic terms in opposition to the outsiders/foreigners, there is no denying the fact that there is a strong tinge of universality in Assamese ethos that has its roots in the humanism of Srimanta Sankaradeva and Muslim saints and preachers. Forces of globalization might encourage the otherwise Janus-faced Assamese community to show its universal face. Ethnic identity in other words, is not something given; it is articulated in course of time.

Corrosion may also be defined as a process whereby it cuts into the ability of community's elite to use ethnicity as a leverage, that is to say, an instrument for promoting its own interests. Naturally, this provokes it to mobilize the community in its favour and to claim for its restitution. If the very basis of the community is jeopardized, how can the elite use it to promote its interests? It therefore has a vested interest in making ethnicity persist over the years. Interpretations—both marxist as well as non-marxist, are replete with instances of how elites in this region have played and continue to play the dirty ethnic game. It does not make much sense to ask them to become saints overnight very like Plato's sermon that Kings ought to be philosophers as well. The point is : Unless otherwise accommodated into the grand scheme of globalization, the elites are bound to grumble against it and frustrate its objectives.

Secondly, in the north-east, 'who initiates' becomes much more important than 'what is being initiated'. The value of an economic programme is judged not by its intrinsic worth—its economic pros and cons that the advocates are seen to be constantly examining but by the nature of the agency that initiates them. Since the government or the state in the broad sense, has already become an object of opprobrium and detestation, the advocates would do well to initiate it through agencies other than the government. The programmes would be acceptable if the agencies are not only friendly but internal to them. Nagas for instance, are known for their antipathy towards any agency that is believed to be outside the boundaries of the community.[13]

The third area that is also in need of deliberate managerial intervention is concerned with the distributive aspect of globalization. Since the viability of globalization critically depends on the positive and favourable response from the ethnic communities, it is obvious that the advantages and privileges that follow upon it are expected to take on an ethnic character in at least two senses of the term : First, if Vanhanen's theory of 'ethnic nepotism' is to be believed, it would be natural on the part of some of these communities to corner and monopolize these privileges and advantages and given that they are not unlimited, they are likely to deprive many others of having a fair share—if at all, of them:

> *The members of an ethnic group tend to favour their group members over non-members because they are more related to their group members than the remainder of the population .... Nepotism is blindly selected because 'nepotistic' individuals in social species have higher fitness than 'non-nepotistic ones' ... There exists a general behavioural predisposition, in our species as in many others, to react favourably toward other organisms to the extent that these organisms are biologically related to the other... Because it principally concerns the strength for scarce resources in limited space and because people with common interests are predisposed to form alliances in this struggle one can assume that, in ethnically severely divided*

societies, such alliances are easily adapted to the pattern of important ethnic cleavages.[14]

The point that is to be kept in mind is that an ethnic community not only seeks to keep up with the Jones' it also wants to have an edge over others. In the eyes of an individual member, there is no community higher than his own.

Secondly and as a corollary to it, insofar as an ethnic community feels deprived, it also intends to catch up with the more advanced communities both of the region as well as outside. The outcome of globalization will be decided by the tug and pull between these two forces. What is interesting to note here is that insofar as a community seeks to catch up with others, it operates within the same framework of social mobility. But a disenchantment with this framework may set in if a community is perpetually deprived of what it considers to be its due. It is this disenchantment that is primarily—though not exclusively, responsible for the switchover from the Assam movement (1979-1985) led by the All Assam Students' Union—All Assam Gana Sangram Parishad combine to the more militant political movement of United Liberation Front of Assam. In a situation where globalization cannot benefit all the communities—at least to an equal extent, the advocates and agencies would do well to take care of its distributive effects. This I think, is the most tangled of all questions having to do with globalization.

These considerations taken together—along with many others which we have not mentioned for obvious limitations of space, constitute the crux of what I called, community-sensitive development : "The solution perhaps lies in initiating community-sensitive economic development.[15]"

References

1. Arunoday Saha, *Industrialization of North-East India—A New Perspective*, paper presented to the Seminar on Constraints to Industrial Development in the North-East, organized by NEICSSR in Shillong, Meghalaya during 26-27 July, 1996.
2. *Ibid.*
3. Nitish Sengupta, Arindam Banik, *Regional Trade and Investment in Developing Countries : The Case of SAARC*, paper presented to

the Seminar on 50 Years After : The Experience of Partition, Decolonization and Independence : Bangladesh, India and Pakistan, organized by MAK Azad Institute of Asian Studies in Calcutta during 12-14 March, 1997.

4. *Ibid.*
5. Partha Chatterjee, "For an Indian History of Peasant Struggle", in *Social Scientist*, 16(11), November, 1988, p. 7.
6. See, for instance, Samir Kumar Das, "Analyzing the Society in Assam : A Plea for Community", in Girin Phukon & N.L. Dutta (ed), Politics of Identity and Nation-Building in North-East India, South Asian, New Delhi, 1997.
7. Samir Kumar Das, "Community and Economic Development in Assam : The Experience of the 1980's", paper presented to the Seminar, *op.cit.*, n. 1.
8. Prof. Amiya Kumar Bagchi while commenting on my paper referred to the role of global capital in reviving and resuscitating ethnic communities all over the world.
9. Samir Kumar Das, *op. cit.*, n. 7.
10. I have been inspired by one of Amitai Etzioni's fairly recent papers in which he has made a plea for managing ethnic factors in the far-off context of the USA. See, Amitai Etzioni, "The Community of Communities", in The Washington Quarterly, Summer, 1996.
11. Donald L. Horowitz, *Ethnic Groups in Conflict*, University of California Press, Berkely, 1985, Chap. 4. Also Leo A. Despres, "Toward a Theory of Ethnic Phenomena", in Leo A. Despres (ed), Ethnicity and Resource Competition in Plural Societies, The Hague, Mouton Publishers, 1975.
12. Leo A. Despres, *ibid.*, p. 196.
13. M.C. Goswami, "Modernization in Nagaland : Retrospects and Prospects", in B.B. Kumar (ed.), *Modernization in Naga Society*, Omsons, New Delhi, 1993, p. 132.
14. Tatu Vanhanen, "Politics of Ethnic Nepotism in India", in Diethelm Weideman (eds.), *Nationalism, Ethnicity and Political Development In South Asia*, Manohar, New Delhi, 1991.
15. Samir Kumar Das, *op. cit.*, p. 7.

Chapter 15

CULTURE AND GROWTH : THE PARADOX OF ECONOMIC DEVELOPMENT

—M.M. Agrawal

In todays world, the consolidated effect of modernity, the picture of man as the rational autonomous individual endowed with free-will is complete. The individual is individualistic : self-interested, egoistic, clamouring for more and more power, wealth and social status. He has stopped thinking about life considered as a whole. There is no overall spiritual meaning to life. His life is divided between purposes which are contingently thrust upon him by his environment, requiring fulfilment with a speed and efficiency which occlude any evaluation of their meaning for life as a whole. Indeed he finds it difficult to apprehend "life as a whole", to consider it as a unity, except chronologically. As McIntyre in his most perceptive discussion of the contemporary scene observes: "...... Modernity partitions each human life into a variety of segments, each with its own norms and modes of behaviour. So work is divided from leisure, private life from public life, the corporate from the personal. So both childhood and old age have been wrenched away from the rest of human life and made over into distinct realms. And all these separations have been achieved so that it is the distinctness of each and not the unity of the life of the individual who passes through those parts in terms of which we are taught to think and to feel."[1] Moreover the very character of 'the social' has changed so much, as many post-modern thinkers have emphasized, that the individual need not even bother about the 'unity of life' and its overall inclusive end to provide a teleological framework for his endeavors. 'The social' no longer demands conduct in which human relationships are informed by virtues. Indeed most social institutions of the past which provided for the cultivation of virtues and the qualities of character in the individual have either totally disappeared or have been rendered underdetermined by the vast changes in the character of relationships sought by the individuals. This is the age of shifting relations of inter dependencies, where even the most basic forms of human bonds—pair relations, sexuality, family, kinship and friendship for example—have become institutionally underdetermined. The individual is faced with the stark reality of a communitarian alienation and competitive insecurity. The notion of rational autonomous subject has been taken to its ridiculous limits—freedom into anarchy, individualism into self-centered egoism, rejection of the substantial self into total fragmentation. The blemishes that have warped our ethical consciousness and disfigured our conscience are many, but perhaps, the most serious one.

Emerges, ironically, though unselfconsciously, from what must be considered as the virtue of modernity. Modernity which brought freedom from the unthinking callous 'authority' of various non-secular traditions went too far and liberated the hidden greed lying curled up in the human heart.

But surely in the culture of greed-satisfaction there is no hope for true fulfilment—economic development as a cultural realization must manifest itself first in the social spaces of intercultural attitudes of acceptance, cooperation and sharings.

Development and Growth

A part of the difficulty in understanding the phenomenon of economic development lies in the conflation of the notions of 'growth' and 'development'. Growth is clearly a quantitative notion. We are witnessing growth all around in population or shall we say in the number of consumers, growth in poverty as well as growth in technical knowledge and production of commodities. But would we call any and every form of growth 'development'? Obviously not, the notion of development is evaluative. So the criteria for this evaluation must come from the axiological resources of the ethno-culture concerned. Thus considerations of ethnic aspirations and relativity of cultural values cannot be ignored.

Economic activity includes the total process of retrieval, production and above all, human fulfilment. None of these aspects can be left underdetermined. Even the lowliest on the social scale, say a beggar, is involved in the process, since he consumes. In the medieval world beggars were very important as people could fulfill their religious duty of charity by looking after their interests. In the present world, however, their existence is considered a nuisance, but the fact that they (or their equivalents) exist despite considerable growth casts a shadow upon economic development, which must take into account the fulfilment of the lowliest.

What this shows is that for a proper understanding of the economic phenomena under the concept of development, we must adopt a holistic perspective upon life. But again, holism should not be misunderstood. It is not the summation of the parts but the 'extra' quality of life generated when economy is in harmony with the rest of life. If economic activities do not tend to contribute to the overall quality of human fulfilment, we would hesitate to consider them as developmental processes. That is, in a holistic perspective economic development unfolds an ethical dimension. Its aspect of 'distribution of wealth' and its goal of 'fulfilment' are both notions which connect with those of 'justice' and the 'good of human life' respectively. However, the following complexity calls for attention. In taking a holistic perspective upon developmental process, whose point of view is to be considered? Obviously, the answer is that all the ethno- cultural groups involved have to be considered. But this is no easy task. In the present intellectual climate where liberal individualism coupled with cultural relativism is commonplace, we have no shared concept of 'justice' or 'human fulfilment'. And the global trends in modern economy will naturally tend to defuse the ethnic perspectives. Moreover, a pluralism of perspectives will tend to obstruct the practical side of the developmental process, leading inevitably to unpredictable social conflicts. All the same the changed scenario of the world economy, in terms of global trade and production activities, seems absolutely to require, for a smooth growth of economy, an essentially conflict free world. Unfortunately we have not got that. We need to evolve and accept a common definition of social justice and human well being. The world economy simply cannot flourish without a universally acceptable paradigm of development. But this is not a theoretical matter. Such a paradigm must be embodied in our consciousness, which in turn, it seems, cannot come about without actual success in achieving global social justice in terms of even economic development. As 'nothing succeeds like success', an agreed paradigm can evolve through what is recognizable as 'economic success' (as it has happened in the case of natural sciences). But this is a paradoxical situation. More specifically, the paradox of economic development is this : Economic development involves growth. The latter, as we have seen, is not a sufficient condition for the former, but it is certainly a necessary condition. But now, given the ruthless dynamism of the free-enterprise economies, for growth to be accelerated, economic enterprises must transcend the cultural constraints in their fields of operation. On the other hand for growth to be evaluated as 'development', it must submit itself to the protocols of cultural aspirations.

No one seems to have the answer to this paradox. There is no theoretical solution to it, for it is not a theoretical problem. One cannot dissolve it but perhaps we can transcend it. This would require an extraordinary intelligence, especially on the part of those who are directly responsible for development: industrialists and politicians. The transcendence in question requires a complex set of practical skills, involving a realistic appraisal and sympathetic understanding of the problems, together with the arts of persuasion, placation, and education. It really amounts to a reorientation of the motivational attitudes from an aggressive pursuit of 'profits' towards a participatory pursuit of common human end of 'progress'.

Development and Self-Transformation

For a long time, and perhaps still is, it has been widely believed that economic development, in modern terms of industrial development, is the key to ending all the ills of social conflicts. It was believed that social conflicts were mere reflections of economic forces released from an economic base, which is not stable not because of internal contradictions of cultural forces but because it is constantly threatened by its own logic of growth. So a transformation of the economic base which removes these contradictions resulting in speedy growth would *ipso facto* bring about a social transformation. Such thinking about development takes a one-sided view of its various ramifications. And it clearly carries structuralist assumptions for explanation in the social sciences. It does not, however, need philosophical arguments in the adjudication of their claims to show that the structuralist model is faulty, for it seems to me surely empirically not true. No one has succeeded in identifying 'bases' (structures) from which deterministic forces emanate. Any suggestion to that effect must also provide for their repeated reidentification, if they are to carry a scientific bite. Moreover it is simply not true that mere economic growth dissolves undesirable social institutions underlining discriminations on the basis of castes, ethnicity, sex and religion etc.

Ironically, economic development does not even eliminate poverty. For as it is well noted, growth does not reduce scarcity, simply because it creates as many wants as it creates goods. Poverty is a by-product of a cultural lag, to say the least.

Once again we are back to taking a holistic view of the whole question of economic development. Economic development cannot take place in isolation from other kinds of development. In the ecology of development all meanings, all conflicts and all forms of growth are interconnected. Simply stated one cannot go ahead of oneself. In so far as development is self-advancement, it must also be simultaneously a process of self-transformation. The identity of the collective is not, and must not remain static. They must evolve towards the common identity of all mankind in which individual ethnic and other identities will naturally find their rightful place. As the ancients have taught us : the enlightened will recognize *Vasudhaiva Kutumbukum*—the mankind is one family.

All the same the desirability of ethno-cultural control both of the quantity as well as the quality of economic growth cannot be undermined. One has to operate within the value-constraints of the cultures concerned. Economy is not an isolated phenomena, a 'hanging garden' for pleasure. It is firmly interwoven within the fabric of the whole of social existence.

It is perhaps the neglect of this factor of culture-sensitivity that has been responsible for the failure of the left economies—a point which perhaps in this context was best understood by the Chinese leader Deng.

Whatever may be the truth in this context of human history, it remains true that politics cannot carry us beyond culture, for the former in its concrete reality is itself a cultural product. To move forward is always to carry oneself ahead.

All the same, in the contemporary world it is not left entirely to individual ethnic entities to go alone and carry themselves forward. As Economics is concerned with the increase and refinement of the total resources of material existence, it has become incumbent upon individual social groups to adopt a participatory attitude towards the processes which are increasingly becoming globalized. For one thing, the contemporary advances in information and knowledge technology has brought cultures and politics of the world at our door steps—powers which economics cannot ignore. And it has made it difficult for them even to choose their own style of participation. Nevertheless, it is always open to individual groups to invoke their value-system and exercise pressure upon the larger whole to which they belong for the direction of progress to be commensurate with their reasonable aspirations. They have to be extremely careful, though. Firstly because the capacity to exercise pressure is always open to political abuse. And secondly, due to the complex and holistic nature of economy, ceiling in one area can easily cripple the momentum in another, thus often becoming counter productive. Unfortunately, many activist groups do not show sensitivity to this aspect of the nature of developmental process.

Again we need an agreed ethics of economic interaction. Here the general social ethic does not provide sufficient practical guidance. It is in the nature of economic activity to maximize profits; so it is no good telling an industrialist to 'love thy neighbour as thyself'. Here the role of cultural politics becomes very important. But it is to be remembered that cultural politics—a respectable perhaps necessary instrument for democracy in a multicultural nation—should not degenerate into ' politics of culture'. The latter easily lands itself to ethnic chauvinism and consequently to anti-developmental attitudes.

In the present climate of free-market economy the pressure of multi-nationals cannot be avoided. Nor can their influence on devouring small scale industries be undermined. Yet this pressure has to be contained by cultural forces, for not only 'small is beautiful', but it is also profitable and relatively more amenable to cultural control. The politics of economics has to be fully alert, and in negotiations should never loose sight of the future-sensitivity we have talked about. It is obvious that in answer to 'who shall invest'? we have to realistically say 'as far as possible indigenous agencies'.

Growth and Individual Responsibility

I have painted a somewhat pessimistic picture of the developmental reality, presenting it as a paradox needing to be transcended. But this is no counsel of despair. For there is a ray of hope, a salvation, if we recognize the fact that underlying the surface diversity or pluralism of ethnicity and culture etc., there lies an extraordinary universality of human needs, anxieties and visions of ethical and spiritual perfections which man can attain. Economic development should enable us to attain these perfections. If only we could tap the resources of this common humanity we would see that all cultures are essentially a quest of Truth, Goodness and Beauty in life. We would then see that seeking development is natural to mankind and economy is the natural material tool for that.

We would then use the tool for what it is meant rather than destroying our own humanity with it. But for this to happen each of us individually must feel responsible. And for this, in turn, man must return to himself and know himself in his essential humanity. In self-knowledge he must discover the sacredness of life, of nature and the wholeness of his inter relatedness with it. He will then be able to act from a feeling of great responsibility for the whole. He will then realize that the promised land of happiness through devotion to material (industrial) growth is a mirage. We must transform the acquisitive culture of conflict and aggressive growth into a culture of sharing and caring and of true human fulfilment.

References

1. Alasdair McIntyre, *After Virtue*, Duckworth, 1981, p. 190.

Chapter 16

Socio-Economic Aspects of Ethnic Identity in North-Eastern India*

—*M.N. Karna*

Ethnic identity is the subjective and symbolic use of certain elements of culture by a group of people to differentiate themselves from other groups. It involves claims to higher status as a group in relation to the other groups. Such self-conscious groups develop their own criteria for inclusion into and exclusion from the group. The use of ethnic identity for pursuing group interests is ethnicity which may be articulated in particular contexts at a particular time. In the initial phase of ethnic mobilization primordial identities are constructive but in subsequent phases the same identity turns into an instrument to seek political and economic advantages.

Identity formation is not the function of a single process. Various endogenous and exogenous forces influence building ethnic affinities and attachments that make identity formation a complex process. While primordial elements such as race, language and religion provide institutional frame, the cultural perception of the community towards other groups leads to the crystallization of identity. In a multiethnic society, the reaction to challenges arising out of attempts by the dominant groups towards assimilation, growing economic competition among different ethnic groups and developmental processes enforced by the state reinforce identity formation. Moreover, the whole process gets a fillip when emerged middle classes

* An earlier draft of this paper was presented in a seminar at Indian Institute of Advanced Study, Shimla, November 1996.

politicize issues of language, culture and even religion to their advantage. Thus identity formation is not the outcome of a single identifiable factor. Multiple factors come together to give rise to identity consciousness. That being the case, identity formation is a historical process the character of which is determined by time and space.

The phenomenon of ethnicity has been analyzed in terms of social approaches. The primordialist approach believes ethnicity as 'given' and takes common descent and culture as the basis of identity formation. The reconstruction of the past and showing its relationship with the present is the most common pattern of identity consolidation according to this argument. Another approach known as 'cultural-pluralist approach' refers to the co-existence of different groups in a society with incompatible socio-cultural structures, belief systems and value patterns. Under the condition, one group is dominated by the other often leading to the situation of conflict. The subjective perception of one group about the other remains different and articulation of such a perception for asserting group identity constitutes the basic assumption of this approach. The third major approach takes up modernization and development as its central concern and argues that ethnic affinities are residual phenomena. They would be dissolved with the expansion of the capitalist market. There is still another perspective which says that ethnic conflict arises from the broader political and economic environments, not from the cultural values of the ethnic groups. This approach emphasizes that ethnic conflict is the result of interactions between leaderships of centralizing states and elites from non-dominant ethnic groups. The Marxist approach, on the contrary, treats ethnicity as a reactionary impulse as against the growth of class consciousness. As such, ethnic consciousness is taken as 'false consciousness'. However, this approach can interpret racial and ethnic inequalities within the framework of dialectical epistemology.

The other related concept, multiethnicity may be briefly examined here. Multiethnicity is a historical fact and is a reality for most of the countries in the present world. Groupings and collectivities based on racial, religious, linguistic and regional identities have extensively grown dissolving ethnic homogeneity of a great number of countries. Population shift and migration have added to the diversity. A close look at the prevailing discussion on multiethnicity shows that the term is usually perceived negatively. It is viewed as a danger to the territorial integrity of a state. But to my understanding, it is not a challenge to the survival of states with multiethnic population. History affirms that states have not only existed but progressed faster with numerous ethnic groups. The people of different ethnic groups have lived together peacefully in one state and strengthened each other with mutual advantage. This multiethnicity is neither a risk factor nor a hazard to the integrity of states.

However, multiethnicity may grow into a grave challenge to the system if the latter fails to accommodate the legitimate aspirations of various ethnic groups. In a situation of multiethnicity there are sections of people which do not form part of ethnic majority. Under such a structural condition, it is possible that even justifiable rights of minorities are ignored and neglected. Their lawful demands and genuine grievances are overlooked more often under the pressure of the ethnic majority. As such smaller ethnic communities remain under the constant threat of deprivation and discrimination.

Moreover, in a multiethnic state, minorities are apprehensive of majority's attempt towards assimilation. There is a constant fear about the loss of tradition, culture, language and even religion of the smaller communities. The oft-repeated idea of 'mainstream' is highlighted by dominant groups to pressurize smaller identities to assimilate to the larger whole. Historical grounds are constructed to show the linkages among various ethnic groups on the one hand, and dominant groups on the other.

II

This paper is an attempt to examine some correlations between socio-economic processes and ethnic identity in the context of multiethnic situation in North-Eastern India.

Whenever and wherever India's north-east is discussed today, the reference perpetually remains terrorism and growing ethnic violence. Sometimes Naga-Kuki conflict comes into focus and in the very next moment continuing influx of people from outside the country becomes the topic of discussion. The recent issue of settling the Chakmas and the Hajongs outside Arunachal Pradesh has already assumed significance particularly in the context of National Human Rights Commission's observation on the question. In all these wranglings tribal-non-tribal/ insider-outsider antagonism invariably occupies the central place. Actually, in these debates the ground realities of the region are either ignored or camouflaged. The portrayal of the north-east today is more mythical than real.

The North-East India stands out for its unique ethnic, cultural, linguistic and religious diversity not to be found in any other region of the country. A large number of scheduled tribes with different religions, with one fourth of all the languages and dialects spoken in the country and strong impact of topographical features on identity formation have multiplied the heterogeneous composition of the region.

The ethnic heterogeneity of the region unfolds a complex feature based on distinctive historical experiences. Out of the seven states as many as four—Arunachal Pradesh, Meghalaya, Mizoram and Nagaland are not only tribal majority states but their culture and economy have features remarkably different from the tribal pockets elsewhere in the country. The three other units—Assam, Manipur and Tripura have a majority of non-tribal plains population but even in these states, the tribal population is substantially more than the national average. However, the similarity among these seven states in terms of numerical strength of ethnic groups does not reflect uniformity with regard to their socio-economic settings and the levels of economic development.

Compared to the other parts of the country, the colonial incorporation of the north-east started much later. While Manipur and Tripura were independent principalities maintaining relations with the British since the late nineteenth century, the colonial ruler annexed Assam in 1826 and subsequently the Naga, Mizo, Khasi, Jaintia and Garo Hills. The North-East Frontier Area came under its control in the second half of the nineteenth century. Under the colonial dispensation certain areas were either 'excluded' or 'partially excluded' from the purview of the then prevailing administrative and statutory control over land and forests. However, an attempt was simultaneously made to utilize the natural resources by establishing links with the process operating outside the region. Under the condition the extension of market links, introduction of money, entry of government officials, traders, moneylenders and shopkeepers created a situation under which the vested interests from outside could grab land through alienation and control. The plains areas primarily inhabited by non-tribals were brought under revenue arrangements that were prevailing in other parts of British India while the tribal dominated hill areas remained under customary land system.[1]

Although by the middle of the nineteenth century, the substantial part of North-East came under the overall control of the colonial authority, no strong linkages were established with the outside market except in the case of tea plantations. The regional economy thus remained out of the orbit of the capitalist path and the people continued to lead a life of relative independence, the problem of poverty and destitution notwithstanding. The dominant mode of agricultural practices in tribal areas characterized by swidden cultivation coupled with a feeble link with the emerging capitalist penetration restricted the transformation of the internal dynamics of the tribal social settings. The strong ties of kinship, the communitarian control of land and the associated social network provided a solid base for building ethnic identity among the hill people. The relative absence of differentiation within the community was the foundation on which social cohesion and group identity could survive making self help and community sentiment relevant and functional to the community. Given the context of agrarian social structure and localized political authority and administration, it is not difficult to ascertain why the vast majority of the tribals in North-East could substantially protect their control over land, preserve their dialects and sustain their democratic structure of social and political organization unlike tribal communities elsewhere in the country. The people no doubt negotiated and sustained their survival strategies in the most uncertain and unfavourable structural conditions but there was no direct threat to their demographic balance and social and cultural systems.

However, the situation started changing swiftly in the subsequent phases of its history. Assam opened up for tea plantation by the middle of the nineteenth century and afterwards exploitation of natural oil, coal, and forests developed at full speed. Such changes in economic activities brought a large number of immigrant labour to the area. While agriculture was almost stagnant due to the slow growth of indigenous population, new economic activities absorbed mainly outsiders. Under the circumstances, indigenous peoples' control over local resources began to decline and the process of land alienation commenced. Simultaneously, the arrival of Christian missionaries and the spread of Christianity in tribal areas during the later part of the nineteenth century not only introduced organized religion but brought about change in the life of the people through the church programmes in the fields of education and health. It was also due to the work of the Christian missionaries that linguistic consciousness emerged particularly in the tribal areas. However, the most significant development during this period was the emergence of educated modernized elite. The constitutional developments during 1920s and 1930s synchronized with the growing political consciousness in the region. The Government of India Act of 1919 provided for declaring the tribal areas as "backward tract" and the Act of 1935 as "excluded areas or partially excluded areas". Only some selected areas were allowed to send representatives to the Provincial Legislature before 1947. The attempt to turn the North-East region into an independent political entity separate from India under the Coupland Plan failed on the eve of independence.

It is apparent from the foregoing discussion that there is some amount of historical continuity in the ethnic issues being raised in North-East today. There is an element of continuity in the tension between centrifugal and centripetal forces between pre-independence and post-independence scenario.

Independence has thus marked the widening of difference between nationalism and ethnicity.

My contention, therefore, is that the phenomenon of identity and its manifestation in deteriorating inter-group relations are rooted in the nature of socio-economic development of the area. Identity is not formed instantaneously but it is the product of a historical process determined by forces unleashed by articulation of social, cultural, economic and political forces. Thus there is no uniform pattern of identity building. It depends upon situational contexts and manifests different sets of characteristics. Moreover, individuals and groups possess multiple identities but out of these the one which suits most to the demand if the given situation generally gets manifest. Numerous expressions of loyalty then follow but not in a fixed order.

Initially, the process of identity formation in North-East was based on the idea of large group formation. Attempts were made to bring several smaller tribal groups together to project a unified identity. Just after independence, the term "hill people" was made popular which was projected as a collectivity comprising hill tribes from different areas of the region. But such an identity could not sustain for long. Another attempt in this direction has been to develop generic terms to include various groups located mainly in a particular geographical territory. The Naga and the Mizo are the suitable attempts that come to mind immediately. Both these ethnic groups consist of several tribes each having distinct dialect, well demarcated territory and ostensible socio-cultural system. However, religious and racial elements have played crucial role in bringing them together. A similar attempt was made in Assam when expansive definition of Assamese identity was provided by showing that Assamese society was formed by assimilating tribals and Aryans. A `discourse of inclusion' has been an important dimension of identity formation.[2]

But such a fusion of groups and collectivities may not be stable due to inherent contradictions and the process of fission sets in under the impact of new forces of change. As such small group identity assertion follows. The emerging situation among the Mizo comes in handy. Several smaller groups, till now forming part of the larger Mizo grouping, have started asserting their separate identity by calling themselves by different names such as Zomi, Zou, Mara, Hmar, etcetra. Among the Nagas uneven pace of economic development among various tribes has led to growing competition among them causing simmering discontent and tension towards relatively developed and larger groups. A counter discourse of the tribals and some other smaller non-tribal groups in Assam against 'inclusion' in larger identity has already a long history now.[3]

It is required to be noted at this stage that by using ethnicity, ethnic groups articulate their demands for increased share in political power, more opportunities for economic well-being and protection of their culture and tradition. As such, these groups function as economic interest groups. Identity is thus adaptive strategy of ethnic groups under the condition of multiethnicity.

Although there is a broad consensus among scholars on the origins and course of the phenomenon of identity in North-East but no adequate attention has been paid to economic and social factors. To my understanding, the deteriorating inter-group relations in the region is primarily reflections of undergoing socio-economic forces which eventually manipulate political and communal situation.

III

Let me briefly discuss the nature of developmental strategy adopted in tribal areas of North-East. The most significant aspect in this context is a hiatus between the proclaimed policy and adopted programmes of development undertaken in the region. While both the national and the regional planning authorities have recognized the historical specificities of the North-Eastern situation, they have failed to adopt suitable alternative strategy that could develop the region without disturbing its ecological balance and peoples' psychology. There is essentially no difference in the strategy adopted here and in the other parts of the country. The central goal of development policy is to use natural resources of the region and almost all programmes are in tune with this objective.

However, its total impact in terms of improvement of economic condition of the people has not only been minimal but more often unfavourable. What happened to the Chotanagpur tribals where a similar strategy was adopted may provide with a good lesson.[4] Such a strategy presupposes a particular type of priority and institutional change that destabilize socio-economic life of the people. The programmes place much reliance upon chosen groups who are expected to participate effectively and contribute towards developmental efforts. In this sense, the adopted strategy contradicts its own policy which states, 'the strategy for development should be dictated by considerations of *benefiting the people as a whole rather than the status group* (emphasis mine). Moreover, the development schemes entail emphasis on the growth of linkages with national and global markets, commercialization of indigenous designs and skills, competitive use of land and forests and far reaching changes in patterns of landownership and property relations. Obviously, it involves establishment of linkages between unequal formations, one highly developed and competitive and the other still in the age of slash and burn cultivation. The former expropriates maximum benefits, the latter increases its dependence on market forces. The fact of the matter is that the planning strategy envisaged here requires an ethos and value **gestalt** entirely unconnected with the socio-economic reality of the region.

Looking at the trends in the North-East, it can be concluded that the seeds of inequality have already been sown because of unfavourable socio-economic consequences of developmental programmes. It has already introduced distortions in the traditional socio-economic systems without an inkling of the prosperous and just social order. 'The forces generated by the nature of developmental planning have completely subordinated the interests of the indigenous people and restricted the local control over resources and gains. It has led to a shift from "the relative independence" to complete "dependence" without even passing through "interdependence". That being the case, the time-tested village solidarity and social harmony have been replaced by differentiated heterogeneous community creating strong vested interests from within the community itself. Most of the new deve–

lopmental schemes have benefited a handful of people who are safely aligning themselves with the dominant groups from outside. What I have been trying to argue is that the path of development adopted here has failed to harmonize its impact with the aspirations and conditions of existence of the people of this area.

In fact, problems such as tribal-non-tribal conflicts, direct secessionist demands based on assertion of ethnic identity, demands for further reorganization of states are all intertwined in the continuing backwardness and underdevelopment of the region. Dominance of non-tribals in trade and commerce, preponderance of non-tribals in modern occupations and professions and continuing influx of people from outside the country continue to be central issues frequently assuming the form of communal tension. It should not be missed that the never ending danger of influx from the neighbouring countries has perpetually caused tremendous fear in the wake of the Tripura experience when a complete reversal of demographic patterns had already taken place. Naturally, the demand for deportation of infiltrators that started with the foreign nationals was subsequently applied even to those who came to this area from other parts of the country. Initially, migrants were absorbed in agriculture but when saturation point was reached the attention shifted to other areas of economic activities.

Thus one of the explanations for the problems of North-East concerns the worsening employment situation in the region to which agricultural stagnation also is said to have made a contribution. This question was rarely highlighted earlier because the types of people who dominated the job market in areas like administration, higher education and public sector undertakings were not available among the local tribals. As a result, in almost all states of the region the number of local tribals in departments/offices like Secretariat, Bank, Post & Telegraph, Accountant General, Electricity Board, Schools and Colleges and so forth has been neglected. These offices have mainly been manned by Bengalis and Assamese. Naturally, these sections of people have been immediate targets in communal tensions, but other non tribal groups have also been enveloped under such a situation.

Another potential area of tension has been trade and business which by and large continue to be under the control of people from outside the region. Whether it is tea industry, wholesale trade, transport sector, saw-mills or even petty retail outlets all are mostly in their hands. Despite restrictions in hill areas business concerns are under *de-facto* control of outsiders through *benami* transactions. The recent trade-license controversy in Meghalaya is essentially the outcome of this feature of the economy.

There is another dimension to the problem. The economy of hill areas cannot be thought without its forest component. The intimate relationship of the forest with the hill dwellers is not only reflected in their economic activities but also in their socio-cultural settings. The complex nature of the forest question involves two basic elements-ecology and peoples' rights. Ever since 1855 memorandum restricting forest dwellers rights, several regulations have been imposed to control the rights and privileges of the traditional users of forests. These measures were taken in national interest but were set aside whenever they came in the way of revenue interests of the government. In the process, neither the people could secure their due benefits nor the ecological balance could be maintained. What is happening in the North-East is more alarming both from the viewpoints of ecology and ownership. Its complexity is further added due to the widespread practice of shifting cultivation. It is frequently argued that the forest cover in the North-East has been depleted primarily because of the continuing practice of *jhum*.[6] As such change in the land use pattern introduced by governmental agencies such as developing terrace farming has already started alienating people from their habitat. Such a scheme comes into direct conflict with the tribal social organization. Wherever land has been released from *jhuming* it has not remained under the control of the villagers. While in some cases, it has been utilized for plantation, in others it has passed into the hands of the dominant members of the community for permanent cultivation. Moreover, the commercial linkages and the contractual system have caused reckless felling of trees even in so called protected and reserved forests. For all practical purposes most of these forests have passed from the hands of local people into the hands of unscrupulous merchants and traders who are engaged in large scale timber extraction for meeting demands of outside industry. Under such a system of forest utilization, the forest dwellers are reduced to the status of casual wage labourers while the state forest department and saw-mill owners become the new proprietors.

IV

The occasion does not permit me to go into the subject in more details. However, I would like to emphasize that disparities in the socio-economic development inevitably result in political fragmentation. Emerging regional elites and newly formed middle class tend to utilize the existing conflict potential for more share in power. Under the circumstances, dividing rather than compromising elements become the primary means of agitation towards this goal. Regional political parties and groups emerge to mobilize large section of the population on issues appropriate to common cultural, linguistic, ethnic, and economic interests in their states. They add to the bargaining power of the states and provide more strength to the periphery in bringing about a balance between the Union and the states. The prevailing situation in North East corresponds to this pattern. Ethnic identity is politically articulated for redressal of perceived or real greviences. These demands are trenchantly voiced particularly under the condition of centralizing drives of national political leadership and growing interventionist practices of the central government.

The growing social tensions alone do not essentially endanger the stability of the society. So long the state is capable of balancing the disparities by arranging a socially endurable distribution of national wealth, conflict and militancy can be contained.

References

1. See for details, M.N. Karna, *"The Agrarian Scene"*, Seminar 366 (The North East) February 1990, pp. 30-38.
2. Kishore Bhattacharjee, "Discourse of Inclusion: A *Brief Note on the Ethnic Situation in Assam"*, Paper presented at the seminar

on Ethnic Situation in North-East India: Fields and Frontiers, Anthropological Survey of India, Shillong, September 13-14, 1996.

3. *Ibid.*
4. M.N: Karna, *"Aspects of Tribal Development in North-Eastern India"*, in Ashish Bose, *et al.*, *Tribal Demography and Development in North East India*, B.R. Publishing Corporation, Delhi, 1990, pp. 7-23.
5. *Report on Development of Backward Hill Areas*, National Committee on the Development of Backward Areas, Planning Commission, Government of India, March 1981, p. 21.
6. This argument has been contested by scholarly studies of P.S. Ramakrishnan. See his paper, *"An Inventory of Forest Resources of the North-Eastern Region"*, in M. Dasgupta, *et al.*, (eds), *Forestry Development in North-East India*, Omsons Publications, Guwahati, 1986, p. 234.

Chapter 17

Ethnic Identity and Development in India's North-East : A Conspectus

—S.C. Daniel

In this paper, I would like to explicate the intimate relation between the concept of ethnic identity and the concept of development with special reference to North-East India. I am well aware of the fact that the seminar is on the theme, "Liberalization, Ethnic Identity and Economic Development in India's North-East." I must admit at the outset itself that I do not have the required expertise and competence in the said areas of specialization. After having had the temerity to enter into the labyrinth of liberalization, ethnic identity and economic development, I am not in sight of any escape route. However, I would like to make an endeavour to analyze the concepts of ethnicity, identity and development, and that to indicate the kind of relationship that these important and significant concepts stand in relation to each other.

Let me take up the concept of ethnicity first. Oxford English Dictionary offers the definitions of the term 'ethnicity' and 'ethnic' as follows. It says, "Ethnicity-heathendom, heathen superstition, ethnic-nation especially non-Israelitish, Gentile nation." (Oxford English Dictionary, 1971). Needless to point out that these Oxford lexicon definitions are heavily value loaded, that too nega–tively. Moreover, these definitions show more than amply, the prejudice and the distorted vision of people who dėfine as thus. Therefore, the original definitions of these terms cannot provide a valid basis for the explanatory, value-neutral terminology since they involve an obvious evaluative orientation. In the past, 'ethnics' were considered to be 'others' on the basis of the categories such as minorities, under–developed, and so on. However, these categories have no longer any meaningful application because of the fact that today everybody is considered to be an ethnic since he or she is a member of some ethnic group or other. Thus, ethnicity has now become constitutive of humanity. Ethnicity no longer signifies marginal group or minority; it signifies pluralism. Ethnic pluralism indicates that there is a variety, in fact, an immense variety, of ethnicities. Given this view, it would be a gross mistake to maintain that there is one, and one and only one type of ethnicity.

What would count as ethnic? It is very important to answer this rather vexing question. It must be pointed out here that there cannot be *the* definition or definition *per se*, or definition *as such* of ethnicity, for ethnicity defies such a definition. However, it will be worthwhile, fruitful and extremely useful to have a working definition of the same, that is, of ethnicity. It is very significant to point out that an ostensive definition of ethnicity is impossible because of the fact that we cannot point out and declare, 'this is an ethnic group whereas that is not an ethnic group'. It is generally accepted and acknowledged that ethnicity is a collectivity which means it has a collective character, or it is a collective whole. Hence, when we talk about such a collectivity, we cannot see objects as such, but only object-indicators, or object-recognitors that are symptomatic or indicative of ethnicity. An ethnic collectivity consists of persons who have one or more common characteristic and occupy a common ethnic base or platform. Persons, who belong to a particular ethnic collectivity, as conscious of their ethnic identities, which consist in their recognition, and valuation of their membership in that particular collectivity.

It is worth emphasizing the fact that there is a fundamental difference between ethnic categories and ethnic groups. And this fundamental difference consists in the fact that ethnic categories are more or less permanent while the ethnic groups are changeable or variable. This is why Robert H. Jackson asserts : "An 'ethnic group', therefore, is a collection of persons who occupy an ethnic platform, recognize and value their common occupancy—share an identity—and are organized and therefore have a common interest in maintaining their association" Sartori, 1984. There are ethnic categories among Khasis, Jaintias and Garos of Meghalaya. And these ethnic categories including various clans are more or less permanent. The important clans of Jaintias are as follows: *(i)* Dkhar, *(ii)* Lyngdoh, *(iii)* Suchiang, *(iv)* Dhar, *(v)* Syngkon, *(vi)* Sutnga, *(vii)* Laloo, *(viii)* Pasi, *(ix)* Passah, *(x)* Bthuh, and *(ix)* Pariat. The important clans of the Khasis are: *(i)* Lyngdoh, *(ii)* Kharkongor, *(iii)* Marwein, *(iv)* Lyndem, *(v)* Diengdoh, *(vi)* Nongsiej, *(vii)* Syiem, *(viii)* Jyrwa, *(ix)* Khongwir, *(x)* Kiri, *(xi)* Rani, and *(xii)* Warbah. And, the important clans of Garos are: *(i)* Marak, *(ii)* Sangma, and *(iii)* Momin. Among the Jaintias there are various ethnic groups such as Coal Mine Association, Jaintia Students Union (J.S.U.), All Narpuh Students Association (ANSA), Timber Supply Association etc. The members of these ethnic groups have different common interests specific to their needs. The needs and interests may change or vary according to the various demands of changing situations.

Ethnicity as a collectivity must be differentiated and distinguished from other collectivities such as caste, classes, and so on. A caste as it stands today is an ascriptive collectivity possessing a generally recognized standing in a large society. However, it does not mean that caste is mere ethnic without ethno centricism. As a matter of fact, caste has become ethnos with a much pronounced ethno centrism, that is to say, caste involves the belief in the inherent superiority of one's own caste and culture especially of higher castes, accompanied by a feeling of contempt for other castes and cultures. On the other hand, social class as a collectivity is a collection of persons, who occupy a base or platform of material inequality. Though caste system and class system as similar to each other in being vertical or pyramidical arrangements of social collectivities, they have the following important dissimilarity. Caste system is based on cultural ranking or gradation while class system is based on material inequality. It must be pointed out that ethnic collectivity is different from caste and social collectivities because of the fact that the former consists of horizontally or parallelly aligned collectivities of which none possesses a generally acknowledged claim to superiority over any other ethnic collectivity. Ethnic groups do not stand for what is advantageous for the individual members of those groups. They, instead, stand for those collective or general conditions that are advantageous and essential to the quality of life of the ethnic community as a whole and the common identity of members.

A proper analysis of the concept of ethnicity must consist in reduction of ambiguity and enhancement of clarity of meanings. Furthermore, we must settle for a minimal definition, which would include only the core or necessary factors to the neglect of peripheral or contingent factors. Perhaps one of those things which is easier said than done. However, I would like to make an endeavour. The core or necessary factors of the concept of ethnicity consist in the following : *(i)* ascription of certain characteristics, *(ii)* plurality, *(iii)* identity, and *(iv)* organization. And the peripheral or contingent factors of the concept of ethnicity are: public authority, political independence, blood relation, hierarchy, inequality, and so on.

A word or two about the concept of culture may not be out of place here since it figures prominently in the ethnicity literature. Some employ 'culture' as a generic term to include within itself more specific terms such as 'religion', 'language', and so on. Some employ it as a specific term along with 'religion', 'language' and so on. Still others use it in both ways, that is, both on a generic term as well as a specific term. If the term 'culture' is used both ways, a logical mistake known as category-mistake will be committed. And this logical error consists in assigning elements to one category, when they actually belong to another category. For example, 'either she bought a left hand glove and a right hand glove or she bought a pair of gloves (but not both)' (Gilbert, 1949). In my opinion, it would be prudent to avoid using the term 'culture' as a generic term as well, since it might lead some people to conflating and identifying it mistakenly with certain specific terms as religion and language. In fact, some people actually do it in order to achieve their own vested interests. For example, some people identity culture with religion. And this enables them to muddle the issue of what has come to be known as 'cultural identity'. They tend to identify culture with religion, and claim that once a person changes his religion, he loses his culture. This leads, according to them, to what they call 'cultural identity crisis'. This view is gaining currency. I believe that time has come to discredit this view once and for all to avoid certain confusion. The above discussion will throw some light upon the relation that holds between ethnicity and culture. Though ethnicity and culture are closely related to one another, they should not be identified with one another since they are two separate distinct specific terms.

There are many ethnic indicators, which include characteristics such as race, colour, language, religion, customs, geographical origin, and so on. It may be reiterated that these indicators are only symptomatic, and not necessary or constitutive elements of ethnic collectivity. It is not exaggeration to say that ethnicity and language are very closely related phenomena. Both ethnicity and language are pluralistic in nature. Needless to point out that there is an immense variety of languages in India including North-East India. However, though there is a tremendous diversity of languages, all languages must have common core, which consists in having a common conceptual apparatus of thinking. The Miris (Miri and Miri, 1984) effectively argue that there is a truly fundamental unity among all languages and that it consists in sharing the basic (central) conceptual framework. Here, basic or central means principal, chief or dominant. It also means that from the basic (central) conceptual framework other related things proceed. Thus, this basic (central) conceptual framework is logically primitive or non-derivative, that is to say, other conceptual frameworks can be derived from it, but it cannot be derived from any other conceptual framework. Miris are worth quoting. They say : "... a unity consisting in the fact that they all share a basic (central) conceptual framework. There may be variation in details, in certain kinds of sophistication and discrimination, but the fundamental structure must be the same. Also, although 'the categories' (*a priori* concepts) might change through history, their central application must remain more or less unaltered, permanent (eternal). Thus, take the concept of time. This may vary widely from language to language—and, therefore, some might say-from culture to culture—but whatever the variation, the centre of the concept must be the same. This centre would consist of distinctions such as before, after, at the same time as, early, late etc. There could be no language, in which one could talk about one's experiences and which, yet, did not have room for distinctions such as the above." (*Ibid.*, p. 159). Let us look at the very intimate relation between ethnicity and language for a while. There has been a 'battle of languages' in India including North-East India. Unfortunately, no sincere attempt has been made to map out the politico-cultural terrain on which this battle is being fought. And this has blinded us to the far reaching consequences of this battle. Increased occupational mobility has created a linguistic dislocation. Therefore, there arises a need to have a proficiency in a language other than the mother tongue. This sort of situation is obtainable in North-East India to some extent. Thus, language as an indicator of ethnicity becomes very relevant here. There has been a threat to various vernaculars of North-East India. And this may lead to certain disadvantages, if the issue concerned is not attended to immediately. Some languages especially English, Hindi and Assamese are mistakenly considered to be superior to languages of North-East India. Some scholars even suspect the uniqueness of certain terms in Khasi language such as *Ka Hok*, *Ka Sang* etc. saying that these terms have been borrowed from other languages such as Sanskrit, Persian, and so on. It is true that some of these terms did not originate in the Khasi language. But it does not prevent these terms from being unique, for their uniqueness does not lie in their origin, but in their different applications and meanings. It would be observed and contrary to facts even for these scholars to deny that these words acquire new applications and meanings entirely from those of their root words.

What is identity? The problem of identity is one of the problem perennials of philosophy. This problem has been agitating the great minds at the highest level since the beginning of philosophy. David Hume, (1811-1877) one of the greatest philosophers in the entire history of Western Philosophy, discusses the problem of identity of an object as well as that of self or person in his *magnum opus, A Treatise of Human Nature* (Selby-Bigge, 1978). According to Hume, identity is a relation. He defines identity of an object as an object is the same with itself. He points out that a single object conveys only the idea of unity, and that the multiplicity of resembling objects conveys only the notion of number. Therefore, he comes to the conclusion that there can be no notion of identity of an object since it must be either the notion of unity or the notion of number or multiplicity. He is of the view that we confound resembling objects with identical ones. He also rejects self-identity or personal identity. In the appendix of *A Treatise of Human Nature* (*Ibid.*), Hume says that he is involved in a 'labyrinth' as regards the self-identity or personal identity after having reviewed it. He admits that he does not know how to correct his former opinions nor to make them consistent. He says that he shall produce arguments for and against proper identity and simplicity of a self or thinking being. He denies proper identity and simplicity of the self. His arguments may be summarized as follows : if we talk of self, we must have an idea of the same. If we do not have any idea of self, our talk or discussion about it will become unintelligible or incomprehensible. All our ideas are derived from the preceding impressions and we have no impression of a simple self. Therefore, we cannot have any idea of a simple self. All our perceptions are distinct. Therefore, all our perceptions may exist separately. This does not involve any contradiction or absurdity. All our perceptions exist distinct and independent; they do not need any simple substances. The self is composed of perceptions. Supposing, he has just one perception, say thirst or hunger. In this case, we cannot conceive of anything but that perception; we cannot have the notion of self or substance. Even the addition of other perceptions cannot give us the notion of a self without perceptions, there cannot be a self. Hume is worth quoting here. He says, "For my part, when I enter most intimately into what I call *myself*, I always stumble on some particular perception or other, of heat or cold, light or shade, love or hatred, pain or pleasure. I never can catch *myself* at any time without a perception, and never can observe anything but the perception. When my perceptions are removed for any time, as by sound sleep; so long am I insensible of myself, and may truly be said not to exist. And were all my perceptions removed by death, and could neither think, nor feel, nor see, nor love, nor hate after the dissolution of my body, I should be entirely annihilated, nor do I conceive what is farther requisite to make me a perfect non-entity." (*Ibid*., p. 252). According to Hume, the notion of identity, whether it be identity of objects or self-identity or personal identity is a fiction or an imaginary principle which arises from the relation of parts. He is certain that 'thought alone finds personal identity' meaning that personal identity does not exist in reality. He sarcastically remarks that the philosophers' remedy to the problem of identity does not cure the malady. I agree with Hume that identity is a relation. But I do not agree with him that identity is a fiction. For example, ethnic identity is neither a fiction nor is it found only in thought; it exists in reality. Ethnic identity, as it has been already pointed out, consists in the persons' recognition, and valuation of their identity in a particular collectivity. Therefore, ethnic identity is the relation between the members and their identification with some common interests.

The concept of development has many an aspect such as economic growth, growth in literacy, welfare of the body, welfare of the mind, and the like. But unfortunately, only economic development is highlighted and aimed at. As a consequence, the other important aspects of the concept of development are not only pushed to the background but also viewed with certain amount of contempt. India Today, a leading Indian periodical, brings out this attitude very clearly when it says, "Ten years ago the goals were more food, water, steel, hospitals. How it is all that plus telephones, TV sets, scooters, cars, and refrigerators". It is true that there has been a very significant increase in the production of food in most of the countries of the world. Needless to point out that India has already made a breakthrough in so far as food is concerned, which was possible due to the invention of certain high yielding seeds especially of rice and wheat. Also, there have been other kinds of growth as well such as growth in health facilities, growth in education facilities, growth in material comforts, and growth in entertainment. There has been a steady increase in the number of hospitals especially private clinics with sophisticated equipments in India including North-Eastern part of India. More and more educational institutions are being established in North-East India. There are many universities in North-East India including four central universities and some national institutions. People of North-East India have an easy access to various kinds of material comforts. There are many good cinema houses in North-East India. Many people possess TV sets, that too colour TVs, VCPs and VCRs. There has been a mushrooming of video and audio parlours throughout North-East India. But in my opinion, all these are only material growths, and then one-sided. These are only instruments of mere physical growth. Sports facilities too have been on the increase to supplement this sort of physical growth. But, what about the welfare of the self or the soul? Probably, this aspect is also being taken care of. The existence of many churches, mosques, and temples in North-East India bear testimony to this fact. However, this sort of development too is one-sided. Therefore, we need to have a unitary concept of development. And this unitary concept of development, I am sure, will bring about peace and harmony among the manifolds of ethnic groups. The importance of physical resources cannot be over emphasized. By physical resources, I mean such things as fertile soil, climate, mineral deposits, food, water, hospitals, clinics, material comforts, and by human development, I mean such things as literacy, skills of work force, administrative skills, various levels of commitment to ethnic groups, society, state, nation, religion, value system and welfare of the self or soul. The unitary concept of development requires both physical as well as human resources. In other words, it includes both physical dimension and spiritual dimension. And this concept of development must be equalitarian in all its aspects, complete and holistic.

The concepts of ethnicity, as it has been already shown, can be connected with each other without much difficulty. But connecting these two concepts, that is, the concept of ethnicity and the concept of identity, with that of the concept of development seems to be an extremely difficult task. However, there seems to be an important connection between these three significant concepts. Ethnic identity can be an important means to achieve development proper or genuine development, which takes care of both the dimensions, the physical and the spiritual. Ethnic collectivities consists of individuals. The development of individuals contribute to the development of ethnic collectivities. The development of ethnic collectivities, in turn, contribute to the development of the nation as a whole. Ethnic identity could also be used by people with vested interests to bring about the so called development as opposed to genuine development, which is based on prejudice and narrow-mindedness. Moreover, the so-called development will inevitably lead to a solipsistic view, because it takes care of only one's own development. We must remember that we all belong to one nation, that is, India, and not that our nation is in us. Any sort of development that is in relation to ethnic identity must be pursued diligently with the notion of development of our dear country as a whole in mind. The parts must contribute to the enrichment of the whole. Otherwise, the dichotomy between 'we' and 'they' would be increased instead of being decreased. In fact, there has been a national convergence of various economic and non-economic measures of the welfare of the Indians. And this national convergence, I am sure, will lead to the global convergence of the said measures.

References

Hume, David, 1978, A Treatise of Human Nature, Selby-Bigge, L.A., (ed), Clarendon Press, Second Edition, Oxford.

Miri, Mrinal and Sujata Miri, 1984, "Unity in Diversity" in Abbi, B.L., (ed), North-East Region: Problems and Prospects of Development, Centre for Research and Industrial Development, Chandigarh.

Ryle, Gilbert, 1949, Concept of Mind, Hutchinson, London.

Sartori, Giovanni, (ed), 1984, "Ethnicity" in Social Science Concepts—A Systematic Analysis, Sage Publications, New Delhi.

The compact edition of Oxford English Dictionary, Volume 1, 1971, Oxford Clarendon Press.

PART FOUR

LIBERALIZATION : IMPLICATIONS FOR BORDER TRADE

Chapter 18

India's North-East and Border Trade with Neighbouring Countries : A Case Study on Indo-Bangladesh Relations

—*C. Joshua Thomas*

India's Northeastern region is identified with various aspects of underdevelopment, such as it is tne house of a number of relatively small ethnic groups constitutionally guaranteed with special status of the scheduled tribes, it is sparsely populated, infrastructurally backward and isolated from the Indian mainstream due to lack of proper transport and communication facilities. These indicators of underdevelopment are further aggravated by some other problems such as *(i)* the problem of immigration from neighbouring countries, *(ii)* the problem of insurgency, *(iii)* the problem of ethnic unrest, and *(iv)* the problem of corruption at all levels. These four problems make the entire region of Northeast as the backward area. On the one hand the Government of India categorized the States in the Northeastern region as special category States and on the other hand both the Union and the State governments provided some noteworthy incentives such as : introduction of capital investment subsidy, power subsidy, interest subsidy, tax exemption, five year tax holiday to industries in 1993-94 budget proposals and transport subsidy for another 5 years up to 2000 AD to encourage industrial development in the region. The paper, firstly, tries to examine a profile on Northeast, its potentiality and its problems. Secondly, the paper makes a plea that since in the sphere of economic cooperation without wider border trade relationship, regional cooperation and development will not gain the necessary and vital economic subsistence and therefore an attempt is made on the feasibility of border trade cooperation between India's Northeast and Bangladesh.

Northeast India comprises seven States *viz.*, Arunachal Pradesh, Assam, Manipur, Meghalaya, Mizoram, Nagaland and Tripura. Located in the Northeastern most corner of India, this region has a great strategic importance since it has common borders with five foreign countries, namely, Bangladesh, Bhutan, China, Myanmar and Nepal. The total geographical area of these seven States is 2,55,083 sq.km constituting 8.74 per cent of the total geographical area of the country. From the point of view of area, Arunachal Pradesh is the largest State and Tripura the smallest.

The density of population in the region is 124 per sq.km. as against 267 per sq.km. for the country according to 1991 Census. This low average density of population is due mainly to the fact that the hill areas of this region are very sparsely populated. But we must hasten to add that the density picture conceals more than it reveals in that the plain areas of the region have a density of population much higher than the national average.

Again among seven States, while Arunachal Pradesh has the lowest density of population (10 per sq.km.) Assam has the highest (285 per sq.km.). Assam's figure is higher than that of the all India average of 267 per sq.km. From the point of view of composition of people Northeast India presents a unique feature in the sense that it is a meeting place of people of a large number of races, castes, creed, religions, cultures, languages, etc. Here we have people from all the States of India and therefore the region can very well be regarded as a miniature of India. However, this region is well-known for being the homeland of a large number of tribal communities most of whom belong to Mongoloid group racially but Tibeto-

Burman families linguistically. The Khasis and the Jaintias of Meghalaya, of course, belong to Mon-khmer linguistic family.

The total number of tribal communities in Northeast India would be around 200 as against 430 for the whole of India. It can, therefore, very well be said that almost 47 per cent of the tribal communities in India hail from the Northeast. According to 1991 Census, out of 315.47 lakh population in the seven Northeastern States the total number of tribal population is 81.42 lakh constituting 25.71 per cent of the total population of the seven States. On the other hand, the Scheduled Caste population in the Northeast is not so significant. The total Scheduled Caste population in this region, is 21.61 lakh constituting 6.85 per cent of the total population. Excepting Tripura and Assam, the other five States have very low percentage of Scheduled Caste population.

Although the level of literacy is not uniform in all seven States, yet in some of the States it is quite high. A statewise statement of literacy in the seven States is furnished below :

LITERACY RATE IN THE SEVEN STATES OF NORTHEASTERN REGION OF INDIA

Sl.No.	*Name of State*	*Male(%)*	*Female(%)*	*Total(%)*
1.	Arunachal Pradesh	51.20	29.37	41.22
2.	Assam	62.34	43.70	53.22
3.	Manipur	72.98	48.64	60.96
4.	Meghalaya	51.57	44.78	48.26
5.	Mizoram	84.06	78.09	81.23
6.	Nagaland	66.09	55.72	61.30
7.	Tripura	70.08	50.01	60.39
	For All Seven States	65.47	50.04	58.11
	All India	63.86	39.42	52.11

It is noteworthy that among all the tribal communities of India, the Mizos of Mizoram have the highest percentage of literacy as per 1991 census.

The treaty of Yandaboo (February 24, 1826) between the East India Company and the King of Burma (Myanmar) formed the Northeast as a part of India. However, Manipur and Tripura were princely kingdoms and they were not a part of greater Assam. During the British rule they were protected kingdoms. These two kingdoms maintained their distinct identity till they were merged with the Indian Union after 1947. By and large all the hill tribes of Northeast India followed a policy of peaceful coexistence, mutual trust and cooperation and friendship. However, the British rulers, reversed the policy followed by the hill tribes and introduced the policy of isolation through Inner Line Regulation in 1873 in all the Northeastern areas except Manipur and Tripura, which imposed restrictions on the movement of the plains people into these areas. Initially, the British administrators treated the hill areas of Northeast as a "Non-Regulated Area" and then declared them as "Backward Tract" (1919) and lastly "Excluded Areas" and "Partly Excluded Areas" (1935). This policy of "isolation" followed by the British and coupled with more recent causes, many parts of Northeastern region now face problem of insurgency and separatist movement.

This region is very rich in natural resources like forest, soil, water, oil, natural gas and minerals etc. According to the recent Forest Survey in India, Arunachal Pradesh has the highest percentage (63) of thick green coverage among all the States in India. With so many perennial rivers and streams, this area has a very great potential for generating hydro-electricity power. Underground water reserve is also quite substantial in the Brahmaputra Valley. In the Barak Valley also oil deposits of sizeable dimension have very recently been found. Coal, limestone, and uranium (in Meghalaya) are important mineral resources of the region. These natural resources are yet to be utilized scientifically.

From the point of view of bio-diversity this area is the richest in India. Owing to very unscientific way of exploiting forest resources, some of the bio-species are in the process of extinction. The world famous one-horned rhinos' homeland—the Kaziranga National Park—is located in Assam. The brow-antlered deer is found in Manipur only.

Most of the people in the Northeastern States, particularly hill dwellers are still practicing shifting cultivation. Alternatives to Jhum cultivation are yet to make an impact on the people. Agriculture, by and large, is marked by mono-crop cultivation with either low level or primitive technology resulting in low yield. Although market economy has penetrated even into the remote tribal areas, the tribal people produce, generally what they need without caring for surplus production. The other sectors allied to agriculture like veterinary, fishery, irrigation and soil conservation, etc., have not been developed to the desired extent although they have greater potentiality. In spite of all these vast resources and potentiality Northeastern region remained backward due to various reasons mentioned elsewhere in this paper.

II

Having discussed the potentiality and the problems of the Northeastern region of India let us move to the second part of this paper on economic cooperation with the neighbouring countries in this region with special reference to Bangladesh.

During the last forty-five years India has witnessed spectacular development in the agricultural sector and achieved nearly four-fold increase in food grain production—from mere 52 million tonnes in 1951-52 to about 190 million tonnes in 1994-95. Production of oil seeds, cotton and sugar cane also rose to manifold. It is worth to note that India is now the second largest producer of fruits, vegetable and dairy products in the world. These have been possible because of technical break through, development of infrastructure, such as communication, power, irrigation etc. and several policy initiatives since independence in land reforms and development (Grassroots Options, 1997).

The Northeastern region virtually remained untouched by these sweeping developments across the Country. It has not only failed to take advantage of benefits of planned development, on the contrary, import of food grains, poultry, fish, meat and dairy products increased year after year. The Department of Agriculture and Cooperation committee reported that the region spends nearly Rs. 700 crore on import of agricultural products and another 1000 crore for poultry products and fish. But the economic situation continued slide. It is a fact that, this region is rich in crop and genetic diversities, abundance of water sources as major assets. But the climate factor, infrastructural inadequacy, biophysical skills had hampered implementation of programmes. Also the region having the longest international boundary along five foreign countries straddling it denied the people access to this traditional market across the border (*ibid.* p. 24). Professor J.B. Bhattacharjee in his Presidential address delivered in the Annual Conference of North-East India History Association held at Jorhat aptly said, "Today, the common character of the region lies, at least in its strategic vulnerability and its economic backwardness. Whereas the total geographical area of the region is 2,55,037 sq. kilometers, it has 4,200 km long international boundary with Burma, Bangladesh, Bhutan and China and it is connected with rest of the country by the narrow `Siliguri neck' of less than 20 km.' (Bhattacharjee, J.B.: 1994, p. 2). Here comes the relevance of border trade with neighbouing countries.

Border trade has special significance to the economies of the Northeastern States due to their peculiar geographical location. The States have a larger border with neighbouring countries than with India. With the exception of the tiny 'chicken-neck' connecting Assam with West Bengal, the rest of the border is shared with Bangladesh, China, Bhutan and Myanmar. This peculiar location coupled with poor infrastructural facilities within the region as a whole had led to a situation where each one of the seven States is looking more to the neighbouring countries than to mainland India for economic relations. On the other hand, lack of infrastructural facilities and the slow pace of industrialization have contributed the scope for promoting exports.

The Government of India has entered into a border trade agreement with the Government of Myanmar on January 21, 1994, and it came into effect on April 12,1995, when Indo-Myanmar border was officially declared open for trade at Moreh in Manipur and other points likely to be opened for border trade are Champhai in Mizoram and Lungwa in Nagaland. On the other hand there is no border trade agreement between India and Bangladesh, however, regular normal trade between India and Bangladesh is going on between India and Bangladesh by regulation trade posts in the States of Meghalaya, Assam and Tripura. An attempt is made in the next part of this paper on the feasibility of economic cooperation between India and Bangladesh.

III

India and Bangladesh share a common border of nearly 1630 kms. covering three Indian States in the Northeastern region, viz., Meghalaya, Assam and Tripura. In view of the immense potential that exists between India and Bangladesh in the fields of trade and economic cooperation, Government of India and Government of Bangladesh had a series of discussions on many common matters. One among such items is the recently signed 30 years Indo-Bangladesh, treaty on sharing of Ganga waters signed on December 12, 1996, during Bangladesh Prime Minister, Sheikh Hasina's visit to New Delhi is a major development in bilateral relations. This water treaty constitutes the most outstanding success of India's foreign policy in recent times precisely because India went out of its way to mend fences with a neighbour whose legitimate water request were conceded in the final count (Chakravarty, 1997).

This 30 years treaty in a sense has opened up prospects of accords on transit, trade and handling of the problem of illegal immigrants from Bangladesh and many more other items. There is no doubt about this that the Northeastern region too stands to gain substantially once India is granted transit facilities through Bangladesh which will reap mutual dividend from such an arrangement.

IV

It is gratifying to note that the Eighth General Conference (Special) of the Northeast Congress(I) committee held at Dimapur, Nagaland (June 22, 1993) gave a forceful emphasis on a scheme for economic development of Northeast wherein the committee remarked: "It is necessary to open up border trade with neighbouring countries—Bangladesh, Burma and the Tibet regime of China—and keep those free from the usual foreign trade formalities.... we consider the demand for a 10 km free trade zone on either side to be highly justified...."

(Administrator, 1994). It further remarks that the "poor economic state of Bangladesh has been a cause of worry in India in more ways than one. Apart from the chronic influx of people in search of work and food, fundamentalist forces find fertile ground for anti-secular and anti-Indian campaign. The problem can be controlled only if the Bangladesh economy can lift itself up at least to the Indian level through cooperation and not by our constructing a concrete wall." (Administrator, 1994).

In a recent study on India's Northeast Resurgent, B.G, Verghese observed: "It would cost India Rs. 450 crores to extend the railway system in Tripura from Kumarghat to Agartala, a distance of 135 km (as proposed) whereas Agartala is barely four kilometres from the Bangladesh railhead at Akhaura and thence to Chittaong, the Northeast's traditional entreport. Many other such rail and road connections could be restored or forged at minimal cost. The benefit to the Northeast would be immense while Bangladesh would earn a tidy sum as revenues for these services which would also generate employment. Indeed, India should and probably would be prepared to assist programmes to strengthen, upgrade and expand the Bangladesh road, rail, inland water and port facilities to the extent these serve Indian needs. Such improvements in Bangladeshi infrastructure would enhance investments and employment opportunities in the country. The new multipurpose Jamuna (Brahmaputra) Bridge at Sirajganj in Bangladesh could provide direct access for Indian traffic from Malda in West Bengal to Karimganj in Cachar, greatly improving the economics of the bridge." (Vergese, 1996).

It is worth to quote here the study on Promotion of Border Trade Between India and Myanmar prepared by the Indian Institute of Foreign Trade for Northeastern Council in 1995: "An attempt has been made in the study to assess the potential of Northeastern States to exports to Myanmar on the basis of the revenue endowments. Opening of border trade is expected to activate the industrialization process of the Northeastern States, taking into account export prospects offered not only by Myanmar but also by other Southeast

Asian Countries." (Study on Promotion of Border Trade Between India and Myanmar: 1995: p. 67). The resource base of Northeastern States particularly of Assam, Meghalaya and Tripura, as identified by the above mentioned report are:

Assam with a geographical area of 78438 sq.kms. and a population of 22.3 million in 1991 is the only Northeastern State having a reasonably good industrial base. Major industries of Assam are tea, plywood, crude oil and natural gas, coal, paper, petrochemicals, fertilizer and textiles. Assam accounts for more than 50% of tea produced in the country. There are 848 tea gardens in the State with as annual average production of 380 million kilograms.The State produces a variety of fruits including pineapples (184,485 tonnes), banana (538,442 tonnes), oranges (56,113 tonnes), and papaya (83,129 tonnes). Sericulture is a traditional industry of Assam. Eri,Muga and Mulberry are special types of silk produced in the State. Muga, in fact, is the monopoly of the State. Forest area covering 22% of the total land area of Assam contributes substantially to the State's revenue. Plywood and safety match industries are the major forest based industries. Handmade paper industry and cane and bamboo industry are the other industries at small and cottage level. Besides, there are more than 300 varieties of medicinal plants and herbs grown in the forest of Assam. Assam produces approximately 5 million tonnes of crude oil in a year, out of the total annual production of 34.4 million tonnes in the country. Natural gas output of the State is 3,740 million cubic meters per annum. It also has rich resources of coal, limestone, china clay, sillimanite, granite, barlys and gypsum. The Assam Industrial Development Corporation (AIDC) had identified potential areas for investment. These are hydro electric power based industries, food processing, floriculture, inland fishery, granite mining and polishing as export oriented industries and infrastructure projects.

The State of Tripura with total land area of 10,486 sq.kms. has a population of 2.7 million. It has an international border running into 839 km with Bangladesh, whereas its national boundary with Mizoram is 109 kms. and Assam 53 kms only. The economy of Tripura is agrarian, with paddy as its main agricultural crop. Other agricultural products are pulses, oil seeds and jute. Some horticultural products including oranges, pineapples, bananas, lemons and arecanuts are also grown in the State. Natural rubber has emerged as an important plantation product in the State. The State also produces 4 million kg. of tea annually. Forest, covering 34% of the total land area of the State contributes significantly to the economy of Tripura. Teak, agar, mahogany and sisu are grown in the forest. Medicinal plants like Nuxvemica are also available in the forests of Tripura. Bamboo-based handicraft industry is one of the main economic activities of the State. Though Tripura has natural gas deposits, it is yet to be exploited commercially. Industries having potential in the State on the basis of its natural resources are fertilizer units for urea and ammonia, power generation, natural rubber products like tyres, tubes and gloves, various processed food items, handmade paper and packing materials.

The State of Meghalaya is predominantly an agricultural economy, and has a total land area of 22,429 sq.kms. and a population of 1.7 million. The main crops of the State are rice, maize, wheat, potatoes, pulses and oilseeds. Other crops like juts, mesta, cotton, ginger, arecanut, betal leaves, pineapple, oranges and guava are also grown in the State. Meghalaya has rich mineral resources like coal, limestone, clay and sillimanite. Coal and limestone are being exported to Bangladesh through its border. Rich uranium deposits are also found in the State, which await exploitation. As the number of resource-based industries is limited, the State is industrially backward. Lack of proper industrial infrastructure prevents capital inflow into industrial sector. (pp. 68-71).

V

Recently, a team of Parliamentary Sub-Committee on Commerce, Government of India, when they visited Northeast India had advised the North-Eastern Council (NEC), to start a full fledged commerce wing headed by an adviser to co-ordinate efforts to promote exports from the Northeastern region to neighbouring countries, specially the South and Southeast Asian Countries. In a sense this indicates, that the

Northeastern region has immense potential to make use of its natural resources and achieve the goal of being economically independent.

Ever since Independence, the Northeastern region, had remained only as a stagnant back water in this eastern most corner of the Indian sub-continent. Even during the British rule, the foreigners were interested only to exploit the resources of the region, specially tea and oil and minerals like coal and also timber. There was no attempt whatsoever to put the region into the right track in which it could grow into an economically viable entity. It is only in the recent years, when militancy had raised its head, that the Government of India took notice of this region. The Commerce Parliamentary Committee had therefore correctly opined that, the Centre had done nothing to promote trade and commerce in the region despite its tremendous potentials.

As mentioned earlier the Indo-Myanmar trade treaty is an eye opener for the border trade and economic cooperation and development for the States in the Northeastern region with the immediate neighbouring countries. A more realistic and dynamic approach is needed from the Indian side, in the promotion of border trade with Bangladesh, if it is to be further expanded into a full fledged export and import activity. Therefore, the government at the Centre and at the State level should expedite the matters to improve the existing road condition on the border area, build a concrete Dawki bridge in place of the present one, improve the infrastructure, including transport and communication net-work which is very poor at the Indian side, more joint venture should be encouraged and efforts should be taken to utilize the port facilities in Bangladesh.

Lastly, we cannot agree more than to the observation drawn by Verghese in his recent study: "The future of the Northeast is inextricably linked with Bangladesh, Nepal, Bhutan, Burma and the lands beyond encompassing the Lower Ganga-Brahmaputra, Upper Yangtze, Mekong growth triangle (BRYMEK). In this design, the Northeast, with Chittagong, awaits rediscovery as a bridge on a lost crossroad of history between proud civilizations of yesterday and vibrant centres of emerging economic opportunity. There must, of course, be an internal resolution of the many ills of the Northeast. On the surface, things do not appear to have got any better there. This is however, no more than that moment of darkness that heralds the dawn. The morning midst may delay but cannot deny the promise of the day as it is touched by the sun which rises in the east." (Verghese, 1996).

References

A Grassroots Options Report, "Two Decades of ICAR in Northeast: Far Away From Farmer's Field and Heart", in Grassroots Options, (Shillong: February, 1997), pp. 19-24.

Bhattacharjee, J.B., "North-East Indian Perspectives in History", The Administrator, (New Delhi: Wiley Eastern Ltd., 1994), Vol. 34, October-December, 1994, pp. 1-7.

Chakravarty, Sumit, "Indo-Bangladesh Treaty on Sharing Ganga Water", Mainstream , Vol. 35, No. 5, January 11, 1997, pp. 28-29.

Indian Institute of Foreign Trade, Study on Promotion of Border Trade Between India and Myanmar, (New Delhi: 1995), p. 67; pp. 68-71. (Sponsored by the North Eastern Council).

Report of General Secretaries to the VIIIth General Conference (Special) of the North-East Congress(I) Coordination Committee held at Dimapur, Nagaland (June 22, 1993), The Administrator, Vol. 36, "A Scheme For Economic Development of Northeast", pp. 43-50.

Verghese, B.G., *India's Northeast Resurgent: Ethnicity, Insurgency, Governance, Development*, (New Delhi: Konark, 1996) p. 386.

Chapter 19

Liberalization, Ethnic Identity and Economic Development : A Case Study of Khasi and Jaintia Hills

—L.S. Gassah

The two oft quoted terms, globalization and liberalization, may not have much serious impact on North-East India as a whole and Meghalaya in particular until very recently. As far as Meghalaya's economy is concerned, the two terms have yet to strike their firm roots. This is due to the fact that industrialization, in the true sense of the term, cannot be said to have its impact on the state and its people. But then, when one analyzes the situation, the experiences, the ups and downs of the tribal economy and trade relations at the grass-root level of the trans-border people, we do find an impact of globalization, though at a different footing.

The necessities of life sometimes know no man-made political boundaries. Partition of the Indian sub-continent had taken place and political boundaries drawn; official movement of people across the border was not permitted. Trade and commerce was also stopped or if allowed, it has to be performed only on the basis of the official trade treaties signed between the two parties—any act beyond the official sanction may be treated as illegal. Against this background, many perplexed issues and questions may emanate as to the condition of the trans-border people. This paper seeks to analyze the issues relating to the questions of liberalization, ethnic identity and economic development with special reference to the Khasi and Jaintia Hills of Meghalaya.

The first part of the paper proposes to deal with the historical background of the close link and relationship between the people of Khasi-Jaintia Hills and that of the plains across the international border of the present nation of Bangladesh. The contact between the Khasi-Jaintia people and that of the plains of Sylhet can be said to have started many centuries back. Regular border trade or 'frontier traffic' was conducted through those *hats* on specific days in a week. During those market days, the population living on both sides of the international border are able to exchange and trade their various products.[1] This contact was easier during the pre-British days as there was no restriction of the movement of the people. Moreover, this earlier contact was possible because the Jaintia kingdom itself extended deep into the southern plains of Sylhet known as the 'Jaintia Parganas'. The Jaintia Rajas (Raja to his subjects in the plains, *Syiem* to his people in the hills) had their personal authority and control over their subjects in the plains. As such, maximum revenue of the kingdom was imposed and collected by the Jaintia *Syiems* from their subjects in the plains. This southern plain territory of the kingdom was annexed by the British in 1835 and the British Political Agent took over the administration of the hills also on the 15th March 1835. The same year, the British abolished the office of the Jaintia *Syiem* but retained the offices of the other traditional chiefs like the *Doloi, Pator* and village headman. Like the Jaintia kingdom, certain areas in the plains of Sylhet were also under the jurisdiction of some of the Khasi States.

The British colonial rule accelerated the process of extraneous domination through the markets that had emerged as the sensitive pressure points in tribal economy. The colonial restructurisation of the socio-economic institutions in the hills of the area under study, was intended to serve the British interests by ensuring the regular flow of income. But the trade relationship between the hills and plains had at times been adversely affected by the retaliatory challenges of both the Khasis and Jaintias who had been known by the British as troublesome marauders upon the plains of Sylhet where they were much dreaded. It was reported that because of these ravages, a line of forts was kept under the hills to check these incursions.[2]

Although occasional raids and skirmishes in the frontier took place between the fierce tribes from the Hills and the plainsmen, business transactions were however carried on when a peaceful atmosphere prevailed. With regard to the Jaintia kingdom, Jaintiapur was its capital in the plains. Jaintiapur also served as an entrepot between the hills and the plains which led to an extensive trade and commercial relationship. Pemberton was of the opinion that a considerable trade in cotton, iron ore, wax, ivory, *paan*(betel leaf) and clothes, was carried on between the plains and the hills... The articles specified were bartered for salt, tobacco, rice and goats.[3] This account gives a clear picture of the trade and commercial dealings transacted between the inhabitants of Khasi-Jaintia Hills and that of the plains of Sylhet during the period as far back as 1834.

The Khasi-Jaintia economy depended much on the markets along the foothills. The increasing dependence on these markets in later years was particularly due to the absence of professional social groups of artisans and craftsmen which stood in the way of effective social formation. It was reported that in the hill districts there were considerable differences in extent in which the tribesmen engaged in trade. Further, in most of these tracts, frontier traffic was a necessary of life, the hills not producing sufficient food for the people to live upon; but in most also it took the simple form of barter, the exports consisting chiefly of cotton, wax, ivory and forest produce, and the imports of rice, salt, dried fish and clothes.[4] But in the Khasi and Jaintia Hills, there was a much more active commerce, and the trade in the commodities like limestone, iron ore, wax ivory and forest produce was kept by the people almost entirely in their own hands. Many of them were adventurous merchants, travelling as far as Dacca (Dhaka), or even Calcutta during the cold season.[5] In particular, the Jaintia traders were adventurous enough in extending their areas of trading as far as Calcutta, Udalguri and Bhutan.[6]

The presence of vast reserves of coal and limestone in Khasi and Jaintia Hills, encouraged the local people to engage themselves in exploiting these minerals even in the past, though it was done in a very primitive way and essentially for their domestic consumption and local supply. Even then, it is well known that individuals had embarked on mining and quarrying with the expectations of large profits, which in some instances at least have been realized.[7] The British authorities right from the time of the East India Company had realized the abundant reserves of coal in the area and with their astute administration and farsightedness, soon embarked themselves on commercial exploitation of it. The coal mines of Khasi and Jaintia Hills were then leased out to Messers Inglis and Company, and others as well, out of which a huge amount of revenue was received annually by the East India Company.

Besides coal, limestone of excellent quality was also found in abundance both in Khasi and Jaintia Hills. The need and demands of the people in the neighbouring area of the plains were therefore provided and immediately fed through the supply of limestone from the hills. The earlier records indicated that lower Bengal obtained nearly the whole of its lime supply from the Khasi and Jaintia Hills. The lime was known as 'Sylhet lime', and obtained by quarrying from the beds of stone which line the base of the mountains along the whole length of the Sylhet boundary. The supply was literally inexhaustible and the wants of Calcutta and of the whole of lower Bengal had been satisfied from these hills from time immemorial.

There were many other essential items produced by the Khasi and Jaintia people which found a great demand and ready markets in the southern plains. The border markets bordering Khasi-Jaintia Hills with that of Sylhet were actually fed by the produce of the hills. Essential items like oranges, betelnuts, betel-leaves and other horticultural crops found ready markets in Sylhet and other border *hats*.

The Khasi-Jaintia people are believed to be the first to have started trade and commerce with the people of the then East Bengal (now Bangladesh) especially that of Sylhet district in the pre-partition period. On the basis of the accounts relating to trade relations and commercial dealings between Sylhet and its highland neighbours, two important features are explicitly noticeable in which the Khasi-Jaintia people contributed to their neighbours in the southern plains; firstly, that they were 'the first from the hills to put their feet on the soils of Sylhet' and secondly, they were 'the first customers of all products' in the plains of that district. This, therefore, explained and confirmed the extent of trade relationship between the people of the two different areas. Morever, trading between them was not a one sided affair but rather there was an equal exchange of goods and commodities from both sides. Thus, besides trade in coal, limestones and oranges, the natural outlet for the latter being the markets in the plains, there were hosts of things supplied to the plains which included big stones for embankments, *silbatas* (grinding stones), potatoes, fresh vegetables and fruits, the hot favourites of Sylhetees, the *satkoras, tezpata,* timber for boat making. In return, the people of Sylhet supplied coarse rice, dry fish, the hot favourite of every home in the hills, fish and a lot of other essential commodities. At one time, the markets of Sylhet were the base for almost all the consumer's goods that went to at least the southern side of Khasi and Jaintia Hills.[8]

During the British rule, the fast development of trade and commerce between the Khasi-Jaintia people and that of the plains of Sylhet was possible and encouraging because of the presence of different means of communication like bridle paths, the use of navigable rivers up to certain points and roads. Though some of these means of communications were in a crude form, they served a useful purpose in transportation of goods and materials to and fro the hills and plains. For example, the road which was declared open by Sir Michael Keane, then Governor of Assam, in 1933, linked Sylhet-Shillong-Gauhati. Since then, this road became the life-line of trade and commerce and a major important link between the hills and plains. Besides this, it also played an important role because of the fact that it connected all the major and important administrative centres, both in the Surma and Brahmaputra valleys. Shillong, then the capital of the province of Assam, as well as the other hill areas were also linked up with both the northern and southern plains of the province. With the opening up of the above mentioned road, communication was easy and saved a lot of time and trouble of traveling between the hills and plains.

The transfer of power in 1947, and the change of administration thereafter, brought a heavy burden and an immense impact on the economic life of the people living in the border areas of Khasi and Jaintia Hills. Their relation in trade and commerce with their counterparts in the plains was drastically disturbed and a severe setback in the exchange of goods and essential commodities took place. There was also a setback of marketing facilities soon after the partition of the country into India and Pakistan and later Bangladesh in 1971.

While trying to analyze the immense impact of the partition of 1947, one writer was of the opinion that the ultimate halt of the entire trade between the hills and the plains in Khasi and Jaintia Hills and Sylhet, was due to the shortsighted policy of the erstwhile government of Pakistan, the policy which was to starve the neighbouring area in India, their avowed enemies, of their normal and legitimate facilities.[9]

The after-effect of partition of 1947 brought untold miseries and hardships to the people living in the Border Areas of the two neighbouring countries who were actually the worst sufferers due to the sealing off and the closure of the border trade and commerce immediately after 1947. This led to a total dislocation of trade and commerce. At a particular period of time, an agreement was arrived at between the Government of India and Pakistan. According to this agreement, certain commodities were allowed for export to East Pakistan by the people of Meghalaya. The items agreed upon for export were candle, Indian ware, earthen ware, turmeric, vegetables of local produce, fruits of local produce, limestone, ginger, spices, hardwood, durgents, betel-leaves, pots, fuel, thatching grass, bamboos, stones, boulders and shingles.[10] From the number of items included under the agreement for export, it looked very promising and encourag–

ing and could surely bring once again the lost grounds and contact. It looked as though the missing link will be brought back again to life and prosperity would come in the way of the people living in the border which had so long eluded them. But unfortunately, this arrangement was purely temporary and shortlived one. It did not bring any relief at all to the affected people of the area under study.

There was an air of expectation for things to improve better and specially in terms of increase in volume of trade and commerce between India and Bangladesh after the liberation of the latter in 1971. The people living in the border areas with Bangladesh expected that better relationship, at least in trade would prevail between the two countries and this would lead to the reopening of the border markets. There was no doubt an attempt between the two governments to officially channelise the trade between the bordering neighbours and exchange their normal necessities through official channels, but this too, as it happened before with the Pakistan government was short-lived and therefore once again belied the hopes and expectations of the people when the whole border was again sealed off and markets across the international border were closed down. The economic prospects of the people therefore came to a near standstill. The precarious condition of trade and the sinking of prices due to the closure of the border markets was noticeable all along the border belt. The volume of trade and output at that point of time, were at bottom level since the economy was oriented towards the Sylhet markets in the plains. An official dossier records that the prices of produce sank to an unbelievably low levels. Worse still, there was no one to lift the produce in the absence of an easy means of transport link and communication with the alternative markets in the rest of India. The people specializing in orchard cultivation were at a distinct disadvantage in learning or initiating any new techniques of cultivation of other crops. With the opening up of a few vital roads, alternative markets were found, but transporting the produce to the focal points posed a great problem. Many a time, unscrupulous businessmen took advantage of the situation. They bought the goods from the local producers and paid them at a throw-away price since there is no other alternative left to them.

The reopening of a few border *hats* for a brief period between December 1970 and March 1971, seemed to suggest the fact that the people living on both sides of the international border shared the same suffering from the closure of the border and markets set up therein. In 1972, there was another agreement signed known as Indo-Bangladesh Trade Agreement, 1972. Article IV of the agreement reads as follows:

> *In order to meet the day to day requirements of the people living within a sixteen kilometre belt of border between West Bengal, Assam, Meghalaya, Tripura and Mizoram on the one hand and Bangladesh on the other and with a view to providing facilities to these people to dispose their goods, border trade shall be allowed in specified commodities in accordance with 'Schedule B' attached to the Agreement.*

The salient features for the operation of the border trade were *(i)* entry of the individual trader was to be regulated by the issue of permit by the local authorities on both sides, *(ii)* only the specified items in given quantities could be exchanged or purchased, *(iii)* border trade would not be subject to the normal export, import and exchange regulations as well as custom formalities, and *(iv)* each trader could carry an amount not more than Rs/Taka 100 when crossing the border from either country into the other. Although border trade between the two countries started in middle of April 1972, in actual effect, it did not take off the ground because firstly it took considerable time to devise instructions for the issue of special permit, which was the principal instrument of control and then finalization of measures on routes, check posts, travel and custom documents and common inspection facilities. However, after a six-month period due to complain by the Bangladesh government of large-smuggling, accordingly border trade between the two countries was suspended with effect from 13.10.1972.[11] Position of the ground realities is however a different story altogether.

The above analysis of the economic situation that prevai-led in Khasi and Jaintia Hills both during the pre and post

British period as well as India's independence, shows the interlink and mutual feeling of dependency of the people living on both sides of the international border on each other. Even after the official closure of the border markets, it is noteworthy to state that economic necessities know no border.The people from both sides of the international border on their own initiative still continue to have unofficial contact and trading.

Economic liberalization must take into consideration this kind of frustration and economic suffocation created by building up walls of separation. Against this background, perhaps the recent initiative taken by both the governments of India and Bangladesh to relieve this frustration is a welcome gesture. The official opening of the trade relations in the border areas of Meghalaya with that of Bangladesh has come at the right time. The recent official delegations from the North Eastern States having experienced the difficulties faced by their own people have done an appreciable act to liberate the people who had suffered economically for a pretty long time. The past experiences of opening up of border markets or trade relations for a short period only and then close them down must not be perpetuated. Past experiences call for a lasting economic liberalization.

The search by the Khasi and Jaintia people for better economic avenues and opportunities led them not only to have some kind of understanding with their counterparts across the international border, be it during the time of the Government of Pakistan or Bangladesh today, but this economic dependency urged or shall we say, even forced them to physically cross the border and look for greener areas of cultivation. Migration of the trans-border people is therefore a two way traffic. The official closure of the international border could not stop them.

There are few pertinent issues which may be raised here regarding the question of ethnic identity of those people who have voluntarily migrated to the then East Pakistan or Bangladesh of today. With the question of ethnic identity, such other issues like adjustment and adaptation of these people in a foreign land, their socio-economic condition and activities, their relationship with their kith and kin in India, the problem of religion as well as their children's education and the whole issue of ethnic identity crisis in a foreign land with foreign culture and religious belief—all these issues need to be analyzed empirically.

Majority of the Khasi-Jaintia people who crossed over the international border to settle down in the then East Pakistan continued to remain there even after Bangladesh came into existence. Almost cent percent of them came from the border villages of Khasi and Jaintia Hills. The people who inhabited the precipitous slopes of Khasi and Jaintia Hills are experts in betel-leaf, betel-nut and orange cultivation. The failure to grow and produce betel-leaf in the slopes and foothills of Khasi-Jaintia Hills due to certain plant diseases, forced these people to look for new cultivable lands. They found the forests and soil of the then East Pakistan and now Bangladesh as better alternatives. This led them to leave their hearths and homes in India in pursuit of their agricultural activities in a foreign land. Though a majority of these people are illiterate, they however did well in their economic activities. The soil and forests of Bangladesh provide them a better opportunity to continue their profession even if it is in a foreign land.

As far as the question of adjustment and adaptation in a foreign land, it does not pose much of a problem. It may be noted that even if these people come from a neighbouring foreign land, they are not much disturbed both politically and socially by the local government. The fact is that they try as far as possible not to get themselves involved with the politics of that country and concentrated only on their economic activities. Secondly, the local government received a good amount of revenue out of the betel-leaf, the production of which is done by the Khasi-Jaintia people. This is another reason why they are not much disturbed by the local authorities.

Though Bangladesh follows Islam as one of its religions, the Khasi-Jaintia people living in that country who are mainly Christians by faith, are not restricted or debarred to continue worship in their own religion. In some of the villages inhabited by the Khasi and Jaintia people where the author visited, found that they have full freedom of worship in their own religious faith. On Sundays, it was found that all the village gates were closed and business transactions stopped; no interference from outside was allowed. In terms of the children's education there are some problems due to the absence of schools where their own vernacular is taught. This is of course compensated by sending their children to schools and even colleges taught either in Bengali or English medium. Few such students have studied even at the University level. This view is of course an impressionistic one, and it is therefore felt necessary to have a more empirical study on this very important aspect.

With regard to the relationship of those people who have crossed the international border to settle in a foreign land with their kith and kin on the other side of the border, the same way of their unofficial economic relationship may be applied. Some of them keep on coming and going or crossing the border in their own way or arrangement without disturbing the custom officials or border security forces. That way, their relationship with their kith and kin on both sides of the border poses not much of a problem.

Crisis of ethnic identity broadly speaking is sometimes unnecessarily created due to hatred of each other either politically or culturally. This hatred also emanated because of the fact that we keep in thinking that our neighbour's garden on the other side of the fence is always greener than that of our own. This may be termed loosely as an ethnic fad.

References

1. For further details see the following research papers by the same author:

   (i) 'Pattern of Economic Change in Jaintia Society', NEHU Journal of Social Sciences and Humanities, Vol. vii, No. 4, Oct-Dec., 1990.

   (ii) 'Effect of Partition on the Border Markets of Jaintia Hills', in *Marketing in North-East India,* (Ed) J.B. Ganguly, Omsons Publications, New Delhi, 1984.

(iii) 'Trade Routes and Trade Relations between Jaintia Hills and Sylhet District in the pre-independence period', *Proceedings of NEIHA* (Ninth Session), Gauhati, 1988.

(iv) 'Impact of Partition and after on the Economic Life of the Border Areas of Jaintia Hills District', Journal of Social Research, Shillong, 1990.

2. *Report on the Administration of North-East India*, Mittal Publications, Delhi, 1984 (Reprint), p. 41 (footnote).
3. Pemberton, R.B., *Report on the Eastern Frontier of British India*, Gauhati, 1966 (Reprint), p. 224.
4. There is a similarity of the Garo situation with that of the Khasi-Jaintia Hills. For details see, Bhattacharjee, J.B., 'Pattern of Economic Change in Garo Society', in *Garo Hills : Land and the People,* (ed), LS Gassah, Omsons Publications, New Delhi, 1984.
5. Note 2, *op. cit.*, p. 29.
6. Gait, Edward, *A History of Assam* (1905), Gauhati 1984 (Reprint) pp. 358-59.
7. Hunter, W.W., *A Statistical Account of Assam,* Vol II (1879), P.R. Publishing Corp., Delhi, 1975, (Reprint), pp. 233-34.
8. Choudhury, A.R., 'Sylhet and its Trade with Highland Neighbours', Souvenir, The Frontier Chamber of Commerce, Shillong, 1972, p. 43.
9. *Ibid.*
10. *Provincial Meghalaya Legislative Assembly Debates,* Vol. II, No. I, 22 Sept., 1970, p. 52.
11. Agnihotri, S.K., 'Border Trade with Bangladesh', *Journal of NEICSSR,* Vol. 17:2, October 1993, Shillong, p. 30.

PART FIVE

LIBERALIZATION : REFLECTIONS ON NORTH-EASTERN SITUATION

Chapter 20

LIBERALIZATION AND THE PROBLEM OF THE NORTH-EASTERN REGION

—Ranjit De

Globalization of economy is a misnomer; in India, of course, globalization, liberalization or economic reform or some other terminologies are being used with equal force. Liberalization or economic reforms and other phrases like structural changes, to some extent, carry some obvious meaning but globalization in India's context or in the context of any underdeveloped country, hardly betrays the truth. In recent years, what have been theoretically proposed and practically introduced, cannot justifiably termed as globalization.

Production has two major factors; one is the capital and the other, no less important factor, is the labour. The liberalization of the so-called structural reform has simply paved the path for the capital's free movement without any national barrier but movement of the labour remained restricted as before. Therefore, globalization of economy is a half truth. Despite this unsavoury reality, loud claims are being made. Many advocates of the new reforms are not only making loud propaganda (often dishonest) but are really inclined to believe that the panacea of the economic ills, the country had suffered so long, lie in globalization of our economy. In their opinion, the closed door economy in the name of self reliance, an ideology strongly nourished during the independence struggle and a kind of regulated economy with licensing control of the industries, etc. in a bid to develop a planned economy, has wrought havoc with country's development. In this back-drop, new orientation of ideology, the slogan of liberalization has been formulated; foreign multinationals and other alien capital has been given free entry into our economy; in many areas, these companies have been allowed fifty one percent equity participation; custom tariff has been drastically reduced with an aim to allow easy entry of the foreign commodities. On top of all, a philosophy of de-regulated economy, *i.e.*, non intervention by the government in the economy in terms of licensing control etc. has been disseminated powerfully. Along with this, a propaganda campaign on the so called inefficiency of the public sector has been unleashed: the result has been to attempt at large-scale dismantling of the public sectors; disinvestment even of many profit earning public sector units has been carried out with impunity.

This philosophy was gaining currency from the early eighties but suddenly from the nineties, during Mr. Narasimha Rao's Regime, the pace of its implementation became tremendous and the theoretical milieu became surcharged with this philosophy, neglecting other schools into the background. A cross-section of critics feel that this shift in policy-formulation has been at the behest of the International Monetary Fund and the World Bank. While others are of the opinion that one should not marvel at the theoretical novelty—the drift is simply into a neo-classical model from the theoretical shackle of the regulated economy.

This write up offers no scope for a theoretical polemic between Keynesianism(regulated economy) and neo-classicism but certainly warrants a debate between the Nehruvian concept which, according to many theorists, are based on the Keynesian recipes and the braggadocio of liberalization, mainly an offspring of the neo-classicism.

There are critics of Nehruvian economy (for want of proper phrase, this popular terminology is used here even though many critics are averse to the term; however the term has come to stay in the vocabulary of the political science and conveys clear connotation to the common readerdom). These critics consists mainly of left and right schools apart from a motley crowd of intelligentsia. The rights were wholesale opposed to the theory and practice of the economy while the left were critical of the half hearted measure that the policy formulation had adopted over time. Despite these criticism, the merit of the Nehruvian economy can be enumerated as follows :

(i) Endeavour to build up heavy industries with a view to overcoming the dependence on Western economy.

(ii) Building up of a public sector, mainly in the area of infrastructure and heavy industries; these heavy industries and public sector units are the biggest source of employment.

(iii) Five-year plans with their aims to abolish regional imbalances; plans not only to have target for development in the public sector but also to facilitate growth of private sectors.

(iv) A certain kind of regulation of the economy through industrial licensing system.

(v) In the fifties, land reform and abolition of landlordism; it is true that land reform was not radical enough and all the vestiges of feudalism was not radically eradicated; but this limited kind of reform also had given fillip to the economy.The broad frame of the reform in economy and the old Nehruvian pattern is somewhat critically placed above. This will help us in understanding the impact of the economic reform on the economy of the North-Eastern Region (if such isolation is permissible in gauging the economic development) and also on socio-political issues. For this, of course, collation of performance between Nehruvian economy and the loud claim of the reform, may provide a clearer picture.

The reaction of the mainland (the terminology is used not from any ulterior motive; the phrase has an innocuous meaning, giving a vague but surer geo-political demarcation) where both industrial development and remnants of medieval or semi-medieval socio-economic institutions are staying in wedlock till date, will offer to the reform effort, can easily be visualized and in fact, clear picture is already available; the big business and the industrial houses have gone the whole hog to welcome the reform; their ideologies are waxing eloquent on the extension of the measures. But unfortunately, the toilers of all shades and hues, could not yet develop any definite view; left-political parties also have elusive views; initially a sharp view was formulated; masses of the people were given to understand that the country's sovereignty is being surrendered and organized resistance was also offered. But since then, much water has flown down the Ganges and a very thin line of demarcation with that formulated by the reform-enthusiasts, has been drawn up now. It has been accepted that in the area where we lack expertise, participation of the multinationals in the joint sectors (*i.e.*, collaboration between the state, Indian capital and the multinationals) is not un-welcome. In this shift there may be an element of pragmatism and wisdom, but common toilers have the feeling of confusion.

The circumstances and the milieu of the North-Eastern Region is basically different from the brief picture of the mainland outlined above. To understand tne North-Eastern situation *vis-a-vis* the reform, one has to travel in retrospect into the areas of historico-economic development which will unfold the unsavoury fact that except distinct areas in the Assam and Barak Valleys, the socio-economic formation of the North-Eastern Region remained tribal for centuries. Even during the British Rule, when the mainland India passed through many phases of change, the society in the North-Eastern Region underwent no change at all. But many sociologist may not make common course with me and they may argue that British rule and the advent of Christianity had imparted mobility to these vegetative societies. This is undoubtedly a misconception for two plain reasons. First, British administration as an avowed policy did not bring about any institutional change. Even the commodity economy made no inroad. Secondly, spread of Christianity could not delve deep into the structural fabric of the tribal institutions. One may even wonder to see that Christianity had to strike compromises with tribal religious institutions. Therefore the argument of social mobility resulting into stratification of the society, is far fetched. But remarkable changes that followed the independence of the country, can not escape anybody's notice. But the investigations of these phenomena have to make a thorough probe into basic factors as given below:

(i) Whether the political policies pursued by the power-that-be, were really conducive to impart dynamism to the hitherto existing vegetative social formation.

(ii) The economic policies of the country as a whole or the specific policy for the North-Eastern Region, if there was at all any, was instrumental for these changes.

The Nehruvian policy towards the North-Eastern Region's tribes was very simple; it immanated from his deep-rooted humanitarian outlook. Along with Verrier Elwin, he formulated policies that would in the least disturb the simple life of these tribes. These policies were the manifestation of his love for these people but betrayed no scientific outlook towards socio-political problems. He forgot that in a fast changing world, the archaic social formation is an anachronism and the sooner it is elevated into modern social formation, better it is for the people. True, often the process of development is painful but history has sanctioned no other alternative.

With regard to the economic policies, one can safely say that no specific emphasis was ever given to the question of development in North-Eastern Region. Even the merits of Nehruvian economy referred to above *vis-a-vis* the economic reform, can not claim any special contribution towards the development in the North-Eastern Region. But the general spurt of the economic development throughout the country during the post independent period, made certain impact on the socio-economic formation of the tribal North-Eastern Region, the commodity economy made fast inroad into the natural economy (or the tribal economy); and this was responsible for coalescing many tribes and elevation of them into nationalities. This is an epoch-making phenomenon. All socio-political ferment for which of late North-Eastern Region has attained conspicuity, may safely be traced to this new development. Unfortunately, this phenomenon was not an end in itself; this gave rise to two factors:

(i) The aspiration for self-assertion of these nationalities within the comity of Indian nationalities.

(ii) The problem of retaining identity in view of the large scale influx of members from other nationalities.

It is true, the vested interest over magnifies the issue but despite this, the reality remains that the threat of being swamped is not unfounded. The problem was combated with the use of political power and even occasionally abusing that power. But this was feasible within the confine of Nehruvian economy only. For the aspiration of economic development, to a large extent, was satisfied through the developments in the public sector. One will certainly not miss that whatever economic development worth its name has taken place in the region, is only in the public sector. This, of course, was not fortuitous nor simply because of the virtues in the Nehruvian model of economic development. There were specific socio-economic reasons. This situation may be explained as follows:

During the post independent era, economic development (capitalist development) in the country was rather fast and this was responsible for the disintegration of the tribal formation, giving rise to stratification in the hitherto existing egalitarian societies; emergence of the social classes, specially a middle class who has severed its relation with older mode of production in the society, was the special feature in this period. Obviously, emerging as they were, these social forces were very weak; they lacked the expertise of entrepreneurship and did not also possess the capital. Therefore, on private endeavour, any development worth-noticing, did not come up in this region. Meanwhile, appearance of the monopoly houses in the mainland and their control over the economy has adversely affected the possibility of development of private entrepreneurship. Therefore, only escape route remained in the development of the public sector enterprises. The regulation of the economy through licensing was of no avail either. In this domain also, the control of the big-business was not less.

One who agrees with me, will obviously reach the conclusion from the above analysis that backwardness and underdevelopment of the North-Eastern Region, is not solely a fallout of willful neglect and wrong policy formulation *vis-a-vis* the problems of development in the region. To a major extent, the causes lie in the historicity of this region.

In my opinion, Nehruvian economy and not the Nehruvian socio-political policies, was a better lever for the uplift of this region. This was all under old dispensation.

Under the new dispensation, under the slogan of globalization, liberalization and structural reform, how the question of the development of the North-Eastern Region in which day in day out, the media and the leadership in New Delhi, express their too much concern, is to be understood, is again a very knotty issue. How far the historical disability of this region described above will go to determine the prospect of development here or as the admirers of the reform often suggest that the socio-cultural structural handicap or for that matter any other disability, can not thwart the pace of development, because the enormous force the reform will generate, will sweep away all hindrance the socio-political backwardness may offer, requires to be analyzed here. Let me take up the issue as follows:

The practical ambience in the country is not yet radically changed though the spiritual milieu is surcharged with the philosophy of the reform, globalization and structural changes in our economy. This is of course, not to suggest that nothing in practice is being done. Many practical steps have already been taken. The process of disinvestment in the public sectors, reducing customs and other tariffs, opening up many areas to the foreign multinationals, allowing them more than 51% of equity participation, convertibility of rupee and many other steps have already been taken and some are on the offing. And on top of all, the philosophy of privatization *i.e.,* the superiority of private sector over the public sectors, are being hurled at us. How far this new orientation in the economic policies will have impact on the development in the mainland, no one can vouchsafe except the reform enthusiast. Now let me turn to the problems of the North-Eastern Region.

Apart from the general impact the country's economy will witness, some major shifts that have been ushered in by this reform, will have very conspicuous effect on the development and the development strategy of the North-Eastern Region. Let me enumerate them below:

(i) Abandonment of mixed economy *i.e.,* development through both private and public sectors. Over emphasis on the private sector and discontinuance of state's intervention and abandoning the concept of welfare economy.

(ii) Opening up the economy to the foreign multi and transnationals.

For understanding the impact of the first reform measure, one can not only rely upon the economic theories but will have to make a thorough probe into the socio-economic institutions of the area. History has long established that the vehicle of industrial development is a social class. If we are prepared to take our lessons from the long course of the world economy, events and periods like industrial revolution, enlightenment and many other which have been standing out in the boldest relief, we will certainly agree that the vehicle of the industrial development is a social class *viz.,* the middle class (bourgeoisie). Indian experience also corroborate this; the middle class were the harbinger of the industrial entrepreneurship in the country. I have already in the foregoing established that North-Eastern Region during the post independent era has undergone considerable change and social stratification in the egalitarian fabric also had taken place. The middle class who were the major vehicle of industrialization has also emerged. But this class here obviously is very weak and yet to develop into a matured force capable of big initiative—social, political and above all economic. This will be vindicated if I analyze the composition of the class in Meghalaya, where this class is by far the strongest compared to its counterparts in other states in the region. The middle class in Meghalaya mainly consists of contractors and suppliers, officials, lawyers, teachers, petty shop owners, businessmen and a handful of quarry owners (coal quarry). If Meghalaya betrays this picture, one can easily visualize what picture the Meghalaya's counterpart can offer. However, the point I want to make here is that the middle class of this region lack the expertise of an industrialist and also ostensibly lack the capital and other qualities. Now, under the new dispensation of market economy, when option is cut throat competition in the arena of entrepreneurship, where do these weak bourgeoisie of the region stand. In this situation, if development (which obviously mean industrial development) is on the agenda, the initiative is bound to pass on to the mainland bourgeoisie and to the foreign multinationals. One may suggest that such developments are welcome; and in fact, many economists are on their toe to welcome this: of late, one of the theorists of globalization of economy of great repute, Shri Kaushik Bose in an article published in the EPW had aired this type of opinion. He wrote:

> *Over the years, a mistaken sense of nationalism among the intelligentsia together with the indigenous businessmen's sense of property right over the domestic market fueled a kind of economic xenophobia.....*(**Economic and Political Weekly, Vol XXVIII No. 48, Nov. 27, 1993**)

The above quote ostensibly suggests a freer movement of the capital without any consideration of ethnicity (to be precise the question of nationality). As I have already in the foregoing made an innuendo on this claim if globalization to the effect that giving up of national or for that matter any ethnic conception, paves the path for freer movement of capital and not that of labour. I now venture to add that the advocates of globalization particularly those nations who are in the forefront of such dissemination like the U.S.A., are most conservative in respect of globalization of labour. Again in this context, I wish to remind the protagonist of the globalization that the concept of nation and national interest are the determining factors of all eco-political issues. May I point an argument for the consumption of Mr.Bose & Co.? Will the U.S.A. allow foreign multinationals to control its home economy?

In the back drop of the above exacerbation, I surmise that an aspiration of the nationalities in the North-Eastern Region to control the home economy must be uppermost in their mind and there is nothing illegitimate about it. But the reform has put the people here in an ambivalent situation. Let me summarize the position.

Development which in the contemporary world, means industrialization in real sense of the term, is the natural aspiration of all people. The people in the North-Eastern Region are also in the same boat. But difficulty for them is formidable; under the new economic policy, if industrialization of the region is meant in right earnest, the economic control will pass into the mainland bourgeoisie or the multinationals. In that case, the option left will be to oppose all industrial development. I can say this a veritable situation where on the one side the tiger and on the other the precipice.

In conclusion, I may suggest that the leaders and the ideologues in the North-Eastern Region will do well if they remember the positive aspects of the mixed economy (Nehruvian Economy) specially the features like development of the public sectors. Capitulation before the wild propaganda will do immense harm.

Chapter 21

LIBERALIZATION IN THE CONTEXT OF NORTH-EAST INDIA : A COMMENT

—Debasish Bhattacharjee

The twin processes of 'globalization' and 'liberalization' are so much discussed and debated that they have become the catchwords in both academic and non-academic discussions. Generally in all discussions, globalization and liberalization are either supported or opposed without an attempt to put them in their historical perspectives. Here in this paper, an attempt is made to put globalization and liberalization in their historical perspective and then to take note of their possible impact on north-east India. This is felt necessary, for things are to be studied in their structured inter-connections and not in isolation.

Globalization is not a sudden development. It is the result of world-wide capitalist development in the post world war period. The over accumulation of productive capital in the metropolitan centers at the end of the boom period resulted in increased competition for profit. This increased competition for profit on its turn put pressure for the expansion of capital beyond the national boundaries.[1] This expansion could be made effective only through integrating the peripheral economy with the world economy dominated by the metropolitan centers. This integration demands what is called 'liberalization'. Liberalization is a process of opening up the national economy through the measures of de-control and de-regulation in order to facilitate the free flow of capital.

The Government of India initiated the process of globa–lization in 1991 and had adopted different measures to integrate her economy with the world economy. While India is trying to integrate her economy with that of the world economy, a question that naturally arises is to what extent her different regions and sub-regions have been integrated with the national economy. This is perhaps the most important question in considering the prospect of development of the north-east in the liberalized era. For, the idea of liberalization is based on the assumption that free market economy would ensure a better economic management by an entrepreneurial class at different levels and it would also ensure the flow of both national and international capital. In other words, the advocates of liberalization argue that free flow of capital and goods in a liberalized era would ensure efficiency and equalization of return. But it is unlikely that north-eastern region will derive much benefits on this count.

To begin with, north-east India, especially its tribal belts, does not have an entrepreneurial class that can reap the benefit of free market. Lack of entrepreneurship in tribal areas is partly because of the policies pursued in reference to the north-east. The tribals of the north-east were mostly cut off from the rest of India. Their social life did not extend much beyond their community and consequently, there was an isolationist attitude which was further reinforced by the legal and administrative policies pursued by the colonial rulers. The tribal economy was primitive agricultural subsistence economy that could hardly produce any surplus. As a result, the entrepreneurial activities were absent amongst the tribals and hardly any tribal was engaged in trading or commercial activities worth the name. Trade and commerce was in the hands of the people from outside the region who, for different reasons, have been parceling out the profit they make through their efforts. Things did not change much even after independence. During the last fifty years of independence north-east India has undergone reorganization hitherto unparalleled and this has resulted in the creation of new power elites on the one hand, and a new economic elite on the other. While the power elites have been engaged in manipulating power, the economic elites have been engaged in making quick fortune through contract, government supply, and through trade in forest and other natural resources. This new rich section preferred trade to production and thus failed to make any effective contribution to the socio-economic re-construction of the region. Besides, the elites have stalled the introduction of land reforms, the pre-condition to generate developmental incentives at the lowest level[2] and have also misused the developmental funds that have been made available to the region. Center, being dependent on such elites in tribal and backward pockets, turned a blind eye to the plunder and loot.[3]

Again, the north-eastern region can hardly attract much national and international capital. This is so, because private investors being guided by profit motive are not likely to be interested in investing funds in a backward area lacking infrastructural facilities. Besides lagging behind the national average in terms of roadways, railways and *per-capita* consumption of electricity,[4] the very geographical location of the region makes it unattractive to outside investors.

Under the present policy regime center is less likely to play a key role in the development of the state as it was the case in the past. Under the system of bureaucratic controls, the center played a key role in infrastructural development. But now the role of the center is increasingly becoming more and more parasitic. The huge volume of taxes that the center extracts would go towards servicing the debts, especially the debts contracted from IMF and World Bank; maintaining the army and paramilitary forces; and maintaining its own parasitic establishments. The state governments of North-East can hardly think of removing the bottlenecks on their own. The reorganization of North-East resulting in the multiplication of states was a decision prompted by political expediency without any consideration of economic viability. None of the states in the North-East is economically self-sufficient nor can generate enough resources to meet its own requirements. Hence the state governments doing much for infrastructure development is out of question.

At the theoretical level, it might be argued that a bulk of the capital can come from private sources. But the socio-political condition of the North-East India acts as disincentive to the private investors. For historical and political reasons outsiders are suspect to the North-East. The system of inner line permit regulates the free movement and the licensing principle is discriminatory in many states. Racial/ethnic militancy poses a continuous threat to the life and property of the people. The business houses from outside the states and the people of racial origin other than the localities are doubly taxed—statutory tax by the state and non-statutory one by the militants and outfits. In many cases, students organizations and militant outfits compel the entrepreneurial/business houses to employ people of their choice. All these results in discouraging fresh investment on the one hand, and making the existing enterprises either to shift outside the region or to limit their operation to the minimum, on the other. This is a paradoxical situation. Over and above, the government and the political leadership of North-East India are yet to come out of their inertia to cope with the policy change undergoing in the era of liberalization. Formerly the role of the state was to plead with the center for aid for its development. With liberalization underway, a state can develop and survive by competing with the other states in attracting big capital. In other words, globalization and liberalization have unleashed an unhealthy competition between states to woo international finance capital and national monopoly capital. While many state governments in the country are trying to outdo each other in providing national and international capital with the maximum of incentives, concessions, cheap raw materials, cheap land, subsidized infrastructure, tax exemption, etc. no such marked attempt is visible on the part of the state governments in the north-east India. Politicians in north-east India are engaged in the game of manipulation of power by dividing people in terms of their racial, linguistic and ethnic consideration.

Hence it is unlikely that North-East India will have a great leap forward in the era of liberalization. It will remain a backward pocket in India, *i.e.,* a periphery within a periphery. But this is not to suggest that the strategy that has so far been pursued in the name of so-called socialist development could deliver better results to North-East India. What is necessary at this juncture of history is not to follow any prescribed design but to evolve a path of development suitable to our needs and circumstances. This is beyond the purview of this paper and also not related to the North-Eastern region alone but to the country as a whole.

References

1. Tanzer, Michael, *'Globalizing the Economy—The influence of the International Monetary Fund and the World Bank'*, Monthly Review, September, 1995.
2. Chaube, S.K., *'Regionalism with Special Reference to North-East India'*, a paper submitted to the UGC sponsored National Seminar, organized by the Department of Political Science, NEHU, Shillong, 1985.
3. Gohain, Hiren, *'Ethnic Unrest in the North-east'*, Economic and Political Weekly, February, 22-28, 1997.
4. The road length per 100 sq. km. of land in NER is only 45.69 km. against 62.8 km. at all India level. Of 62,486 km. of railway gauge at all India level in 1992-93, NER's share was only 2524.83 km. (only 4.3% of the total railway length of the country). Per-capita consumpation of electricity in NER is only 118.48 KW against 330.60 at the national level (Basic Statistics of NER, 1995).

Chapter 22

Economic Liberalization and India's North-East : Reflections on Some Socio-Political and Environmental Crisis

—S. Sengupta

A lot of development programmes have been implemented in India since 1947. Albeit there have some progress, yet the rate and nature of progress are far from satisfactory. Owing to improper implementation of those developmental programmes over the last 50 years, there has been a steady growth of a group of neo-political elites, a group of neo-affluent class and a rise in the group of middle class people in the country. The last group is comparatively larger than the other two above mentioned groups and due to their perpetual economic problems they suffer from a sense of chronic insecurity. Besides there are a large number of poor people. As per the estimates of the Planning Commission, 21.68% of rural population and 11.55% of urban population during 1993-94 lived below the poverty line (**The Hindu: 6/ 1/1996**). The picture becomes different if the approximate number of population in each above stated class is taken into consideration. As Kurien (1996) has reported, the upper layer of the Indian population (who are affluent) consists of about 6 crore people. About 25 to 30 crore people belong to the middle class and the lowest layer of lower income and poor people consists of about 55 to 65 crore. Economic disparity has increased among different sections of population due to inequal distribution of the national wealth (Dandekar and Rath-1971, Sinha-1993).

This type of socio-economic development of the plains region of India has also affected the hill region of the North-East India. Seven states of this region are mostly inhabited by many small indegenous communities. Their societies too now have experienced the growth of the above stated economic classes in their traditional apparently non-stratified egalitarian social systems.

According to Myrdal (1968), a state may be termed as a "soft state" if it shows the following features:

(i) inconsistent formulation and application of state policies and laws,

(ii) circumvention of laws and regulation by the government officials,

(iii) the secret collusion between civil servants with politicians, military, etc. against the public interest, and

(iv) the use of corruption to secure objectives other than those officially sanctioned.

Apart from being a state of 'functional chaos', Myrdal opined that, since attaining her independence from the colonial subjugation India has exhibited all the characters of a 'soft state'. If India is a soft state, on the basis of above stated features, then considering the present politico-economic condition one may say that the entire North-Eastern India is the softest part of it. Due to its geographical location and some other factors, the entire North-Eastern India is economically backward. Different plans that have been implemented for the all-round development of this region have not yielded the desired results. They did not keep pace with the population increase in this region (particularly among the indegenous communities) and did not help in the employment generation for the common people. Tremendous pressure of unemployment, specially among the educated middle class section of the population, has given rise to many types of political agitations and the entire region has become very sensitive politically.

Besides 'HIV', apparently many of the small indegenous communities of the North-Eastern India seem to be very much infected by 'HITT' virus now (H=hatred, I=intolerance, T=territorialism, and T=terrorism). It causes a special type of morbid condition. People have become parochial and in their every political agitation they repeatedly bring forward the issues of ethnic boundaries, restoration of their traditional cultures and so on. No fruitful attempt has so far been undertaken to pacify or settle these political agitations politically for a permanent peaceful solution. Governments have used either armed forces or have pumped huge amount of money to appease them. As a natural outcome of these strategies, a good number of underground organisations have been formed here. They run a kind of parallel administration in certain areas where they have their own control. From the point of biology, this particular phenomenon can be described as klepto-parasitism (klepto = taking things which belong to others; parasitism = phenomenon of living on others for survival). In the animal kingdom, there are certain creatures who do not do anything to collect their food. They steal it from others and in some cases by using force. These creatures are known as klepto-parasites. This is to some extent true in many North-East Indian states. So long a person pays protection money to the representatives of the underground organisations (does not matter to which ethnic or linguistic community he belongs to) he is safe and can carry on his business. He, on the other hand, recovers his money by charging higher price for the goods from the common poor and middle class people. This situation indeed demonstrates 'power comes out of the barrel of gun'.

Klepto-parasitism has caused many undesirable effects on the entire region. It is gradually pumping out a considerable portion of the capital of the North-Eastern India to the foreign countries. For their survival, the underground organisations have to spend most of their money for purchasing arms, ammunitions and explosives from abroad and for maintaining their hideouts and training camps in the foreign countries. It brings a lot of miseries in the life of the common people of the state who are innocent and very often get subjected to the searching and combing operations of the armed police as well as paramilitary forces. Economic development of this region also gets thwarted.

For economic development, Indian planners, political leaders and the economists generally give more importance on industrialization. Let us systematically discuss the factors why during the last 50 years, no notable industries could be set up in this region. Development of industries depend on many factors, *viz.*, capital, skilled labour, sufficient raw material, land, and so on. In the North-East India capital is absent. So is the condition of the skilled labourer, without whom no modern industry can run profitably. If they are brought from the other states, the local population will not appreciate that and their anger will give rise to hostile political agitations. Basing on the natural resources of this region, it is also very difficult to set any big industry here. The last big hurdle is land. Due to state regulations nobody from the other states of India can purchase land in the tribal areas and start an industry.

Like other parts of India, political leadership in the North-East India at present is passing through a great crisis as they are affected by factionalism, individualism, careerism, corruption, parliamentary opportunism, adopting wrong style of doing public works, etc. All these factors together are responsible for the backwardness of the entire North-East India.

II

The developmental policies, that have been implemented in India since 1947, have mostly benefited the upper strata of the society comprising of the rich people. The benefits hardly trickled down to the lower strata in desirable manner. Apart from improper implementation the said developmental policies also had some defects at their formulation stage. They had been conceived by the experts who were either foreign trained or had depended heavily on the development model of the other developed countries without giving much thought on socio-economic and geo-political situation of the different Indian states. So in a country like ours, we must be very careful about economic liberalization policy. It also requires careful analysis of the class character of the persons who prescribe "Economic Liberalization" for the economic development of India.

The members of the ruling class in India at present are strongly advocating of the importance of 'economic liberalization'. This is perhaps necessary for them to remain in power and enjoy their affluence. Because "power" now emanates from the International Monetary Fund, the World Bank and the Multinational Corporations. In India, the ruling class is consisted of the politicians (many have corruption charges against them), industrial/commercial capitalists (who give donations to political party funds during the elections so that they may influence the national policies for the maximisation of their profit), and bureaucrats.

Economic liberalization means a market driven economy where state has minimum control. It's effect on developing economies is disastrous as it does not ensure any steady growth in terms of employment for the growing number of unemployed youths or in the distribution of national wealth equally among all the classes of people, particularly among the poorer sections (Assad, 1996).

It is true that poverty, as reflected by the low standards of living, can be alleviated through increase in the industrial and agricultural production as well as better management of human resources. All these activities require constant monitoring and improvement. For example, any industry requires its technology to be updated regularly. Otherwise, the factors like increase of population, depletion of natural resources and the desire of having more profit would make them useless. It requires huge amount of money and necessary infrastructure for research and development (R&D).

It is not the fact that the MNCs will invest to establish all sorts of industries which are required for the real economic development of our country. On the contrary, they will prefer to set up those industries and to manufacture those products that have a good demand in the markets of the developed countries. For that they will use our natural resources as raw material and engage our industrial labourers at a cheaper rate. They will also use automation in order to manufacture more products in short time by employing lesser number of workers. Naturally they will not generate much employment for the large number of educated unemployed youths of our country. By exporting those products, our country can earn some foreign exchanges. But the MNCs will take away major share from that earning, firstly as royalty for their "patent" or "technology" and secondly as the dividend of the profit as the business partners. Kurien (1996:95-96) has made a detail analysis of the effects of liberalization on India's economy. His findings may be summarised as given below:

(i) Over 75% of foreign capital that has come into India, has been into portfolio investment and its role there has been to claim a share of the profit already being made by the Indian enterprises.

(ii) Imports have been growing at a faster rate. The present indications are that on trade account there is most likely to be a huge deficit by the end of the present financial year (*i.e.,* 1996-97).

(iii) Foreign debt has increased significantly and the World Bank has cautioned that the servicing of the debt and repayment obligations may begin to exert pressure on balance of payment (BOP) in 1996-97 and beyond.

(iv) Comfortable foreign exchange position has not prevented the rupee from depreciating in terms of the major currencies of the world.

(v) Very little or nothing has been done to redefine the role of the state and that of the public sectors in the proposed new economic policy.

From the historical perspective, considering the discussion stated above, we may interpret the economic concept of 'Liberalization, Privatization and Globalization" (LPG) as a neo-colonialist form of exploitation of the poor and developing countries by the industrially developed countries of the northern hemisphere. In the feudal era, they depended upon the slaves brought from poor countries. They took the help of colonialism to get raw materials when they had industrial development. Now in the post-industrial era with the same motive those countries are preaching about the usefulness of LPG for the third world countries. It is a matter of great pity that our ruling class and a part of our best intellectuals and academicians are now canvassing for LPG. It would definitely generate more socio-economic and political problems along with ecological imbalances.

III

In the previous sections, a brief discussion has been made about the general geo-political situation of all the north-eastern states of India and why this entire region is not industrially developed. Besides that, a preliminary discussion has also been made about the nature of LPG. If we take these two pictures into consideration, it is very difficult to say what North-East India will gain from the economic liberalization policy. But it can be said that something must be done very urgently for the improvement of the economic conditions of the people of this region. Otherwise, more political disturbances along with more developed form of klepto-parasitism may be predicted for the states of North-East India in the years to come.

References

Assad, M., 1996, *Attack on multinationals: Re-enactment of Gandhian Violence*, E.P.W. (May 18, 1996: 1184-86).

Dandekar, V.M. and Rath, N., 1971, *Poverty in India*, E.P.W. (1971, Vol. VI, No. 1-2).

Kurien, C.T., 1996, *The Real Impact: Who is Paying the Price*, Frontline (February 9, 1996:95-96).

Myrdal, G., 1968, *Asian Drama*, Vol. II, 895-900, Penguin Books, Great Britain.

Sinha, S. (ed.) 1993, *Anthropology of the Weaker Sections*, Concept Pub. Company, New Delhi.

The Hindu, dated 6.1.96, *(Quoted from Kurien-ibid)*.

Chapter 23

Impact of Liberalization on Industrial Development of India's North-East

—Debjyoti Bhattacharya

With the advent of technology, the world is gradually becoming a small place, the economy is becoming more and more integrated and the role of a centrally operating market force that cuts across all geographical and ethnic barriers is becoming more and more pronounced. Following this trend, if we extrapolate over the scale of time, we can visualize the entire world as a single economic zone with the various local economies playing their respective roles as the components of the whole. Needless to say that the level of industrialization of any area will determine its status in and the benefits from the integrated global economy.

In such a setup, what will be the status of India's Northeast ?

To have an idea of that we have to know the present industrial scenario of this region: its strength and weakness.

The Present Situation

To get an idea of the level of industrialization of any area one may look into two aspects:

[i] The volume of industry in money terms

[ii] The nature of industries of the area.

Let us consider the volume first.

In Search of a Simple but Powerful Indicator

As an indicator of volume of industrialization we shall use Central Excise (CEx) duty collected from this region. The reason for taking this indicator is briefly discussed below.

There can be various indicators that can throw light on this aspect. Of them, the one that comes to mind in the very beginning, is the total industrial output of the area under consideration over a certain period of time, expressed in money terms. But this indicator, in its simplest form, fails to show the value addition done by the local industries. Let me give an example.

Suppose a person is manufacturing iron plates. He has to buy iron ingots, Now suppose value of the plates he has made in one year is Rs. 1 crore. This will include:

[i] Amount utilized in buying the ingots [say 0.5 crores]

[ii] Cost of labour and power & miscellaneous [say 0.3 crores]

So the net value addition by the industry comes down to 0.2 crores only. This will not be reflected if we take the total industrial output in money terms as an indicator. Now, barring the expenses on inputs, the other overheads being mostly local, purging the input cost off the total output in money terms will make the indicator powerful enough to be used as an indicator of volume of industrialization of an area, in the situation where the inputs are coming from outside. This is not required in case of industries using local inputs only.

Central excise duty, as an indicator, addresses both the situations with equal competence. This is a duty levied and collected on manufactured goods. The duty already paid on inputs [if those are manufactured or semi manufactured] is taken care of by a very interestingly designed set of procedure called MODVAT.

Actual duty is collected on the value addition done by the particular firm producing the final product. MODVAT also takes care of the amount paid on capital goods required by the firm. If the inputs used are local or primary in nature, not coming through some other manufacturing process, MODVAT scheme simply ignores it and allows the duty structure to reflect that. In essence, CEX duty, as an indicator, takes out all the monetary effects of the forces that are from the outside of a region but keeps intact the money value of the local resources and the value addition factor of a firm. Hence Central Excise duty collected from an area gives a rough but workable idea of the volume of industrialization there.

Table 1 shows the amount of Central Excise duty collected [including Chess] in the North-Eastern India annually, for last seven years along with the percentage increase over the previous years.

Table 1

TABLE SHOWING REVENUE & PERCENTAGE GROWTH OF REVENUE

Year	*Revenue [Crores]*	*% Increase Over Last Year's Figure*
1990-91	708.68	
1991-92	725.38	(+) 2.36
1992-93	711.91	(-) 1.86
1993-94	669.21	(-) 6
1994-95	740.75	(+) 10.7
1995-96	780.98	(+) 5.47
1996-97	763.95	(+) 1.41

Source : Central Excise Department Data.

The total revenue coming from CEX duty to the national exchequer is approximately 40,000 crores. The approximate contribution of the NE region in this is about 2% which is not a mean achievement by any standards.

The real area of concern is depicted by the third column of the table. The rate of increase in revenue in recent past is not at all encouraging. If we add to it the fact of inflation over this period, the picture becomes even more dismal. This can also be taken as the level of non responsiveness of the industrial sector here to the liberalization process which has been in full swing during this period.

A look at table II will give some more ideas about this non-responsive nature.

Table 2

TABLE SHOWING PERCENTAGE OF REVENUE PAID BY VARIOUS INDUSTRIES. (1995-96 FIGURES)

Name of Industry	*Type of Industry*	*Percentage of Revenue Paid*
Crude Oil	Dependent on Non-Recurring Natural Resources	56.01
Petrochemicals	As Above	16.16
Synthetic Fabric		5.76
Organic Chemicals		2.59
Wood Products	As in Row I	7.51
Cement		1.56
Paper		6.69
Total		96.28%

Source : Central Excise Department Data.

Contribution from the rest of the industries together is 3.72% only.

Table 2 shows a few more things.

[i] In terms of duty payment, the largest industry here is production of crude oil, followed by the petrochem industry. The rest is negligible.

[ii] Contribution from engineering, electronic & other modern industries is microscopic.

Observations

[i] Though the volume of industrialization as indicated by the duty and cess collected from the various industries

is considerable, most of it is coming from industries with a very fast eroding base, like Crude oil production, petrochem industries etc.

[ii] Basic industries that can be used to develop infrastructure are absent. (Example, big iron and steel industries)

[iii] Our largest revenue paying industries are totally dependent on non recurring natural resources, which is not sustainable in the long run.

[iv] Modern industries, like electronics, chemical industries etc. have only a microscopic presence and contribution.

[v] Impact of liberalization till now remains unfelt as far as establishment of new industries and increase in the volume of existing industries are concerned.

WHY SO ?

We shall address this question from the point of view of different but complementary industrial sectors.

1. **Basic Industries**. This requires massive investment. Naturally investors will look for places having two main facilities, *i.e.*

(i) Cheap & efficient transport & communication system and

(ii) Easy availability of power.

Transport

Transport is not cheap in this area. Consider an industry functioning in, say, Tripura. What will be the cost factor of bringing the produce in a far away market unless there is a huge local requirement ?

An easy solution appears to be transport subsidy. But in a rapidly growing privatised economy this kind of Governmental backing may not be of much help in the long run.

Power Supply : The Vicious Circle

Power situation is also not very promising. Establishment of basic industries needs adequate power supply as a pre-condition. At the same time, establishment of big power plants will be feasible only when there are takers *i.e.* big industries. One is complementary to the other. In a market based economy, each one grows on the pre-condition of the existence of the other. If both are absent, the absence of each hinders the growth of the other, thus forming the never ending vicious circle.

2. **Consumers goods industries**. These are labour intensive industries. They require comparatively less capital, employ more persons and there is always a guarantee of a good local market provided the type of industry is rightly chosen. Also, knowledge of local tastes & practices helps a local producer in customizing the goods accordingly, and can give him some mileage over his big brother making the same thing somewhere far away, bringing the products all the way down and selling it on his doorsteps.

Agreed, that to get a good foothold, a consumer goods industry requires a very aggressive marketing strategy and flexibility to adapt very fast to changing tastes and time, but compared to the formidable task or creating an infrastructure for basic industries and luring in big investors in the face of an already existing massive infrastructures of many Indian States, this task looks simpler and highly feasible given the available human and natural resources of this part of the country.

WHICH INDUSTRIES ARE SUITABLE ?

Naturally a question will arise as to what kind of labour intensive industries will be best suited for this area ? Two kinds of goods appears to be suitable:

(i) Essential (*i.e.* non luxury) consumer durable.

(ii) Agro based products.

In case of the first one, competition in the area of luxury consumer durable (say, Colour. TV sets) and luxury non durable (like nail polish, chocolates) very high and it will be difficult for a new entrant to lure in buyers out of the grasp of the bigger players in the field. Factors like brand fidelity and prestige bias will put tough hindrances in the way.

Essential consumer durable (say chappals, steel furnitures, radio sets, ball point pens and other writing instruments, dress material suitable to local tastes & culture, etc.) when locally made, will sell, as this will have an appeal to the larger chunk of the lower income group who are devoid of most of the biases as mentioned above, or even when they are influenced by the stronger advertisement campaigns of the bigger houses, are forced to shy away from purchasing them regularly due to disparity between their purchasing power and price tag.

In case of agro-based products, India's North-East appears to be highly suitable due to favourable climatic and other conditions. Some never thoughts are required in this zone. Tea has remained the major cash crop of the region. Spices & horticultural products could be two items with a huge value addition factor, they would not require the huge capital investment required for tea, but the profit margin in these items is quite high. Once this pattern of industries grow, this will create the environ and demand for the basic industries; and once the market senses the feasibility of such industries, the rest will be automatic.

Subject Index